TEACHING AND LEARNING STEM

A PRACTICAL GUIDE

Richard M. Felder
Rebecca Brent

JB JOSSEY-BASS™
A Wiley Brand

Published by Jossey-Bass
A Wiley Brand
One Montgomery Street, Suite 1000, San Francisco, CA 94104–4594—www.josseybass.com

Jossey-Bass books and products are available through most bookstores. To contact Jossey-Bass directly call our Customer Care Department within the U.S. at 800-956-7739, outside the U.S. at 317-572-3986, or fax 317-572-4002.

Wiley publishes in a variety of print and electronic formats and by print-on-demand. Some material included with standard print versions of this book may not be included in e-books or in print-on-demand. If this book refers to media such as a CD or DVD that is not included in the version you purchased, you may download this material at http://booksupport.wiley.com. For more information about Wiley products, visit www.wiley.com.

Library of Congress Cataloging-in-Publication Data

ISBN 9781118925812 (Hardcover)
ISBN 9781118925836 (ePDF)
ISBN 9781118925829 (ePub)

Cover image: © agsandrew/iStockphoto
Cover design: Wiley

Printed in the United States of America

FIRST EDITION

HB Printing   10 9 8 7 6 5 4 3 2

THE AUTHORS

Richard Felder, PhD, is Hoechst Celanese Professor Emeritus of Chemical Engineering at North Carolina State University, where he has been a faculty member since 1969. He is a coauthor of *Elementary Principles of Chemical Processes* (fourth edition, Wiley, 2015), which has been used as the introductory text by roughly 90% of all chemical engineering departments in the United States and many abroad since it first appeared in 1978, and he has authored or coauthored more than 300 papers on process engineering and STEM education. He has won numerous awards for his teaching, research, and publications, including the International Federation of Engineering Education Societies Global Award for Excellence in Engineering Education (2010, first recipient) and the American Society for Engineering Education Lifetime Achievement Award (2012, first recipient). A bibliography of Dr. Felder's papers and reprints of his columns and articles can be found at www.ncsu.edu/effective_teaching.

Rebecca Brent, EdD, is president of Education Designs, Inc., a consulting firm in Cary, North Carolina. She has more than 35 years of experience in education and specializes in STEM faculty development, precollege teacher preparation, and evaluation of educational programs at precollege and college levels, and she holds a certificate in evaluation practice from the Evaluators' Institute at George Washington University. She has authored or coauthored more than 60 papers on effective teaching and faculty development, and coordinated faculty development in the NSF-sponsored SUCCEED Coalition and new faculty orientation in the Colleges of Engineering and Sciences at North Carolina State University. Prior to entering private consulting, Dr. Brent was an associate professor of education at East Carolina University, where she won an outstanding teacher award. In 2014, she was named a Fellow of the American Society for Engineering Education.

Separately and together, Drs. Felder and Brent have presented more than 450 workshops on effective teaching, course design, mentoring and supporting new faculty members, and STEM faculty development on campuses throughout the United States and abroad. They co-directed the American Society for Engineering Education National Effective Teaching Institute from 1991 to 2015.

We dedicate this book to Charlotte and Wilson Brent, in loving memory of their lives well lived.

CONTENTS

PART TWO
Teaching courses

PART THREE
Facilitating skill development

TABLES, FIGURES, AND EXHIBITS

FOREWORD

FOR MANY UNIVERSITY professors, teaching is like being handed the keys to a car without being taught how to drive. The result? Even experienced professors can wind up driving with their pedagogical parking brakes on. They steer forward clumsily, unaware that there's an easier way, and ignoring the smoke emerging from the tailpipe.

This book is hands-down the best instruction manual for professors in science, technology, engineering, and mathematics that you can find. Husband-and-wife team Richard Felder and Rebecca Brent write in an exceptionally clear, non-stuffy voice that makes this a book you can read even at the end of a busy day. A simple glance at the table of contents or index will rapidly take you to what you might need to find at the moment—either before or after you've read the whole book.

The book is packed with special features, which include brief interlude essays that give you a sense of what your students are thinking, succinct summaries of key practical insights from neuroscience, and concrete suggestions based on solid research and decades of experience. Everything is backed with loads of references, so you can easily explore as deeply as you choose.

Books on teaching in the STEM disciplines often center on one discipline—physics, say, or engineering. Few comprehensively encompass teaching in STEM fields ranging from biology and chemistry to theoretical mathematics. This book takes a broad-ranging approach that enables readers to pluck the best insights from a wide variety of STEM disciplines.

And it's a great thing—there's never been a stronger need for a book that lays out the foundations of good teaching at university levels in the STEM disciplines. Worldwide, STEM jobs are like mushrooms—popping up at far higher rates than many other types of jobs, yet not enough candidates for these jobs are graduating from our STEM programs. In fact, often only a small percentage of high school seniors are interested in pursuing STEM careers. Many of those students fall by the wayside as they bump against the challenges of STEM studies.

But as Richard Felder and Rebecca Brent lay out in this remarkably engaging book, there are ways to work smarter as instructors—ways to help improve students' desire and ability to master tough material. This book can help you open important career opportunities for your students, even as you help improve and increase their skills that address profound national and international needs. You will also find that releasing the parking brake of less-than-adequate teaching will make your life as a professor more fulfilling and enjoyable.

Learner-centered approaches go all the way back to the Greeks, the Buddha, and various traditions of the Far East, and have recently been taken up again in the STEM disciplines by expert teachers and researchers such as mathematician Robert Lee Moore and physicists Eric Mazur and Carl Wieman. There is a reason for the continued popularity of learner-centered teaching techniques by the best and most famous teachers—such approaches do much to stimulate student success. This book contains up-to-date practical information about how to apply these techniques in the STEM disciplines.

On a personal note, I first met Rich and Rebecca at the very beginning of my teaching career and was lucky enough to attend a workshop they taught on learner-centered teaching, which is the pedagogical framework of their book. That workshop changed the whole focus of my teaching and enabled me to understand learning in a whole new, deeper way. You'll find that your own understanding of learning will be greatly enriched as you read this extraordinary book.

—Barbara Oakley, PhD, PE
Professor of Engineering, Oakland University, Rochester, Michigan
Visiting Scholar, University of California, San Diego

Author of *New York Times* best-selling book *A Mind for Numbers: How to Excel in Math and Science (Even If You Flunked Algebra)*, and co-instructor of *Learning How to Learn: Powerful Mental Tools to Help You Master Tough Subjects*, one of the world's largest massive open online courses, for Coursera-UC San Diego.

PREFACE

WHY ANOTHER "how-to-teach" book, and why us as the authors? Our answers are in our stories.

(Rich's story) *When I started my academic career in chemical engineering at NC State back in prehistoric times, I had the same training in teaching that most college professors get: none. Not knowing that there were alternatives, I fell back on the only teaching model I had, which was how my professors had taught me. Unfortunately, no one ever taught them how to teach either, and so for the first fifteen years of my career I did what all my colleagues did—gave nonstop lectures and tests that were always too long and drastically curved course grades so I wouldn't end up failing most of the class.*

You could take my lecture notes to the bank. The derivations were complete and correct, my delivery was clear and occasionally entertaining, and most students left the lectures thinking they understood everything. The result was that I got high ratings and won some awards. There were just two minor hitches. After the lectures the students struggled for hours to complete assignments that involved problems similar to the ones I worked in class, and many of their exam grades were pitiful. Most who failed blamed themselves, figuring that if they couldn't do well with a teacher as clear as I was, they obviously lacked what it takes to be an engineer.

Most of them were wrong—a lot of the blame for their failure was mine. When I was developing and polishing those lecture notes—finding clear ways to express difficult concepts, coming up with good examples of every method I was teaching—I was really learning that stuff! The problem was that I was then feeding my students predigested food. They didn't have to go through the intellectual labor of working some of it out for themselves, which meant that they never really understood it, no matter how clear it may have seemed in the lectures.

Most STEM professors never read education literature, and I was no exception. It was years before I learned that excellent research has been done on alternative teaching methods, some of which have been found to

*promote learning much better than traditional methods do. I started try-
ing some of those alternatives and found that they worked beautifully in
my courses, and I subsequently met some pedagogical experts who helped
me sharpen my understanding. One of them became my professional colleague and the coauthor of this book and my wife—Rebecca Brent. (Who
says educational research doesn't pay off?)*

(Rebecca's story) *I've been a teacher since my earliest preschool days
spent "teaching" a neighbor child her letters, and early on I made education the focus of my career. I loved learning about how people learn and
creative ways to facilitate learning. I began my professional life as an elementary school teacher, and then got my doctorate and became a teacher
educator at East Carolina University. It was fascinating for me to watch
my students as they first began to teach and put all the education theory
I had taught them into practice on a daily basis. I also worked on a faculty
team to develop training programs for people in non-academic professions
who wanted to change careers and become teachers. It was then that I
realized that passing along a few, well-chosen techniques could go a long
way toward helping people to become effective instructors. When Rich
and I began to give workshops to university STEM faculty, I found that
the approach held up. We could help people understand something about
how their students learn, get them to think carefully about what they
wanted their students to be able to do and how they could evaluate the students' ability to do it, and offer some simple ways to get students engaged
in class, no matter how many of them were in the room. Some workshop attendees tried a few of our suggestions and started to see effects on
their students' learning, some made major transformative changes in their
courses and saw correspondingly significant impacts, and a few now give
excellent teaching workshops themselves, which delights us.*

*In our workshops, we review teaching methods that have been proven
effective by solid replicated research, most of which are relatively easy to
implement. Our goal in this book is to share those methods and some of
the supporting research with you.*

The first chapter of the book contains a short introduction to some
of what educational research has revealed about effective teaching and
learning, a preview of the book's contents, and some suggestions for how
to use the book. The chapter is a quick read and introduces ideas we will
return to periodically in the rest of the book. Following that are chapters
that deal with methods for designing and implementing effective courses
and helping students acquire and improve their skills at problem solving,

communications, creative and critical thinking, high-performance team-work, and self-directed learning.

There are several things we don't intend the book to be. One is a compendium of everything anyone knows about teaching. Writing something like that would take more time than we have and reading it would take more time than you have. It's also not a scholarly treatise on the theories behind the methods we have chosen to cover. Plenty of books out there review the theories and we will point you to some of them, but our emphasis will be on nuts and bolts of the practice—what the methods are, how to implement them, and pitfalls to avoid when doing so. We'll also share findings from modern cognitive science that provide good clues about why the methods consistently work as well as they do.

The book draws extensively on journal articles we have authored or coauthored. Most notably, the interludes between chapters are almost all based on our "Random Thoughts" columns that have appeared in the quarterly journal *Chemical Engineering Education* since 1988. We are grateful to Managing Editor Lynn Heasley for granting us permission to modify and reprint the columns.

We have not been shy about asking for help, and so we have a long list of colleagues who previewed and critiqued chapter drafts, shared course materials, and provided invaluable encouragement. Rather than elaborating on what most of them did and making this preface longer than some of the chapters, we will simply express our deep thanks to David Brightman, Lisa Bullard, Jo-Ann Cohen, Marc Cubeta, Jackie Dietz, John Falconer, Stephanie Farrell, Elena Felder, Gary Felder, Kenny Felder, Mary Felder, Cindy Furse, Susan Geraghty, Jeff Joines, Milo Koretsky, Susan Lord, Misty Loughry, Nicki Monahan, Michael Moys, Mike Prince, Julie Sharp, Kimberly Tanner, Dan Teague, John Tolle, Thomas Wentworth, and Carl Zorowski.

We will, however, single out two individuals, without whom this book would not exist. From the moment she learned that we were planning a book more years ago than we care to contemplate, the superb author and educator Barbara Oakley functioned as our principal cheerleader, critic, and nudge, repeatedly and good-naturedly assuring us that the world desperately needed this book when we doubted ourselves, red-inking our occasionally pedantic and hyperbolic prose, and gently prodding us back into action when not much from us was showing up in her in-box. Eventually things reached a point where we had to keep pushing on—we couldn't have lived with the guilt we would have felt over disappointing Barb. Words can't begin to convey our gratitude.

And words are equally inadequate to thank our editor, Maryellen Weimer, the long-time guru of *The Teaching Professor* newsletter and author of *Learner-Centered Teaching*. Having a professional icon like Maryellen working with us was somewhat intimidating—it was as if we had set out to compose a symphony and learned that Mozart would be advising us. Fortunately, besides being one of the top authorities on higher education in the world, Maryellen is also one of the finest editors and nicest human beings. She gave us a steady stream of impeccably good advice, without ever trying to impose her views or her voice on our writing, and Rich has even forgiven her for siding with Rebecca every single time the coauthors disagreed about something.

And finally, we want to thank Kenny, Joyce, Elena, Leonicia, Gary, Rosemary, Mary, Ben, Jack, Shannon, Johnny, James, and Cecelia for putting up with our frequent disappearances in the final stages of writing this book. At the top of our very long list headed by "*When we finish this &#ˆ *%& book, we will…*" is "*be more reliable parents and grandparents.*" We hope that by the time the thirteen of you are reading this, we will have started to keep that resolution.

Richard Felder
Rebecca Brent

INTRODUCTION TO COLLEGE TEACHING

1.0 Welcome to the University, There's Your Office, Good Luck

As everyone knows, skilled professionals routinely receive training before being certified to practice independently. Electricians, machinists, and chefs get preliminary instruction and then serve for months or years as apprentices. Accountants, psychologists, physicists, and physicians spend years earning degrees in their fields, and the physicians spend additional years in supervised internships and residencies. It would be unthinkable to allow people to practice a skilled profession without first being trained for it, especially if their mistakes could cause harm to others … unless they are college faculty members.

The standard preparation for a faculty career is taking undergraduate and graduate courses in your discipline and completing a research project on a topic someone else has defined. Once you join a faculty, your orientation may consist of nothing but the heading of this section, and perhaps a half-day or a day on such things as health and retirement benefits and the importance of laboratory safety. The unstated assumption is that if you have a degree in a subject, you must know how to teach it at the college level.

Anyone who has ever been a college student knows how bad that assumption can be. What student has never had a professor who taught at a level ridiculously above anything the students had a chance of understanding, or put entire classes to sleep by droning monotonously for 50- or 75-minute stretches with no apparent awareness that there were students in the room, or flashed PowerPoint slides at a rate no human brain could possibly keep up with?

Instructors like these unfortunately abound on college faculties. If you teach like any of them, no matter how much you know and how accurately you present it, you probably won't enjoy looking at your students' test scores or your end-of-class student ratings. Being an excellent or even just a competent teacher requires knowing many things graduate school doesn't teach, such as how to design courses and deliver them effectively; write assignments and exams that are both rigorous and fair; and deal with classroom management, advising problems, cheating, and an uncountable number of other headaches teachers routinely encounter. Figuring out all those things on your own is not trivial. Although there is something to be said for trial-and-error learning, it's not efficient—and in the case of teaching, the ones making the errors are not the ones suffering the consequences. Many new faculty members take years to learn how to teach well, and others never learn.

It doesn't have to be that way. Proven methods for teaching effectively—that is, motivating students to learn and helping them acquire the knowledge, skills, and values they will need to succeed in college and their professions—are well known. Many of those methods are not particularly hard—you can just learn what they are and then start using them. That doesn't mean they make teaching simple: teaching a course—especially for the first time—is and always will be a challenging and time-consuming task. The point is that teaching well does not have to be harder than teaching poorly. The purpose of this book is to help you learn how to teach well.

1.1 Making Learning Happen

Brainwave: What Goes on in Our Brains When We Learn?

Learning is shorthand for encoding and storing information in long-term memory, from which it can later be retrieved and used. According to a widely-used model of this process, new information comes in through the senses, is held for a fraction of a second in a sensory register, and is then either passed on to working memory or lost. Once in working memory, the information is processed, and after a fraction of a minute (or longer if the information is repeated), it is then either stored in long-term memory or lost.

The chances of a new sensory input getting into long-term memory vary dramatically from one input to another. The inputs most likely to make it relate to (1) *threats* to the learner's survival or well-being. In descending order, the next most likely inputs to be stored are those with (2) *strong emotional associations* for the learner; (3) *meaning* (relationship to the learner's interests, goals, prior knowledge, and past experiences); and (4) *sense* (comprehensibility).

It follows that if teachers present information irrelevant to anything students know and care about and it makes little sense to them, there should be no surprise if the students later act as if they never heard it. It never made it into their long-term memory, so for all practical purposes they *didn't* hear it. Moreover, even if information makes it into long-term memory, unless it is reinforced by rehearsal (conscious repetition), the clusters of nerve cells that collectively contain it are weakly connected and the information may not be easily retrieved.

In short, *the more new information has meaning and makes sense to students, the more likely it is to be stored. Once stored, the more often the information is retrieved and rehearsed, the more effective the learning is* (Sousa, 2011, Ch. 3).

Think about something you're really good at. It might be soccer, auto mechanics, chess, piano, physics, Java programming, or anything else. Go on—we'll wait.

Now think about *how* you got good. You might think of courses you took but you probably won't. You're much more likely to think about making your first awkward and unsuccessful efforts, getting feedback from someone else or learning from your mistakes, and trying again. If you persisted, you eventually started to succeed. The more practice and feedback you got, the better you got, until you reached your current level.

That's how people learn. Mastery of a skill comes mainly from doing things, noticing and reflecting on the results, and possibly getting feedback from someone else. If we learn anything by just reading a text or watching and listening to someone lecturing at us, it generally isn't much, and the chances of retaining it for very long are slim. The truth of that message has been recognized for a long time.

> One must learn by doing the thing; for though you think you know it, you have no certainty until you try. (Sophocles)
> What we have to learn to do, we learn by doing. (Aristotle)
> You cannot teach a man anything: you can only help him to find it within himself. (Galileo)
> No thought, no idea, can possibly be conveyed as an idea from one person to another. (John Dewey)

Modern cognitive science and decades of classroom research studies demonstrate that Sophocles and those other sages were right. People learn by doing and reflecting, not by watching and listening. Unfortunately, starting in about the sixth grade and continuing through college, most classes are taught primarily by lecturing. Traditional education is consequently uninspiring and ineffective for most people, and for some it becomes a serious and sometimes permanent deterrent to lifelong learning.

Fortunately, there are excellent alternatives to pure lecture-based instruction. We will describe many of them in this book, starting in the next section of this chapter. They are not traditional in STEM (science, technology, engineering, and mathematics) education, but they have all been validated by extensive research, and many STEM instructors have discovered them and used them successfully. There's even more good news:

To teach effectively you don't have to use every teaching method known to be effective, and you shouldn't even think of trying to implement too many at once.

If you try to change how you teach too drastically, you and your students may be so uncomfortable that the class turns into a disaster, the student pushback can be overwhelming, and you'll never want to do anything new again. Instead, start with one or two relatively simple alternative methods, such as active learning, and introduce new methods gradually, never moving too far out of your comfort zone. If you take that moderate approach, your teaching and your students' learning will steadily improve, which should be your goal.

Becoming a more effective teacher doesn't require throwing out everything traditional.

We won't be telling you, for example, to abandon lecturing and make every class you teach an extravaganza of student activity. We *will* tell you to avoid making lecturing the only thing that happens in your class sessions. Introduce one or two activities in the first few sessions so you and the students can get used to them, and gradually increase their frequency. As you continue to use the method your confidence will rise, and your use of active learning will probably rise with it. The same thing is true for the other teaching methods we will discuss. Again, the key is to take it easy!

You're not going to win them all, and you don't have to.

Even if you use the most effective teaching methods known to education, many of your students will not get top grades and some will fail. That doesn't mean you failed as a teacher. How well students do in a course

depends on much more than how their instructor teaches: it al
on their aptitude for the subject, how interested they are in it
they are willing and able to work on it, how important their cou
to them, and an uncountable number of other factors. We suggest that
your goal as a teacher should not be to have 100% of your students
achieve your learning objectives, because that's generally neither possible nor even desirable. Not everyone was born to be a scientist, engineer,
or mathematician, and if all of your students fully meet your objectives you
may be setting the bar too low. Rather, your goal should be to enable as
many as possible of your students with the required aptitude, motivation,
and work ethic to succeed in your course and transfer what they learn to
other courses and eventually to their careers. *That* you can do.

1.2 Learner-Centered Teaching: Definition, Warning, and Reassurance

The great philosopher and educator John Dewey said, "Teaching and
learning are correlative or corresponding processes, as much so as selling
and buying. One might as well say he has sold when no one has bought, as
to say that he has taught when no one has learned" (Dewey, 1910, p. 29).

That statement may seem obvious but it isn't to everyone. If you look up
the word *teach* in a dictionary, you will find variations of two completely
different concepts:

1. *Teach:* To show or explain something.
2. *Teach:* To cause to know something.

By the first definition, if everything the students are supposed to learn
in a course is covered in lectures and readings, then the instructor has
successfully taught the course, whether or not anyone learned it. By the
second definition, if students don't learn, the instructor didn't teach.

Many STEM instructors subscribe to the first definition. "My job is to
cover the syllabus," they argue. "If the students don't learn it, that's their
problem, not mine." They use *teacher-centered instruction,* in which
the course instructor defines the course content; designs and delivers
lectures; creates, administers, and marks assignments and tests; assigns
course grades; and is essentially in control of everything that happens
in the course except how the students react and achieve. The students
mainly sit through the lectures—some occasionally asking or answering
questions and most just passively observing. They absorb whatever they

can, and then do their best to reproduce it in the assignments and exams. That model pretty much describes STEM higher education as it has been practiced for centuries throughout the world, despite the fact that it is incompatible with what we now know about how people actually learn.

John Dewey, whose quote began this section, clearly believed in the second definition of teaching—to cause learning to occur. That definition lies at the heart of what is now called *learner-centered teaching (LCT)*. The teacher of a course still sets the broad parameters of instruction, making sure that the learning objectives and lessons cover all the knowledge and skills the course is supposed to address, the assessments match the objectives and are fair, and the course grades are consistent with the assessment data. The difference is that the students are no longer passive recipients and repeaters of information but take much more responsibility for their own learning. The instructor functions not as the sole source of wisdom and knowledge to them but more as a coach or guide, whose task is to help them acquire the desired knowledge and skills for themselves.

Weimer (2013, Ch. 2) surveyed the voluminous research literature on the various forms of learner-centered teaching and observed that properly implemented LCT has been found superior to teacher-centered instruction at achieving almost every conceivable learning outcome. We will use LCT as a framework for the rest of this book. In later chapters we'll discuss specific LCT techniques—what they are, what research says about them, how to implement them, what can go wrong when you use them, and how to make sure it doesn't. Before we preview the book in the next section, though, we'll warn you about something you might find troublesome when you launch into LCT for the first time. When you make students more responsible for their own learning than they have ever been, they will not all leap to their feet and embrace you with gratitude! Weimer (2013, p. 199) offers the following cautionary words:

> Some faculty [members] find the arguments for learner-centered teaching very convincing. With considerable enthusiasm, they start creating new assignments, developing classroom activities, and realigning course policies. By the time they've completed the planning process, they are just plain excited about launching what feels like a whole new course. They introduce these new course features on the first day, sharing with students their conviction that these changes will make the class so much better. And what happens? Students do not respond with corresponding enthusiasm. In fact, they make it very clear that they prefer having things done as they are in most classes. Teachers leave class disheartened. The student response feels like a personal affront.

If you have not used learner-centered teaching yet, the resistance you may encounter from some students the first time you try it may be a shock to your system. You may envision your student ratings plummeting and your chances for advancement on the faculty shrinking, and it can be easy for you to say "Who needs this?" and go back to traditional lecturing.

If you find yourself in that situation, fight the temptation to retreat. Several references on learner-centered teaching methods have discussed the phenomenon of student resistance: why it's there, what forms it might take, and how instructors can deal with it (Felder, 2007, 2011a; Felder & Brent, 1996; Seidel & Tanner, 2013; Weimer, 2013, Ch. 8). We won't go into detail about it now but will explore the issue later when we get into active learning, cooperative learning, and other learner-centered methods. For now, just be aware of the possibility of student resistance to LCT, and be assured that you can minimize or eliminate it if you take the measures we'll tell you about. If your need for immediate reassurance is urgent, check out any of the five references just cited, and then relax.

You may also hear from some of your faculty colleagues that LCT doesn't work. If you do, cheerfully offer to share with them the research that proves it does (we'll provide you with plenty of it). That offer usually ends *that* discussion.

1.3 What's in This Book?

A graphic organizer of the book is shown in Figure 1.3–1.

Here are the main topics covered in the chapters.

Chapter 2.

Writing course learning objectives (statements of how the students will demonstrate their mastery of the knowledge, methods, skills, and attitudes or values the instructor plans to teach) and using them to achieve *constructive alignment,* in which the course lessons, activities, assignments, and assessments of learning all point toward the same goals.

Chapter 3.

Preparing to teach a new or redesigned course for the first time. Writing a syllabus and formulating a course grading policy. Getting the course off to a good start.

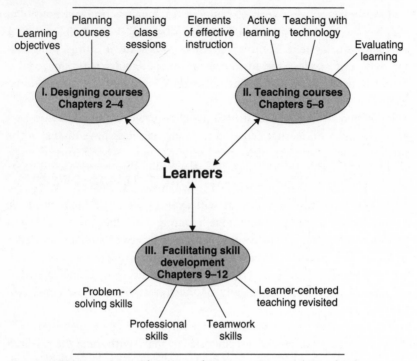

Figure 1.3–1: Elements of Learner-Centered Teaching

Chapter 4.

Planning individual class sessions.

Chapter 5.

Teaching effectively and continuing to improve.

Chapter 6.

Getting students actively engaged in class, no matter how large the class is.

Chapter 7.

Teaching effectively with technology. Blended learning (combining face-to-face and online instruction), flipped (inverted) classrooms, and online courses.

Chapter 8.

Evaluating how well students are acquiring the knowledge, skills, and conceptual understanding specified in the course learning objectives.

Chapter 9.

Helping students develop expert problem-solving skills. Problem-based learning.

Chapter 10.

Helping students develop skills in communication, creative thinking, critical thinking, and self-directed learning. Project-based learning.

Chapter 11.

Helping students develop skills required for high-performance teamwork (time and project management, leadership, conflict management, and various interpersonal skills).

Chapter 12.

Revisiting learner-centered teaching and wrapping up.

1.4 How to Use the Book

Our goal is to describe some proven teaching methods—mostly relatively easy ones that don't require major preparation time and a few that present greater challenges—and to prepare you to implement those methods. There's one small problem, though. Let's look at a point we made earlier in this chapter:

> Mastery of a skill comes mainly from doing things, noticing and reflecting on the results, and possibly getting feedback from someone else. If we learn anything by just reading a text or watching and listening to someone lecturing at us, it generally isn't much, and the chances of retaining it for very long are slim.

That's true for our students, and it's also true for you as you work to become a better teacher. If you start out intending to plow through this book from cover to cover, you'll be inundated by a flood of information coming at you faster than the human mind can absorb. You may pick up a few useful ideas but they may not lead to significant changes in your teaching, and you could easily decide to stop reading before you even get close to finishing.

Instead of reading the book like a novel, treat it more like a reference work. We have made the chapters and many individual sections in them reasonably independent, so you can jump in almost anywhere and just start reading. Here are some ideas for when and how to do it:

Take the book out at the beginning of each course you teach, look through a section you haven't read recently or at all, find a couple of new ideas to try, and try them.

Give them a fair chance to succeed—don't just do something once and decide that it didn't work, because it usually takes some repetition before teachers and students become comfortable with unfamiliar teaching strategies.

During the course, when a question, problem, or need arises, find out which part or parts of the book deal with it and check them out.

For example, if you just gave an exam and the results were terrible, go to Chapter 8 to get some ideas about what you may have done wrong, even if you haven't read what comes before it. (You may not have done anything wrong—sometimes students just don't study.)

When the course is finished, search for information about things that might not have gone as well as you would have liked.

Figure out what you want to change when you teach the course again, and put the changes in your class session plans to remind yourself to make them.

In short, read the book *actively* to get the most out of it.

Okay, we're ready when you are. Enjoy!

PART ONE

DESIGNING COURSES

Suppose you're a professor of microbiology and your nephew is a senior in high school interested in enrolling in microbiology at a nearby university. Your sister asks you what you think of the microbiology department at that university, and you find their website and check out the department curriculum and descriptions of the courses. Your ability to evaluate the program now might be better than it was before you looked, but not much better.

A curriculum (basically, a list of course titles), catalog descriptions of the courses in it, and course syllabi are all condensed statements of what teachers are supposed to teach. After you have read them, you still know very little about what students should be able to *do*—define, explain, calculate, derive, model, critique, design, and so on—after passing each course (*learning objectives*). When instructors practice *learner-centered teaching*—an instructional approach defined in Chapter 1—they formulate learning objectives and use them as cornerstones of course design, delivery, and assessment. When this approach is adopted, the objectives give program evaluators, prospective students, high school guidance counselors, the program faculty members, and the students themselves a clear picture of exactly what the program is trying to achieve and what its graduates should be prepared to do.

Part I of the book outlines the basics of planning an effective course. Chapter 2 describes how to write learning objectives that address basic knowledge and high-level thinking, problem-solving, and important non-technical professional skills. Chapter 3 suggests ways to minimize the massive time and effort usually required by a new course preparation or major course redesign and to get off to a good start in the first week, and Chapter 4 discusses how to plan what you will do in the rest of the course. The graphic organizer in Figure I-1 provides an overview of the structure of this set of chapters.

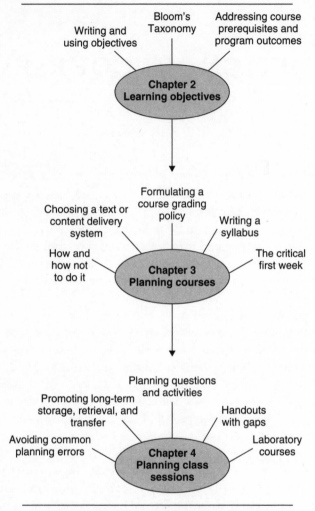

Figure I-1: Graphic Organizer of Part I

INTERLUDE. WHAT DO THEY
NEED TO KNOW?

Interviewer: Good morning, Mr. Allen. I'm Angela Macher—project
engineering and human resources at Consolidated Nanoproducts.

Senior: Good morning, Ms. Macher—nice to meet you.

I: So, I understand you're getting ready to graduate in May and you're
looking for a position with Consolidated ... and I also see you've
got a 3.75 GPA coming into this semester—very impressive. What
kind of position did you have in mind?

S: Well, I liked most of my engineering courses but especially the ones
with lots of math and computer applications—I've gotten pretty
good at Excel with Visual Basic and MATLAB with Simulink, and
I also know some JAVA. I was thinking about integrated circuit
design or something like that.

I: I see. Well, to be honest, we have very few openings in design and
programming—we've moved most of our design and
manufacturing to China and Romania and most of our
programming to India. Got any foreign languages?

S: Um, a couple of years of Spanish in high school but I couldn't take
any more in college—no room in the curriculum.

I: How would you feel about taking an intensive language course for a
few months and moving to one of our overseas facilities? If you do
well you could be on a fast track to management.

S: Uh ... I was really hoping I could stay in the States. Aren't any
positions left over here?

I: Sure, but not like ten years ago, and you need different skills to get
them. Let me ask you a couple of questions to see if we can find a
fit. First, what do you think your strengths are outside of electrical
and computer engineering?

S: Well, I've always been good in physics.

I: How about social sciences and humanities?

S: I did all right in those courses but I can't say I enjoy that stuff.

I: I see ... (stands up) OK, Mr. Allen—thanks. I'll forward your
application to our central headquarters, and if we find any slots
that might work we'll be in touch. Have a nice day.

This hypothetical interview is not all that hypothetical. The job
market in technical disciplines—especially in developed countries—is
changing, and future graduates will need skills beyond the ones that
used to be sufficient. An implication for STEM education is that a lot
of what we're teaching is the wrong material. Since the 1960s, we have
concentrated almost exclusively on equipping students with analytical
problem-solving skills. In recent years a significant number of business
and industry spokespersons (see, for example, Prichard [2013]) argue
that most jobs calling for those skills can now be done better and cheaper
by either computers or skilled workers in developing countries—and if
they can be, they will be. They also predict that STEM graduates with
certain different skills will continue to find jobs in developed countries:

- o Creative researchers, developers, and entrepreneurs who can help
  their companies stay ahead of the technology development curve
- o Holistic, multidisciplinary thinkers who can recognize opportunities
  in the global economy and formulate strategies to capitalize on them
- o People with strong communication, management, and teamwork
  skills who can establish and maintain good relationships with
  coworkers, clients, and potential clients
- o People with the language skills and cultural awareness needed
  to build bridges between companies in developing nations, where
  many manufacturing facilities and jobs are migrating, and developed
  nations, where many customers and consumers will continue to be
  located

The question is, are we helping STEM students develop those increasingly important attributes? In relatively few cases—mostly small colleges
with strong liberal arts programs that emphasize project-based learning
(Prichard, 2013) and some individual STEM departments—the answer is
"yes," but in an overwhelming majority of STEM programs, it is "not
really." We still spend most of our time and effort teaching our students
to "derive an expression relating A to B" and "given X and Y, calculate
Z," but we rarely provide systematic training in the abilities that future
graduates will need to get and hold jobs. Why don't we? Because people
as a rule are reluctant to leave their comfort zones, and faculty members are no exception. Most of us can solve equations in our sleep and

feel comfortable teaching students to do it, but we're not so sure about our ability to tackle multidisciplinary problems that require creativity and critical thinking, let alone our ability to teach anyone else to do it.

An effective first step in teaching high-level thinking and problem-solving is to formulate *learning objectives*, statements that define targeted knowledge and skills in a way that is clear to instructors and students. How to do that for basic knowledge and high-level skills is the primary subject of Chapter 2. How to then teach the students to meet those objectives is the subject of the rest of the book.

2

LEARNING OBJECTIVES: A FOUNDATION OF EFFECTIVE TEACHING

2.0 Introduction

Here are two dialogues you can hear variants of every day on every campus. Let's first eavesdrop in the student lounge, where several students are talking about their upcoming physics exam.

George: Buffo's first test is next Monday. I haven't had him before—can you just plug into formulas or does he make you do derivations and all that?

Ming-Hua: No telling. Jackie has copies of Buffo's old tests, and last fall a lot of the problems were straight substitution but a couple of times Buffo threw in things he never talked about in class.

Kelly: Yeah, I had him last spring and he pulls problems out of nowhere all the time, and he even makes you write paragraphs about stuff and marks you down for grammar mistakes! Whatever you do, don't ask him what you're responsible for on the test. He just gets mad and gives you a sermon on how bad your attitude is … we had a 600-page textbook and according to Buffo we were supposed to know everything in it.

George: Forget that—no time. I'll just look over the homework problems and the old exams and hope it's enough.

Now let's step across the hall to the faculty lounge and hear what some of those students' instructors have to say.

Professor Harwood: All these students can do is memorize—give them a problem that makes them think a little and they're helpless.

Professor Buffo: I don't know how most of them got to be sophomores. After my last exam some of them went to the department head to complain that I was testing them on things I never taught, even though the chapter we just covered had everything they needed to know.

Professor Harwood: I don't know how they even got out of high school—most of them couldn't write a coherent shopping list, let alone a project report or even an abstract.

Professor Kreplach: It's this whole spoiled generation—they want the grades but don't want to work for them!

Things are clearly not going quite the way either group would like. Many STEM instructors give assignments and tests that require skills they believe they have taught—high-level problem-solving skills, critical or creative thinking, or any of the professional skills discussed in the preceding interlude—and then get frustrated when the students fail. The students come to believe that their primary responsibility is not so much to learn as to guess what their instructors want them to know. When they guess wrong and their test grades show it, they resent the instructors for being unreasonably demanding or unclear in their expectations, and the instructors conclude that the students must be unmotivated, lazy, or ignorant, and clearly unqualified for their intended professions. The instructors are generally wrong: the correlation between grades in college and professional success is close to zero (Cohen, 1984; Donhardt, 2004; Stice, 1979).

Making education a guessing game has never been shown to promote knowledge acquisition or skill development. Common sense says and many references (e.g., Ambrose et al., 2010; Felder & Brent, 2005; Weimer, 2013) affirm that the clearer instructors are about their expectations, the more likely their students will be to meet those expectations. This chapter introduces a powerful way to communicate your expectations to your students. It involves writing *learning objectives*—explicit statements of the types of tasks the students should be able to complete if they learn what you intend to teach them. If you write learning objectives and use them appropriately, your course will be in *constructive alignment* (Biggs, 1999) with lessons, class activities, assignments, and tests all pointing toward the same knowledge and skills. You will also get few complaints about the tests being unfair, even from students who did poorly. Most important, many more students who are capable of succeeding as STEM professionals will be able to complete the tasks specified in the objectives, especially the kinds of tasks described in the interlude that require high-level problem-solving and professional skills.

This chapter addresses these questions:

○ What are learning objectives? Why should I write them?
○ How should I write objectives to make them as useful as possible?
○ Should I share my learning objectives with the students? If I share them, what's the most effective way to do it?
○ What is *Bloom's Taxonomy of Educational Objectives?* How can a working knowledge of the taxonomy help me improve the level of learning in my class?
○ What are *program learning outcomes* and what is *outcomes-based education?* How can I write course learning objectives to address specified outcomes, such as those required for program accreditation?

2.1 Writing and Using Course Learning Objectives

Learning objectives are explicit statements of what students should be able to do (define, explain, calculate, derive, model, critique, design, etc.) if they have learned what their instructor has attempted to teach them (Felder & Brent, 1997, 2003; Gronlund, 2008; Mager, 1997). Objectives usually begin with a phrase such as "By the end of [this lecture, this month, Chapter 6, the course], students should be able to ..." or "To do well on the next exam, you should be able to ..." followed by the statement of a task. Examples are given in Table 2.1–1.

All instructors write learning objectives. If you have ever taught a course, you wrote them, even if you never heard of them. You just didn't call them *learning objectives*; you called them *exams.* When instructors make up exams is often the first time they start thinking seriously about exactly what they want their students to be able to do that demonstrates whether and how well they learned the course content. That's too late. Failure to create objectives well ahead of assessments leads to the disturbing situation in which instructors put problems on tests without

Table 2.1–1. Illustrative Learning Objectives

To do well on the next midterm exam, you should be able to:

o label the [engine parts, types of rocks, emission spectra, clouds] in a series of photos.
o perform one-tailed and two-tailed hypothesis tests on sample means and variances.
o integrate algebraic and trigonometric functions and perform integration by parts.
o outline how adenosine and dopamine contribute to caffeine dependence or addiction.
o define [moment of inertia, vapor pressure, photosynthesis, geologic time] in terms that a nonscientist could understand.
o interpret a magnetic resonance image.
o critique an op-ed column that deals with the subject of this course.
o predict the output of an Excel/VBA spreadsheet from known values, formulas, and subroutines in selected cells.
o describe how stem cell research might result in therapies for a specified disease.

first adequately teaching the students to how solve such problems. For complex material, a lecture or reading and an example or two are generally not enough for the required techniques to sink in. It takes extensive practice and feedback.

In the introduction, we observed that well-written learning objectives enable instructors to achieve *constructive alignment* in a course. Here's how it works:

o Review the knowledge you want your students to acquire and the skills you want them to improve in the course. Write detailed learning objectives that address the targeted knowledge and skills.
o Design lectures, in-class activities, and assignments that illustrate and provide practice in all of the targeted skills, and create assignments and exams that test students' mastery of the tasks specified in the learning objectives.
o Share the objectives with the students, ideally as study guides for exams and other course assessments. Continue to refer to them in your lessons and assignments.

○ When the assessments show that many students are failing to meet an objective, consider modifying the corresponding lessons, activities, and assignments to provide more practice and feedback in the task(s) specified in that objective.

This process is iterative, usually taking several offerings of the course to arrive at satisfactory objectives, lessons, and assessments. It should be carried out again whenever the course content is modified.

2.1.1 Scopes of learning objectives

Learning objectives may have any of three scopes. Examples of each one are given in the following paragraphs for a course on differential equations or applied mathematics.

Course-level objectives.

At one extreme, objectives can be very broad and cover in a few statements the knowledge and skills the course is designed to help the students develop. Example: *Students completing this course will be able to model physical systems with equations involving derivatives and integrals, solve those equations, and apply the solutions to describe or predict system behavior.* Well-written course-level objectives in a syllabus indicate what the course is about far better than the usual bulleted list of topics can do, and they can also help establish the relevance of the course to students' goals and interests.

Individual lesson objectives.

At the other extreme, objectives may describe what students should be able to do after a single class session. A set of one to three lesson objectives written on the board at the beginning of a class can help students anticipate what's coming, keep them focused during the class, and provide a convenient reference point for a concluding summary of the lesson. Example: *By the end of class today, you should be able to solve separable first-order differential equations.*

Section-level objectives.

Objectives may also list student capabilities after a specified section of the course has been covered, as in "Students who have finished Chapter 4 of the text should be able to ..." or "To do well on the next exam, you should be able to ...." Example: *To do well on the next exam, you should be able to model a physical system with a first-order ordinary differential equation, solve the equation, and apply the solution to describe or predict the system behavior.* Section-level objectives can play a powerful role in determining the quality of a course and the learning it produces.

2.1.2 Two keys to effective objectives: Clarity and observability

For learning objectives to be effective, the actions they specify must be *clear* to the students and *observable* by the instructor. For an objective to be considered clear, students should be able to read it and say with confidence, "Yes, I know what that means and I can do it" or "No, I can't do that—and I'd better learn how before the exam." (It should not be so specific, however, that the students know exactly what you're going to ask.) One of the main purposes of writing learning objectives is to communicate your expectations to the students. That purpose is defeated if the students can't determine whether or not they can accomplish the specified tasks.

An objective is observable if instructors can either watch the students doing the task or see the results of their having done it. If you're not sure about the observability of a particular task, ask yourself whether you would ever include it in an assignment or exam. If the answer is no, the task is probably not observable and the objective is flawed. As a clarifying exercise, glance over the objectives in Table 2.1–1 and convince yourself that they would all (probably) be clear to students who have completed the relevant sections of the course and (definitely) be observable to the instructor.

The requirement of observability rules out the use of such words in objectives as *know, learn, understand,* and *appreciate.* (We refer to those verbs as the *forbidden four.*) Knowing, learning, understanding, and appreciating are unquestionably vital goals for any instructor, but they are not suitable terms to put in learning objectives. You cannot directly observe students understanding a concept, for example, and it would make no sense for you to ask them to understand something on an assignment or test. For you to know whether or not they understand, they must do something observable, such as explaining or deriving or critiquing something or solving a problem, that *demonstrates* their understanding or lack of it. The things you might ask them to do would be your learning objectives for that particular concept.

The following examples show unacceptable, weak, and good learning objectives that address the general goals specified in the unacceptable versions.

Examples of Unacceptable, Weak, and Good Learning Objectives

Example 1. By the end of the first set of experiments in this lab course, you (or "the students") will ...

Unacceptable: learn how to design and conduct experiments (*unobservable*).

Weak: be able to *design* an experiment and *analyze* the results (*probably too vague*).

Good: be able to
(a) *design* and *carry out* an experiment to measure a dependent variable as a function of one or two independent variables and perform an error analysis of the data.
(b) *explain* in terms a bright high school senior could understand the meaning of the experimental results.

Example 2. By the end of this course, you (or "the students") will ...

Unacceptable: understand the requirements of multidisciplinary teamwork (*unobservable*).

Weak: be able to *function* effectively on a multidisciplinary project team (*vague—could mean many different things*).

Good: be able to
(a) *function* effectively as a team member on a multidisciplinary project team, with effectiveness being determined by instructor observations, peer ratings, and self-assessment.
(b) *explain* the roles of the different disciplines in the project and *judge* their relative importance.

2.1.3 Using objectives as study guides

Here is a one-question quiz. Of all the questions students commonly ask, which one do instructors dislike most? Think about it—we'll give you five seconds.

If you answered "Are we responsible for ____ on the exam?" you get an A. Many faculty members become indignant at the very thought of that question. "They should be able to figure out what's important for themselves," they fume. "Nobody ever told me what I was responsible for on my tests. Today's students are ..." and you can fill in the rest yourself.

It's not quite that simple, however. Instructors often assign hundreds of pages of readings, give examples in class, and assign homework problems ustrate some—but not nearly all—of the material in the readings, ...en put problems on a test with solution methods that may have been illustrated only once on an assignment or not at all. Students who guess that such problems might show up will do well, and other less lucky students with an equal mastery of the course material who guess wrong might fail.

That's a terrible way to assess students' learning. A better way that we strongly recommend is to write comprehensive section-level objectives and share them with your students in the form of study guides at least a week before each exam. Students are likely to pay attention to study guides, which cannot be said for any other form in which objectives might be given to them. The next brainwave suggests why learning objectives in general and study guides in particular have a great potential to improve learning.

Brainwave: Practice Improves Skills; Focused Practice Improves Targeted Skills.

In the brainwave in Section 1.1, we saw that when an item of knowledge or a method is first "learned," the information is stored in long-term memory as a linked network of nerve cells. The more the information is rehearsed (consciously repeated), the stronger the network becomes, the less effort is required to subsequently recall the knowledge or implement the method, and the more knowledgeable or skillful the learner can be said to be in whatever was learned.

Students learn more and retain their knowledge longer when they engage in *deliberate practice* focused on clear and specific goals than when their study is more diffuse (Ericsson et al., 1993). Think of a tennis player trying to improve her game. She has a great serve and a strong forehand, but her backhand is weak and uncontrolled. She practices three hours a week. She will improve her game more by concentrating her practice on her backhand than by practicing all of her strokes equally. Similarly, a pianist struggling to master a difficult sonata will profit more by rehearsing the hardest passages repeatedly than by practicing the entire piece again and again.

By the same reasoning, students should concentrate hardest on studying the concepts and practicing the methods that are most challenging to them. Explicit learning objectives help them achieve that concentration, increasing their chances of mastering all the knowledge and skills that their instructors are attempting to help them develop.

Relative to athletes and musicians, STEM students are at a disadvantage. The tennis player knows that if she doesn't improve that backhand, she won't go very far in high-level competition, and the pianist knows exactly which passages need most of his attention. STEM students don't have that knowledge. They are usually not given clear statements of which parts of the vast body of knowledge in the text and lectures they are likely to be tested on, and they don't find out where their major weaknesses are until the test is over, which is too late. A comprehensive list of objectives on a study guide can help your students make sound decisions about how best to focus their attention—and you will then get a much better idea of how well they have learned what you want them to know.

Rich believes that of all the teaching techniques he experimented with over the course of his career, giving students study guides had the clearest positive impact on his students' learning. Here's his story:

> I was teaching the introductory chemical engineering course on chemical process principles shortly after I learned about learning objectives and decided to try something before a scheduled midterm exam. This particular exam covered some difficult material, and the average grade on it had always been low. I wrote learning objectives and put them in a study guide ("To do well on this exam, you should be able to...."), deliberately including some high-level conceptual questions and particularly challenging types of problems in addition to the usual exam content. When I made up the exam, I drew from the guide and deliberately included more high-level material than I had ever included before, and yet the class average was ten points higher that it had ever been. Students who lacked the basic ability for the course or who hadn't done the homework or studied for the exam still failed, but the others learned the material better than their counterparts in earlier semesters ever did. I've routinely done the same thing in every course I've taught since then, and the improvements have steadily increased—presumably because I've gotten better at writing objectives and addressing them in my teaching.

Study guides for a first-year statistics course and a third-year chemistry course are shown in Tables 2.1–2 and 2.1–3. Note that the guides are not lists of questions that will be on the exam but rather a comprehensive list of *types* of questions that *might* be on the exam. Some students don't take study guides seriously before the first midterm, but once they see that every question on the exam could have been anticipated from the study guide, all serious students pay close attention to the guides for the rest of the course.

Thought Question

Sometimes instructors resist the idea of giving students study guides for exams, fearing that they will be making things too easy for the students and lowering standards of teaching quality. How could you give study guides without lowering standards and perhaps even raising them?

Table 2.1–2. Illustrative Study Guide 1

MAT 245 Statistics I

STUDY GUIDE FOR TEST 1

This will be a closed book test. You should bring a calculator; an inexpensive one that does arithmetic is sufficient. Laptops will not be needed or permitted.

For Section 2.1, you should know how to do the following:

- Identify the *explanatory* and *response* variables in a study.
- Draw a scatterplot for two quantitative variables.
- Interpret a scatterplot by describing the form (linearity), direction, and strength of the relationship between two quantitative variables, and by identifying any outliers.

For Section 2.2, you should know how to do the following:

- Estimate the value of the correlation r from a scatterplot.
- Describe the strength and direction of a linear relationship between two quantitative variables based on the value of the correlation r.
- Explain the properties of r listed on Pages 103–104 of the text.
- Describe how you would use Fathom to compute r for a set of data.

For Section 2.3, you should know how to do the following:

- Draw a graph of a straight line when you are given its equation.
- Describe the quantity that is minimized by the least-squares regression line.
- Calculate the slope and intercept of the least-squares line from the means and standard deviations of x and y and the correlation r.

Table 2.1–2. (*Continued*)

- Use the equation of the least-squares line to predict y for a given value of x.
- Interpret the slope and intercept of the least-squares line in the context of a particular dataset.
- Interpret the value of r^2 in the context of a particular dataset.
- Explain the dangers of extrapolation.
- Describe how you would use Fathom to compute the equation of a least-squares line and draw it on a scatterplot. Given Fathom output for those operations, interpret it.

For Section 2.4, you should know how to do the following:

- Compute the residual for a particular observation.
- Predict the effect of outliers and influential observations on the least-squares line.
- Explain why association does not imply causation.

For Section 2.5, you should know how to do the following:

- Summarize data on two categorical variables using a two-way table.
- Use the marginal totals (or percentages) to describe the distribution of each variable separately.
- Use appropriate conditional distributions (row or column percentages) to describe the relationship between two variables.

For Section 2.6, you should know how to do the following:

- Explain what it means for variables to be confounded.
- Explain how an observed association between two variables can be a common response to a third variable.
- Explain how an observed association between two variables can involve confounding with other lurking variables.

Source: Reprinted with permission of Dr. E. Jacquelin Dietz, professor emerita of mathematics and computer science, Meredith College, Raleigh, NC.

Illustrative Study Guide 2

CH 312: Physical Chemistry I

UDY GUIDE FOR SECOND MIDTERM EXAM

The test will cover through Section 6.3 in the text. To do well on it, you should be able to do the following:

1. Define an ideal gas. Given any three of the variables P, V, T, and n for an ideal gas, calculate the fourth one.
2. Given the temperature and pressure of a gas, determine whether the ideal gas law is a good approximation.
3. Sketch a phase diagram (P vs. T) for a single species and label the regions (solid, liquid, vapor, gas). Use the diagram to define the vapor pressure, the boiling point and normal boiling point, melting and sublimation point temperatures, and critical temperature and pressure. Explain how P and T vary with time (increase, decrease, or remain constant) as the specified path on the diagram is followed.
4. Explain the following statement from a weather report in terms a first-year student could understand: "The temperature is 75°F, barometric pressure is 29.87 inches of mercury, the relative humidity is 50%, and the dew point is 54°F."
5. Given an equilibrium gas-liquid system with a single condensable component (A) and liquid A present, a correlation for the vapor pressure of A as a function of temperature, and any two of the variables y_A (mole fraction of A(v) in the gas phase), temperature, and total pressure, calculate the third variable using Raoult's law.
6. Given a mixture of a single condensable vapor, A, and one or more noncondensable gases, a correlation for the vapor pressure of A as a function of temperature, and any two of the variables y_A (mole fraction of A in the gas phase), temperature, total pressure, dew point, degrees of superheat, and relative, absolute, and percentage saturation (or humidity), use Raoult's law to calculate the remaining variables.
7. Suppose you ran an experiment to measure the variables calculated in Step 6 and the values were significantly different from the calculated ones. Identify up to ten possible reasons for the discrepancies, including assumptions made in the calculations.
8. Given the description of a familiar physical phenomenon involving more than one phase (such as mist forming at the surface of a pond), explain it in terms of concepts discussed in this course. Given an explanation of such a phenomenon, evaluate its scientific soundness.

2.1.4 Why write objectives?

Section-level learning objectives serve several functions besides making excellent study guides for exams and helping instructors bring their courses into constructive alignment. A good set of objectives helps you achieve the following two important goals:

Evaluate the importance of course material and identify candidates for either reduction in coverage or elimination from the course.

As you look through your course content attempting to determine what students might be expected to do with it (i.e., as you write learning objectives), you will find some material that stumps you, forcing you to ask "Why am I teaching this?" The material may have been important once but is now obsolete, or perhaps it's one of those "nice-to-know" topics you enjoy teaching as opposed to the "need-to-know" topics that are fundamental to the course. Consider dropping course material for which you can't write good learning objectives, which will give you more time to help students develop the skills you consider most important.

Communicate the course content to others who might benefit greatly from the knowledge.

Catalogs and syllabi offer generalities about topics and skills taught in a course, whereas learning objectives spell out the breadth and depth of coverage of each topic. Comprehensive sets of objectives can be invaluable to instructors about to teach the course for the first time, and they also tell instructors of subsequent courses what knowledge and skills their students should have acquired in prerequisite courses. If objectives are assembled for every core course in a curriculum, a departmental review committee can easily identify unwanted duplication and gaps in coverage and take remedial steps.

2.1.5 Objections and responses

Learning objectives come in for a fair amount of criticism from time to time. Following are two commonly raised objections and responses to them:

Giving students learning objectives and study guides is spoon-feeding them.

Students really appreciate study guides, which is nice but it's not why we provide the guides. Our job is to prepare the students to be professionals. Professional scientists, mathematicians, statisticians, and engineers of every description are given specific assignments—problems to solve or processes or products or programs to design or optimize or troubleshoot.

Once they know what they are expected to do,, they go out and learn whatever they need to do it, getting help if necessary. Giving students study guides simulates that process by spelling out what students have to prepare themselves to do. It doesn't make things easier for the students unless the objectives are not challenging enough.

But figuring out what you need to learn is an important skill, and I want my students to have it.

Of course it's important, but STEM professionals figure it out once they know what their assignment is, which is different from guessing what they might need to know and preparing for it just in case. When you give your students learning objectives, they've still got to figure out how to meet the objectives and then make sure they have the necessary facts and procedures and the required thinking and problem-solving skills to do it.

Again, a study guide is not just a list of questions you might ask on the test but a comprehensive list of *types* of problems you might ask, including some problems that require high-level analysis, critical thinking, and creative thinking. Students who are incapable of working at those high levels or who don't do the required studying won't be able to solve those problems, even if they have the study guide. If students can answer any test question you ask based on one of those objectives, they have obviously mastered the objective; if they can't answer a question, they have not mastered the objective. In both cases, they deserve the grade they earn.

2.2 Bloom's Taxonomy of Educational Objectives

As Tables 2.1–2 and 2.1–3 illustrate, different learning objectives place dramatically different intellectual demands on students. Some call for memorization, others for routine application of principles and methods introduced and illustrated in the course, and still others for high-level problem solving. Beginning in the 1950s, a team of educational researchers led by Benjamin Bloom of the University of Chicago sorted objectives into three domains—*cognitive* (intellectual outcomes including acquisition of knowledge, conceptual understanding, and thinking and problem-solving skills) (Bloom & Krathwohl, 1956); *affective* (emotional outcomes including development of interests, attitudes, and values) (Krathwohl et al., 1984); and *psychomotor* (motor skill outcomes including carrying out laboratory and clinical procedures) (Simpson, 1972). For each domain, a hierarchical set of levels was defined.

Most teaching and assessment in technical courses involves objectives primarily in Bloom's cognitive domain. Exceptions include courses that

explicitly seek to develop students' values (such as courses that te
ethical reasoning), which would bring in affective considerations, and
courses that teach students to operate equipment or perform laboratory
or clinical procedures, which would involve psychomotor skills. We will
only consider the cognitive domain in the remainder of this chapter.
(*Note*: Another excellent system for classifying objectives and values that
encompasses cognitive and affective categories is Dee Fink's *Taxonomy
of Significant Learning* [2003].)

In 2001, the levels of Bloom's cognitive domain were reorganized and
renamed (Anderson & Krathwohl, 2001), with the results shown in
Figure 2.2–1. The level labels are enclosed in boxes, and next to them
are brief explanations and action verbs that might precede objectives at
each level.

The bottom three levels of the cognitive domain (remembering,
understanding, and applying) are often referred to as the *lower-level*
(or *lower-order*) *thinking skills*, and the top three levels (analyzing,
evaluating, and creating) are the *higher-level (higher-order) thinking
skills*. Most activities generally classified as *critical thinking* fall into
Level 5. Objectives at all six levels are illustrated in Table 2.2–1.

Notice that the action verb at the beginning of a learning objective is
not a sure indicator of the level of the objective. For example, *explain* is

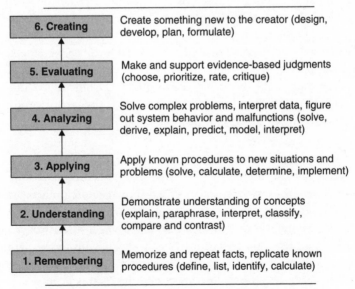

**Figure 2.2–1: Bloom's Taxonomy of Educational
Objectives—Cognitive Domain**

nple Learning Objectives at Different Bloom Levels

ng: *List* [the first ten alkanes]; *state* [formulas for
of simple algebraic and trigonometric functions]; *identify*
)al organs in a cutaway view of a frog].

ling: *Explain* [the function of a comparator in Java
in terms a nonprogrammer could understand]; *compare and
contrast* [bacterial and viral infections], *interpret* [the output
from a SIMULINK simulation]; *outline* [the four stages of team
functioning].

3. **Applying:** *Calculate* [the probability that two sample means will
differ by more than 5 percent]; *draw and label* [a free-body
diagram for a cantilever supporting a distributed weight]; *solve*
[a second-order ordinary differential equation with specified initial
conditions].

4. **Analyzing:** *Explain* [why we feel warm in 70°F air and cold in 70°F
water]; *predict* [the response of an organism to a specified change
in environmental conditions]; *carry out* [a proof by mathematical
induction of a specified result]; *model* [the dynamic response of a
first-order system under PID control].

5. **Evaluating:** *Specify* [which of several given C++ codes is better for
achieving a specified objective, and explain your reasoning]; *select*
[from among available options for expanding production capacity
and justify your choice]; *critique* [an oral project presentation using
criteria presented in class].

6. **Creating:** *Formulate* [a procedure for synthesizing a benzene derivative with specified side groups]; *brainstorm* [possible reasons why a
tissue-engineered skin replacement might not function as designed
when scaled up]; *design* [an experiment or process or product or
code that meets given specifications].

given in Table 2.2–1 as a possible key word for Level 2 (understanding)
and Level 4 (analyzing). "Explain in your own words the concept of electrical conductivity" is Level 2, while "Explain why a treatment protocol
for a metabolic disease works using the concepts of converging metabolic
pathways and enzyme inhibition" is probably Level 4—unless the explanation can easily be given by paraphrasing the textbook, in which case
it's Level 2. Most of the key words given in the table could also be used
to begin objectives at several levels.

The following exercise will give you some practice in classifying objectives using Bloom's Taxonomy. Before you try it, note that sometimes only the instructor who formulated an objective can say for sure whether it falls into, say, Level 3 (straightforward application of a routine method to a new problem) or Level 4 (going beyond procedures that are straightforward to the students in the course). We will just ask you to speculate based on what the objective seems to call for the student to do and then compare your speculations with ours (given at the bottom of the exercise). If your speculation disagrees with ours, it doesn't mean that yours is wrong—just try to think of what we might have had in mind when we chose our response.

Exercise

Speculate on the Bloom levels of each of the following objectives:

1. Explain and distinguish between meiosis and mitosis using terms that your grandparents (who have no scientific training) could understand.
2. Design an egg container that could be dropped from a height of three meters onto a concrete surface without breaking the egg.
3. State the numerical value of a specified color in the resistor color code.
4. Grade a sample lab report using the grading criteria discussed in class and explain your reasoning.
5. Given a null and alternative hypothesis for a problem involving means or standard deviations, select the statistical test you would use and explain your reasoning.
6. Evaluate the indefinite integral of a function of a single variable. (This one could be any of three levels, depending on the function.)
7. Given a case history of a patient, state the physiologic, pathophysiologic, and pharmacologic factors that could modify a drug response in that patient.
8. Calculate the voltage drop V(volts) across a resistance R(ohms) through which a current I(amps) flows.

Authors' responses: 1—understanding; 2—creating; 3—remembering; 4—evaluating; 5—evaluating; 6—remembering, applying, or analyzing, depending on the complexity of the function; 7—analyzing; 8—remembering (substituting variable values into a simple formula).

Previously in this chapter we recommended making your learning objectives clear and observable and giving them to the students in the form of study guides for tests. Here are three more suggestions. First, identify the Bloom levels of all the objectives you write. Then do the following:

If some course material is purely at Level 1 (remembering), put it on a handout, include it on the study guide, and minimize the time you spend on it in lectures.

We are not discounting the importance of memorization. All fields have a core body of definitions, methods, and concepts that practitioners simply must know to be able to function effectively. In some disciplines, such as health and other biological sciences, that core is vast. By all means, keep it in the course and include it in quizzes and exams, but don't spend valuable class time on it. The time you save will be much better spent on higher-level material for which your guidance is needed.

If you haven't already done so, include some Level 2 items (explain in your own words) that address concepts students may be able to apply without understanding them.

Examples of such concepts are derivative, weight, metabolism, statistical significance, and—in several different subjects—induction.

Make sure there are at least a few higher-level objectives on your list (analyzing, evaluating, and creating). Provide plenty of practice and feedback on tasks specified in those objectives, in class, and on assignments, and make sure you include similar tasks in your tests and other assessments.

If you teach but never test high-level skills, many capable students won't bother doing the work necessary to acquire and improve the skills. If you test at high levels but don't provide adequate practice and feedback at those levels in and out of class, many students capable of functioning at those levels will fail to develop the required skills.

2.3 Addressing Course Prerequisites and Program Outcomes

Let's say you've done everything we've recommended in this chapter so far. You've written clear and observable learning objectives that address all the knowledge and skills you want your students to acquire and shared them with the students as study guides. You've designed your lessons, activities, and assignments to provide practice and feedback on the skills, and you've tested the students on the content of the objectives. On average, your students have done significantly better than they ever did when you taught the course without writing and using objectives (at least that's what we're betting will happen). You're done, right?

Sadly, no—there are two other important issues we haven't considered yet. We don't teach in a vacuum: our courses belong to curricula—sets of courses that students must take to get a degree, most of which have other courses as prerequisites. Instructors of courses for which yours is a prerequisite will presume that their students have acquired certain knowledge and developed certain skills in your course. You have a responsibility to those colleagues to teach that knowledge and those skills, and so they should be included in your learning objectives.

Moreover, you may teach in a program that subscribes to *outcomes-based education (OBE)*. In OBE, the faculty of a program reaches consensus on a set of *program learning outcomes*—knowledge, skills, and attitudes that the students are supposed to acquire by the time they graduate. If your course is supposed to address one or more learning outcomes, you have to take them into account when creating your learning objectives. The objectives in turn should guide the design of your course instruction and assessment, as depicted in Figure 2.3–1.

OBE is dynamic, with outcomes, objectives, instruction, and assessment informing one another and continually being adjusted in an effort to improve learning. Outcomes-based education is becoming increasingly common throughout Europe (Cedefop, 2009; European Higher Education Area, 2014) and in engineering curricula in the United States (Accreditation Board for Engineering and Technology [ABET], n.d.; Felder & Brent, 2003) and other countries that are signatories of the *Washington Accord* (International Engineering Alliance, n.d.). A problem faced by most STEM programs involved in OBE is that the outcomes they have decided to adopt (or they have been required to adopt by their accrediting agencies) include knowledge, skills, and values they have never systematically addressed in their curricula.

For example, ABET (the organization that accredits engineering programs in the United States) specifies certain outcomes that must

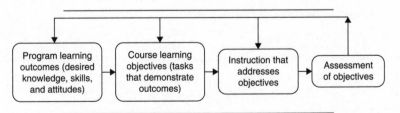

Figure 2.3–1: Course Design in Outcomes-Based Education

be adopted by all programs seeking accreditation. Some of these outcomes can be addressed without making any changes in the traditional engineering curriculum (e.g., the abilities to solve engineering problems by applying principles of engineering, science, and mathematics, and to design systems that meet specified needs). Other outcomes involve knowledge and skills that most of the faculty members were never trained in, including experimental design, teamwork, problem identification and formulation, professional ethics, and self-directed learning. If and when you find yourself teaching in an outcomes-based program with such outcomes, you could not be blamed for asking, "How am I supposed to write learning objectives for skills I'm not sure I have myself, and then how do I teach my students to develop those skills?"

Fortunately, others have faced that problem, worked out solutions, and wrote about them. Felder and Brent (2003), Shuman et al. (2005), and Svinicki (2010) suggest learning objectives and teaching and assessment methods that address the ABET outcomes. The methods were developed in the context of engineering education but should be applicable to all STEM disciplines. Some of them are outlined in Chapters 10 and 11 of this book.

2.4 Ideas to Take Away

○ *Learning objectives* are explicit statements of observable actions students should be able to complete if they have acquired the knowledge and skills their instructor has attempted to teach them. They may be applicable to an entire course, a section of a course (such as the period between midterm examinations), or an individual class session.

○ Sharing section-level objectives with students as study guides for exams increases the likelihood that the students will learn to meet the objectives.

○ Some learning objectives in courses should fall into one or more of Levels 4 (analyzing), 5 (evaluating), and 6 (creating) of Bloom's Taxonomy. The more practice the students get in high-level thinking and problem-solving skills, the greater their expertise in those skills will be by the time they graduate.

○ Course instructors should not waste valuable class time on material entirely at Level 1 of Bloom's Taxonomy (remembering, memorization of facts), which students are perfectly capable of learning on their own. If the material is not essential for the students to know, consideration should be given to dropping it from the course. If it is important, the students should be given a list of what they need to memorize for the test, and class time should be devoted to higher-level material that requires explanations, examples, and opportunities for practice for most students to understand it.

2.5 Try This in Your Course

In the course you are teaching now or the next one you teach, identify a body of material that students always find difficult. Then do the following:

o Write a comprehensive list of learning objectives that includes every type of question you might conceivably ask on an exam covering the material, and put the list in the form of a study guide for that exam (see Figures 2.1–2 and 2.1–3 for illustrations).
o Give the study guide to the students or post it online one to two weeks before the exam is to be given, and tell students that all of the questions on the exam will be based on objectives in the study guide.
o Prepare the exam, drawing on the study guide for each question, and give and grade it.

If the students perform better on average than you have ever seen them perform on a test on the same material, consider making this strategy part of your regular teaching practice.

INTERLUDE. GOOD COP/BAD COP:
EMBRACING CONTRARIES IN TEACHING

I've come to suspect that whenever any ability is difficult to learn and rarely performed well, it's probably because contraries are called for—patting the head and rubbing the belly. Thus, good writing is hard because it means trying to be creative and critical; good teaching is hard because it means trying to be ally and adversary of students; good evaluation is hard because it means trying to be subjective and objective; good intelligence is rare because it means trying to be intuitive and logical. (Elbow, 1986, p. 234)

So says Peter Elbow (1986) in *Embracing Contraries*. The theme of this excellent book should resonate with most faculty members, who commonly feel pulled in opposite directions. We're compelled to spend most of our time on the professional activities (teaching and research) that count toward tenure, promotions, and raises, but we also know we should carve out more time for our health and relationships. If we are researchers, we want to let our graduate students do some floundering and learning by experience, but we also need to produce results quickly for our funding agencies, which requires giving detailed direction. In those and many other respects it feels as though we have to be particles and waves simultaneously and we don't know how: we can either be excellent particles and mediocre waves or vice versa, but not both.

Teaching involves a particularly challenging contrary, which Elbow is eloquent about:

The two conflicting mentalities needed for good teaching stem from the two conflicting obligations inherent in the job: we have an obligation to students but we also have an obligation to knowledge and society. Our loyalty to students asks us to be their allies and hosts as we instruct and share: to invite all students to enter in and join us as members of a learning community. We [also] have a responsibility to society—that is, to our discipline, our college or university, and to other learning communities of which we are members—to see that the students we certify really understand or can do what we teach, to see that the grades and credits and degrees we give really have the meaning or currency they are supposed to have. (Elbow, 1986, pp. 142–143)

Elsewhere in his book, Elbow labels those two roles *coach* and *gatekeeper,* and he observes that both roles are essential but we can't play them simultaneously. His solution is to alternate between them. Switching between student advocate and guardian of standards—good cop and bad cop—lets us serve comfortably in both capacities. It's easier to set high standards if you know you're going to be helping the students attain them, and it's easier to enforce the standards once you've made them clear and have given the students every opportunity to meet them.

How can you perform this juggling act? Start a course as gatekeeper by spelling out rigorous requirements and grading criteria and then put on your coaching hat and announce, "Those are the specific criteria I will use in grading; that's what you are up against... but now we have most of the semester for me to help you attain those standards. They are high standards but I suspect all of you can attain them if you work hard. I will function as your ally" (Elbow, 1986, p. 155).

In Chapter 2, we recommended writing learning objectives and setting the bar high for what you want your students to achieve (gatekeeper) and then sharing the objectives with the students as study guides for your exams (coach). In Chapter 3 we'll discuss how to formulate course policies and procedures and a rigorous but fair grading system (gatekeeper), and also how to find out about your students' prior knowledge and experience, goals, and interests, and use that knowledge to motivate them to do their best in your class (coach). You'll continue to see those contrasting themes played out throughout the rest of the book. We'll look at gatekeeper topics such as designing and grading tests, and coaching topics such as getting students actively engaged and equipping them with the skills they will need to do well on the tests. Besides outlining how to carry out those tasks, we'll offer ideas on how to do them efficiently, fulfilling the gatekeeper and coach roles and still managing to have a life. It's theoretically possible.

3

PLANNING COURSES

3.0 Introduction

Think of a two-word phrase for a huge time sink that can effectively keep faculty members from doing all the other things they need and want to do. Go ahead—we'll wait.

You can probably come up with several possibilities, such as *proposal deadline, curriculum revision, safety inspection, accreditation visit*, and *reserved parking*. (The last one is posted at the only open space you find on campus minutes before you're supposed to teach a class, with small print that says "Reserved for the Deputy Associate Vice Provost for Dry Erase Marker Procurement.") But the phrase we have in mind is *new prep*—preparing for and teaching a course you've never taught before or undertaking a nearly complete revision of an existing course. Anyone who has not done it cannot possibly imagine how much time and effort it takes to create a syllabus and class session plans and handouts and slides and assignments and projects and tests. You can spend every waking hour for months on it, neglecting your research and your personal life, and the course might still be ineffective and your student ratings low!

When you find yourself struggling with a course that's new to you, try not to give yourself a hard time about it or to question your fitness for the profession, but recognize that instructors are always stressed by new preps. We'll give you some strategies in this chapter that may not eliminate the stress but should help make it manageable. Use those that look reasonable to you, try to avoid the mistakes we will warn you about, learn from the experience, and look forward to the significantly easier time you'll have when you teach the course again.

This chapter will focus on questions to address before you begin a new or redesigned course and in the first week or two of classes.

o Why and how should I base my course design on my learning objectives?
o What is a reasonable time to devote to preparing a course? How can I approach that target?
o How do I choose a text? Formulate course management and grading policies? Write a syllabus?
o What can I do in the first week to help ensure that my course will be effective?

Finding good answers to these questions can go a long way toward establishing yourself in the gatekeeper and coach roles in your course (see preceding interlude).

Let's begin with how *not* to approach a new preparation or major redesign of a course and go on from there.

3.1 Three Steps to Disaster, or, How Not to Approach Course Preparation

Here are two course preparation scenarios you either have faced already or will sooner or later face:

Scenario 1: You are getting ready to teach a course for the first time— either a brand-new course in your department or one that has been taught but never by you. If you're lucky, you have several months to prepare for it; if you're not, your department head "asks" you to teach it a week before the first day of class.

Scenario 2: You're scheduled to teach a core course you have taught before that desperately needs a major revision. The content and pedagogy go back for a decade or more and are sadly obsolete, or the grades have been abysmal and the students are threatening to revolt, or someone (the department head, a faculty committee, or you) has decided to offer the course online or to use blended learning (a combination of live and online instruction).

Here are the elements of a common but supremely ineffective three-pronged approach to either of those situations:

1. **Go it alone.** Colleagues in your department or friends at other schools may have taught the course and done it very well, but

you believe it would be an imposition to ask them if you can use some of their materials (syllabi, class session plans, online tutorials and screencasts, assignments, tests, etc.). Instead, set out to create everything yourself from scratch.

2. **Try to cover the entire subject in your lectures, and be prepared to answer any question any student might ever ask.** Assemble all the books and research articles you can find and make your class session plans a self-contained encyclopedia on the subject.

3. **Go for perfection.** Proofread and correct your session plans as many times as it takes to weed out every possible error and point of confusion, and make your PowerPoint slides models of clarity, style, and visual beauty.

Here's what's likely to happen if you adopt this plan. You'll spend an outlandish amount of time planning class sessions and making up assignments and tests. You'll start neglecting your personal life and (if you're at a research university) your research just to keep up with the course preparation, and if you're unfortunate enough to have two new preps at once, you may no longer have a personal life to neglect. Your class session plans will be so long and dense that to cover everything crammed into them you'll have to lecture at a pace few—if any—human brains can maintain. You'll have no time for interactivity in class, and you'll have to skim some important material or skip it altogether. The students' frustration and complaints will mount, and the final course evaluations will not bring you much joy.

There's a better way.

3.2 A Rational Approach to Course Preparation and Redesign

Preparing new courses and redesigning old ones will never be easy or fast, but there are several ways to keep those tasks under control.

Keep your learning objectives close at hand.

In Chapter 2 we tried to persuade you to write learning objectives that define the knowledge, skills, and (possibly) attitudes you want the students in your course to acquire. The message now is that as long as you went to the trouble of writing objectives, you should use them to guide the course design. Hold that thought for a moment—we'll get back to it.

Avoid content overload.

Robert Boice (2000) spent many years examining the career paths of new faculty members. He found that most of those he studied spent nine hours or more preparing for each hour of class they taught. That's roughly thirty hours of preparation a week per course, plus whatever time it took to write and grade assignments and tests and meet with students outside class. You can do the math for two or more courses! Despite all that preparation, the gloomy scenario sketched in the previous section generally played out: the courses were overloaded with content, the students were not actively engaged in class, and the end-of-course evaluations ranged from below average to terrible.

Boice also observed that instructors who limited their class preparation time dramatically improved their teaching effectiveness and—if they were also involved in research—their research productivity. Based on his observations, he proposed this guideline: *set as a target an average of two hours or less of preparation for each hour of class time.* If you are teaching a new course or redesigning an old one, you probably won't make that target very often and you may sometimes find yourself spending as much as three to four hours for each hour of class. When you teach a course for the second time and thereafter, however, you should have little trouble meeting the two-to-one guideline. In any case, if you find yourself regularly spending five or more hours of preparation per hour of class, things have gotten out of hand.

To minimize content overload, bring your learning objectives back into clear focus, look at each body of material you plan to cover, and decide which of two categories it fits into: *need-to-know* (directly addresses one or more of the objectives) or *nice-to-know* (only marginally related to the objectives). *Concentrate your preparation time on need-to-know content.*

Use existing course materials and readily available digital resources.

Consider asking colleagues who are good teachers and have taught the course you're preparing to teach if they would be willing to share course materials with you. Most good teachers will cheerfully agree to that request. You can further reduce preparation time by downloading online materials such as class session plans, handouts, photos, and links to videos, screencasts, simulations, case studies, and interactive tutorials. You can find such resources using general digital resource libraries (which in 2016 include Google and Bing Images, YouTube, Wikimedia Commons, Khan Academy, MERLOT, and the National Science Digital Library), or enter "[type of resource][topic]" into a search engine such as Google or Bing to find subject-specific resources. When possible, adapt the materials to your course by eliminating content that doesn't address your learning objectives and inserting new content that does. You may still be spending lots of time on course preparation but not nearly as much as you would if you create everything yourself from scratch.

Resources in digital repositories like those just listed are sometimes copyrighted. The obvious question is, can you download and include them in your class session plans without getting permission? The answer—at least in the United States—is a qualified yes. Under the *fair use doctrine* of US copyright law, reproduction of copyrighted material without permission is permitted for certain applications, including teaching (US Copyright Office, n.d.). For example, if a downloaded copyrighted photo will only show up on a slide you show in class, there should be no problem, and if it shows up in slides posted on a password-protected course website or in class handouts, it should still be acceptable. If you put it in something you publish or distribute widely outside of your class, the issue becomes murkier. A campus librarian can either help or point you to the right person on your campus to answer questions about copyright issues.

Curb your perfectionism.

You can easily spend two hours preparing a perfectly fine class session and then another six hours polishing it, rewriting and rearranging session plans, and tinkering endlessly with slides to make them look prettier. Don't! The first time you teach a course you should have one overriding goal: *survival*. "Good enough" is good enough. All of that extra polishing time will make relatively little difference in the quality of the course and would be much better spent working on that proposal or paper you keep putting off or taking an afternoon off to spend with your family or work out at the gym. During that first course offering, spend five to ten minutes in your office after every class session noting changes you'd like to make in the session content and presentation materials, and make the changes sometime before you teach the course again. If you approach course modification in this moderate way, in the long run your courses will be better, and so will your research productivity, career advancement, health, and well-being.

Try to minimize new course preparations.

If you are a new faculty member, there is one more step you can take to keep new course preparation from consuming all the time you have. Some department heads burden their newest faculty members with several new preps in their first one or two years. If you find yourself in this position, politely ask your head to consider letting you teach the same course several times before you move on to a new one. If you can do it truthfully, add that you're trying desperately to finish and submit one or two new research proposals that semester. It might not work, but as Rich's grandmother said when told that chicken soup doesn't cure cancer, it couldn't hurt.

Thought Question

Look through the class session plans of a course you teach. Can you identify a body of nice-to-know content that does not directly address your learning objectives and few students are ever likely to use, or content that would be easy for someone to look up if they needed it? If you can, how might you strengthen the course by either dropping or reducing that material?

Table 3.3–1. Questions for Evaluating a Text or Content Delivery System

o How well does the text (or system) match my course learning objectives? (From now on we will just say *text* but will mean *text or system*.) Does the order of topics match the order I want to use?

o What do published reviews of the text say?

o Has anyone I know used the text? If so, how do they feel about it?

o (Pick a couple of topics you don't already know very well and read the text on them.) Is everything clear? Would it be clear to my average students?

o Are all methods described in the text illustrated by clear worked-out examples?

o Are there lots of visuals—pictures, schematics, charts, plots—or is it all words and equations?

o Does the text contain an appropriate blend of theory and applications?

o Are there self-tests or chapter-end questions to help students with studying?

o Are the text problems mostly simple drills, mostly long and difficult brainteasers, or (ideally) a good blend of both?

o Are there enough problems for me to vary the assignments from term to term?

o What support materials are available to instructors and students? Instructor's manual? A bank of test questions? A set of slides? Screencasts or simulations or interactive tutorials? What is the quality of the support material?

o How much does the text cost? Are there alternatives just as good that are more economical?

3.3 Choosing a Course Text or Content Delivery System

Throughout most of the last century, instructors picking a text had to ask only one question: "Which of these competing books does the best job of presenting the content I plan to cover and gives me lots of good questions and problems to assign?" That question still needs to be asked, of course, but now there are others to ask. For example, "Should I use a traditional paper text or an e-book, or an online content delivery system with a paper-based supplement, or just assign readings or online lessons and not have a text at all? Should I choose an existing text, or custom-design a text that combines material from several resources, or have my notes bound into a paper or electronic course pack and use that as the text?"

Once you have answered those questions, we recommend that you ask the additional ones shown in Table 3.3–1 and take the answers into account when making your decision.

3.4 Formulating a Course Grading Policy

A critical course-related question—generally the most important question to students—is, how will course grades be determined? You should have a detailed answer ready before the semester begins. A grading system stitched together while the course is in progress inevitably leads to a flood of complaints from students unhappy with their grades—complaints to the instructor, his or her department head, and possibly higher-level administrators. Regardless of the outcome, the instructor won't enjoy the experience and neither will the administrators.

3.4.1 What should count toward the course grade, and by how much?

As a general rule, *there should be no surprises in course grades.* When you work out your grading policy in advance and put it in the course syllabus, and the students know what they earned on all of your assessments, they should be able to consult the syllabus and determine what their course grade will be. You may still get complaints, but your response can now be that you are just implementing the policy you announced in class on Day 1, which generally ends the discussion.

There are acceptable options for almost every grading policy decision you will have to make. Table 3.4–1 lists and offers suggestions regarding some of the decisions. Ultimately you must make your own decisions, though, taking into account your own philosophy about grades and the cultures of your university and department.

Table 3.4–1. Course Grading Policy Decisions

Question	Options
How much should midterm exam and short quiz grades count in lecture courses?	The sum of weightings assigned to midterm exam and quiz grades may vary from 25% to 75% or more, depending on what else counts toward the course grade (such as homework, projects, final exam, extra-credit assignments, improvement, and attendance).
Should the lowest midterm exam grade be dropped?	Consider counting the lowest midterm grade a fraction of each of the others—say, half—so that all students have an incentive to study for and take all of the tests. A good alternative is to replace the lowest midterm grade with the final exam grade if the latter grade is higher.
How much should the final exam count?	If the final is comprehensive (covering the entire course content), it may count toward the course grade by anywhere from 20% to 50%, possibly more. If it only covers material since the last midterm exam, it should count the same as each of the midterms. Allowing the final exam grade to substitute for the lowest midterm grade (see previous question) is a good approach to rewarding students who finish strong in the course.
How much should homework assignments count?	Most instructors view homework assignments as primarily formative (giving students practice and feedback on the knowledge and skills they will later be tested on) and secondarily summative (contributing toward the course grade). If that's your philosophy, count the assignments from 10% to 20%, rarely more (no matter how grumpy students are about it).

Table 3.4–1. (*Continued*)

Question	Options
Should the homework credit change if students work in teams?	If collaboration is allowed or required on homework, don't weight the homework grade too heavily—no more than, say, 15%. You might also require students to get a passing average grade on individual exams before counting the homework grade. This will keep students who fail the exams from passing the course on the strength of their team homework grades.
What about other performance measures?	If labs or projects are a part of the course, then they should count for an appropriate percentage of the final course grade. Find the ranges that your colleagues use to give you a sense of what's appropriate. You might also count attendance or participation (we don't).
When should I give an incomplete?	At every university we know of, *incomplete* means that there were serious extenuating circumstances that prevented students from completing the course requirements, such as that they were in the hospital during the final exam and can prove it. Not doing as well as they would like doesn't qualify.
What do I do about seniors who failed my course and would graduate if they passed it?	Don't respond on the spot when the student approaches you. First find out what the university policies are regarding this situation; then let the student's advisor know what's happening and confer to come to a fair decision.

3.4.2 To curve or not to curve?

When the weighted average numerical grades are the final course grades, once the numbers have been calculated there is nothing left to do. When the course grades are categorical, however (e.g., A, B, C, D, and F; or A+, A, A–, B+, B, ... , F; or 1, 2, 3, 4, and 5; or first class honors, second class honors, third class honors, pass, and fail), the last step is to translate the numerical grades into categories, which leads to the question that heads this subsection. We will use letter grades as the basis of our discussion.

Curving grades (more formally, *norm-referenced grading*) means sorting weighted average numerical grades into several ranges, and awarding A (or A+) to students with grades in the highest range, B (or A) to students in the second range, C (or A–) to those in the third, and so on to F in the lowest range. Two systems are commonly used to determine the ranges: (1) pre-specified percentages of the numerical grades are designated to receive each letter grade, such as the top 10% get As, the next 20% get Bs, and so on; (2) gaps between several adjacent weighted-average numerical grades are selected as range boundaries, so that numerical grades above the first gap get As, those between the first and second gaps get Bs, and so on.

The opposite of curving is *absolute grading* or *criterion-referenced grading*, in which specific numerical grades are preselected as range boundaries—for example, all numerical grades of 92 and higher earn As, all grades from 80 to 91.9 earn Bs, and so on. When absolute grading is used, it is theoretically possible for every student in a class to earn an A (or an F); when grades are curved, the letter grades are necessarily distributed across the entire range from A to F, whether the class was strong or weak.

We strongly advise against curving course grades, for the following reasons:

What's Wrong with Curving Course Grades?

o Course grades should reflect only level of mastery of learning objectives, but they don't when curving is used. The same mastery level could earn an A in a particularly weak class and a C in a particularly strong one.

o When grades are curved, students with very low performance levels may get passing grades and move on to subsequent courses for which they are unqualified.

o Course grading should be transparent to the students. It isn't if grades are curved: even when students know all their grades on assignments and tests, they cannot predict their course grade unless they know how everyone else in the class did.

o As research to be cited in Chapter 11 shows, authorized cooperation on assignments leads to greater learning for weak students (who get the benefit of being tutored) and strong students (who experience the deep learning that results from teaching someone else). Curving discourages cooperation. If Joan helps Jan, she could end up with a lower numerical grade than Jan gets, and if grades are curved she could get a lower course grade as a result. When absolute grading is used, there is no downside to cooperation.

Absolute grading avoids those deficiencies of curving, but it has two potential drawbacks of its own.

Problem: Grades on a test are abnormally low, and you take some responsibility for it.

Solution: Adjust the test grades.

Before you make any adjustments to test grades, ask yourself if the test was fair (not too long and no inadequately-taught material on it). If the answer is yes, the test grades should stand. If you take some responsibility for the low grades, however, you can adjust them. Section 8.3.4 suggests several test grade adjustment strategies that help all students—unlike curving course grades, which helps some students and penalizes others.

Problem: Minor numerical course grade differences translate to major letter grade differences.

Solution: Include *gray areas* below criterion levels for letter grades.

In a pure criterion-referenced grading system, there are hard boundaries between letter grades, so that a student whose weighted-average grade is 80 gets a B in the course and the student with 79 gets a C. It is acceptable—and in our opinion, desirable—to put *gray areas* below each boundary value. For example, suppose that all students whose numerical grades are 92 or higher are guaranteed As in the course. The range from, say, 88 to 91.9 might be designated as a gray area. A student whose numerical grade falls in that range could get either an A or a B (or an A– or B+ if those grades are given), depending on other criteria that the instructor has specified such as the number of extra-credit assignments attempted or the grade on the final exam. Remember, however, that there should be no surprises in course grades. If you adopt this practice, be sure to spell it out in the syllabus.

3.5 Writing a Syllabus

The course syllabus functions as a travel guide, indicating the territory to be covered on the journey from the first day of class to the final exam, the resources needed for the trip, and the traffic rules that must be observed along the way (O'Brien et al., 2008). Items commonly found in syllabi course descriptions and course-level learning objectives; dates ... assignments are due and tests will be given; statements of course policies regarding such things as attendance, use of electronic devices, and cheating; resources for students taking the course; and specifications of how late assignments and missed exams will be handled and how the final course grade will be determined. An illustrative syllabus for an engineering course that contains all of those elements (including a course grading scheme that includes gray areas and a set of policies regarding team projects) can be seen at www.ncsu.edu/felder-public/cbe205site/205syl.pdf.

If you are teaching a course for the first time, the task of preparing a syllabus can be daunting. A good way to start is to find one of your colleagues (preferably a good teacher) who has taught the course before and use his or her syllabus as a starting point for yours. You can also find sample syllabi for almost any STEM course by entering "syllabus college [course subject]" into a search engine, and start with a syllabus that appeals to you. In addition, some institutions prescribe information and statements about academic integrity and students with disabilities that must be included in all syllabi. Before writing a syllabus for your course, find out if your institution has such prescriptions, and if it does, follow them.

3.6 The Critical First Week

In the interlude preceding this chapter, we drew on the work of Peter Elbow (1986) and observed that we have to juggle two conflicting roles as college teachers—*gatekeeper* and *coach*. As gatekeepers, we set standards high enough to certify that our students are qualified to move on to subsequent courses and our graduates are qualified to enter their intended professions, and as coaches we equip the students to meet and surpass those standards. What we do in the first week of a course to establish ourselves in those roles can have a profound effect on how the entire course goes.

Here is one way to start off a course:

> Good morning. I'm Professor Tweedley and this is Chemistry 102. You all picked up copies of the syllabus when you came in. Be sure to read it carefully—it spells out my policies regarding grading, attendance, lateness, missed exams, and especially cheating, which I have a very low tolerance for, as some of you will no doubt discover the hard way. Now, last semester you learned about atomic structure, the periodic table and various properties of atomic species, some combining rules for chemical reactions, and different ways to look at acids

and bases and how they react. This semester we'll do some more quantitative stoichiometric analysis and examine the thermodynamics and kinetics of reactions. To begin, suppose we want to neutralize 4.4 liters of a 2-molar sodium hydroxide solution with a 3.5-molar sulfuric acid solution. The stoichiometric equation is....

Are you starting to feel a bit uncomfortable? You can bet that many of Tweedley's students are—in the first minute of the course he has probably intimidated half or more of them. He clearly establishes himself as a gatekeeper from the very beginning, without giving the slightest hint that he also views himself as a coach. As soon as the first class session is over, some students who might be perfectly capable of doing well in the course will start scouring the university website for alternative courses and possibly alternative majors.

Early in every course, many students ask themselves several important questions, consciously or unconsciously:

o How hard is this course going to be? Will I be able to handle the tests? Is the material something I really want to learn and understand, or do I just need to learn enough to get the grade I want?
o Is this teacher someone I respect and whose respect I want to earn?
o Will class sessions be worth attending every day, or can I learn what I need to without coming? When I'm in class, do I need to stay on top of things, or can I just sit in the back and do some texting and maybe grab a quick power nap without missing anything important?

The students in Dr. Tweedley's class will come up with tentative answers to those questions in that first lecture, and the odds are high that Tweedley would not be pleased with their answers. Unless he does something in the next one or two lectures to establish his credentials as a coach, the course could turn out to be a disaster.

There are effective ways to get a course off to a good start that quickly establish you as gatekeeper and coach. We will offer several ideas in five categories: establishing good relationships and communications with and among the students (coach), establishing clear expectations (gatekeeper), motivating the students to learn what you will be teaching (coach), carrying out a test of prerequisite knowledge and skills (coach and gatekeeper), and beginning to use formative evaluation (coach). The point is not to adopt all the suggestions at once: instead, treat the list as a menu, initially picking a small number from each category and adding others as you gain experience.

3.6.1 Establish good relationships and communications with and among your students

In a landmark educational research study, Alexander Astin and his colleagues collected data on 24,847 students at 309 different institutions to determine the effects of a host of factors on the students' college experience (Astin, 1993). A massive multiple regression analysis led to the conclusion that the most important factor was the quality of the interactions between students and faculty, followed by the quality of interactions among students. *The better students' relationships with their teachers and classmates, the better their college experience is likely to be.* Lowman (1995), Hawk and Lyons (2008), and Meyers (2009) present substantial research validation of the positive effects of a caring instructor.

Establishing good relationships with and among your students in the first week of a course is crucial to getting the course off to a good start. Here are several ideas for doing it, starting with the two most important ones:

Introduce yourself.

Tell the students something about your background, especially as it relates to what you will be teaching. This is a chance to express your enthusiasm for teaching the course and your desire to help the students learn it. If you have worked in industry, consulted, or done research related to the course subject, mention it. You might also say something about your personal interests to let the students know you have a life outside the classroom.

Learn as many of your students' names as you can.

Being able to call your students by name, in class and in the hall, conveys a message that you view them as more than just faces with ID numbers and increases their motivation to do well in your course. If you have three hundred students in the class you probably won't be able to learn all their names, but learn as many as you can—the effort you're making will be noticed and appreciated. Table 3.6–1 offers several effective name-learning techniques.

Other strategies for learning names are suggested by Morris et al. (2005).

Learn something about the students' goals and interests.

Linking your course content with your students' goals and interests helps motivate them to learn. As part of the first course assignment, ask them to submit a short autobiographical sketch or a cover letter and CV

Table 3.6–1. Learning Students' Names

- Download the students' photo IDs from the electronic class roll and study them in your office.
- Give the students tent cards to display during class. On the first day of the semester, end the class a few minutes early, have the students come up in groups of four holding tent cards with their names, take digital photos of them, and study them in your office.
- On the first day of class, pass a sheet of paper down each row of the classroom and have the students write their names, inserting Xs for empty seats. Prepare a seating chart, use it to call on students, and study it in class during activities and exams.

for the type of job they would like to have after graduation. Compile lists of their talents, hobbies, and career goals and refer to the lists when looking for applications of course material.

Have your students anonymously hand in statements about why they're taking your course and rumors they've heard about it.

The student grapevine is powerful but not necessarily accurate, and students often form opinions about courses based on false or exaggerated rumors. Getting those rumors on the table will help you uncover and address misconceptions and fears. For example, if students in your course have heard that a ridiculously high percentage of the class always fails, you might calm them down by showing a grade distribution from a previous semester. (If the rumors are true, skip this technique.)

Have students write their expectations of you.

Students will be more likely to try to meet your expectations if they believe they are being met halfway. Ask them to write what they expect from you, either as a small-group exercise on the first day of class or in the first homework assignment. Most of them will come up with reasonable expectations, such as that you will come to class on time and prepared, respond to their online questions, and grade and hand back assignments and tests reasonably quickly. Identify the expectations you feel you can commit to and state your commitment in class.

Use active learning.

Many dropouts in the early years of college can be attributed to students feeling isolated (Astin, 1993; Seymour & Hewitt, 1997; Tinto, 1993). *Active learning*—getting students to work in small groups on brief course-related activities during class—is a powerful technique that helps students develop connections and leads to more learning than traditional teaching methods generally produce. (Chapter 6 provides details on how to do active learning and pitfalls to avoid when doing it.) In the first group activity in the course, tell the students to introduce themselves before they start working on the assigned question or problem.

Establish effective communication with the students.

In a good class environment, students feel comfortable interacting with the instructor—volunteering ideas in class, exchanging greetings in the hall, and asking for help when they need it. Unfortunately, many students are intimidated by instructors. If all you do is tell them on Day 1 that they should feel free to ask questions in class and come to you during office hours, you will never hear a word from most of them, and some who are perfectly capable of succeeding may fail because they didn't get help when they needed it. Table 3.6–2 lists several additional things you might do to open communication channels.

Table 3.6–2. Enhancing Communication with Students

□ *Ask each student in your class to send you a text or e-mail message in the first week.* Once they have done it, it will be easier for them to contact you when they have questions or comments.

□ *Unless the class is huge, set up five-minute office appointments with all students in the first week.* Introduce yourself, chat briefly about their interests, and answer any questions they might have. Once they have found their way to your office, they will be more likely to come for help when they need it.

□ *If students are not coming to your office for help, hold office hours in places where they congregate, such as lounges or study areas.* Put a sign on your table that says "BCH 303—need help?" or something like that.

□ *After your first test, if the class is not too large, have the students pick up their graded papers from you in your office and spend a few minutes chatting with them.* If they did poorly, explore how they prepared and what they might do differently on future tests.

□ *Hold virtual office hours.* Designate certain hours during the week when you will be available online to respond to students' questions through texts, video chats and other social media, online discussion forums, or e-mail (if there still is such a thing by the time you're reading this). Whichever method you use, you will hear from some students who wouldn't dream of coming to your office.

3.6.2 *Establish clear expectations*

Making clear what you expect from your students helps you establish yourself in the instructor's gatekeeper role. Several ways to do it follow.

In the first class session, briefly discuss your course policies.

You don't have to cover every detail mentioned in the syllabus, but take some time to go over the most important and unusual policies. Potential topics to stress include grading (what counts and by how much?) and policies regarding absences and tardiness, late homework, missed exams, cell phone and personal computer use in class, and how you would like to be addressed (Professor, Doctor, Mr. or Ms. Jones, or Robin). Regarding the last of those issues, if you are relatively young or new to teaching or female in a male-dominated field, consider telling students—particularly undergraduates—that you wish to be addressed by your title. Instructors who go on a first-name basis with their students sometimes have trouble commanding respect.

Early in the course (but not on the first day), be explicit about your definition of cheating and your policies for dealing with it.

Cheating has existed on campus as long as there have been campuses, but it's now as much a part of student culture as all-night cram sessions and sleeping through 8 a.m. classes. In recent surveys of more than a thousand undergraduates, 80% of the respondents at 23 institutions reported that they cheated at least once in college, 33% of the respondents in engineering reported cheating on exams in the previous semester, and 60% did so on assignments (Carpenter et al., 2006, 2010). In other studies, 49% of the engineering and science students surveyed reported engaging in unauthorized collaboration on assignments and 75% copied homework solutions from bootlegged instructor's manuals (Bullard & Melvin, 2011). There is no reason to expect that students who take unethical shortcuts in school will stop doing it later in life—for example, when they conduct plant safety inspections and design toxic waste treatment facilities—and in fact studies have shown that they don't stop doing it (Carpenter et al., 2010).

The following suggestions to minimize cheating and deal with it when it occurs (Felder, 2011b) are based on the work of Carpenter et al. (2010) and Bullard and Melvin (2011):

1. *Define in a handout what you consider cheating and what kinds of collaboration are acceptable, and discuss your definitions early in the course.* Students' definitions of cheating are likely to be

different from yours, and unless you make yours explicit, the students will grant themselves remarkably broad latitude.

2. *Consider giving the students a role in defining cheating and setting consequences.* If they help make the rules, they will be more likely to abide by them.

3. *If your university has an honor code, support and enforce it.* Codes don't eliminate cheating, but they have been shown to reduce it.

4. *Follow your institution's formal procedures for dealing with cheating.* Fight off the temptation to handle it yourself when you detect it. If you don't use the university system, the students you catch may not do it again in your class, but they are likely to do it in other courses and possibly cheat their way to a degree.

5. *Do everything possible to make your assessments fair.* If you give tests so long or confusing that only the top students in the class can pass, or assignments so long that students can only complete them by neglecting their work in other courses, the students feel they are being cheated and many have no reservations about returning the favor.

3.6.3 Motivate students to learn what you will be teaching

In the brainwave in Section 1.1, we stated that information students take in through their senses is more likely to be stored in their long-term memories (that is, learned) if they have an interest in it and they can connect it to existing stored content. To get a course off to a good start, you should consequently try to link new course content to material the students should know and might care about. Here are several ways to do it:

Show a graphic organizer, pointing out connections between course topics and students' prior knowledge (Bellanca, 1992; Dansereau & Newbern, 1997; Kiewra, 2012; Nilson, 2007).

Most students will get much more from a visual overview of the course than from the usual bulleted list of topics in the syllabus. Briefly go through the organizer in class and suggest how the topics to be covered build on topics in previous courses. Illustrative organizers are shown in the introductions to each of the three parts of this book.

Briefly describe applications of course material to important technological and social problems. Even better, get the students to brainstorm possible applications themselves.

You will frequently hear STEM students complaining bitterly that they don't see what many of their courses have to do with the "real world," by which they mean the world of their experience, interests, and goals.

Their feeling is illustrated by the following comment from a senior in engineering:

> I remember in some of my math classes I would get so frustrated because, honestly, when am I ever going to have to find the volume of a tetrahedron? It's very helpful to know that what I'm learning is real-world applicable and I will be using the concepts I learned in class when I'm actually out there. On the first day of controls class, Dr. _____ used a shower as an example of a controlled system and we figured out what the actuator, sensor, and so on would be ... and now I can't ever take a shower without thinking about controls.

If students can't envision ever needing or wanting to use what is being taught in a course, the only thing left to motivate most of them to study and work hard is grades. For some students that's enough, but for many others—including some of the brightest students on campus—it isn't. (Read about Michelle in the interlude preceding Chapter 8.) Take a few minutes at the start of your course and of each new topic to establish the relevance of the content to important systems and problems.

Perform a demonstration or show a video of one.

A striking experiment or simulation can spark interest in a subject and remain with students long after details of the course content have faded. You can usually find good ones by entering "_____ demonstrations" (where _____ is the subject you are teaching) into a search engine. To get the full benefit of a demonstration in class, describe what you are going to do or show, have the students predict what will happen, and then do or show it. Afterwards discuss why the outcome was what it was and where those who predicted incorrectly went wrong.

Bring in practicing professionals to talk about how they use course material.

Students are concerned about what they'll be doing after they graduate, and they welcome information that might give them clues about their future. Department alumni and corporate recruiters are often pleased to visit classrooms and share their experiences. Talk with the visitors ahead of time and suggest points you would like them to make about your technical course content and any professional skills you plan to stress, such as communications and teamwork.

Pose an open-ended real-world problem that requires a significant amount of course material to solve, and give the students several minutes to brainstorm in small groups what they would need to know to solve it and how they would begin. Have one member of each group record the group's

work. When the allotted time has elapsed, have them sign their work and then hand it in to you.

You can make up a new problem with the desired attributes, pull one from the last chapter you plan to cover in the course text, or find a relevant case study (National Center for Case Study Teaching in Science [NCC-STS], n.d.). Obviously most students beginning the course won't know exactly how to approach the problem—although you might be surprised at how far some of them get—but that's not the point. After you stop them, have them sign their work and turn it in. (You won't be grading it.)

You can do several things after that. As the course progresses, relate each new topic to the opening problem to help the students understand how each part fits into the whole. When students clearly perceive a need to know new material, they are much more motivated to learn it than when it is presented in a vacuum. The knowledge of how what you are about to teach is needed to make progress on a significant problem can provide that motivation.

Then, near the end of the course get the students into their original groups, give them the same problem, and again ask them to outline how they would approach it. Now they can and will fill sheets of paper with what they have learned. Stop them after the allotted time, give them back their first-day work and have them compare their before-and-after solutions. The comparison will give them a gratifying indication of how much they have learned in the course (which won't hurt your end-of-course evaluations one bit).

3.6.4 Test prerequisite knowledge and skills

When you teach a course that builds heavily on previously-taught material, you have a dilemma. Should you just assume that all of the students taking your course have a solid grasp of the prerequisites? You'd better not! Some students may have taken the prerequisite course years ago and have long since forgotten it, or some of the prerequisite content may be really hard or was rushed through so very few students ever really understood it, even though they managed to pass the course. The question is, how can you help students catch up with what they missed in the prerequisite course without spending a lot of class time on it or reteaching material most of them know?

One answer is to first make clear to the students which prerequisite material they need to know, and then give them some time to relearn it if they've forgotten it or never mastered it in the first place. The following outline describes an effective way to achieve both goals.

Test on Key Course Prerequisites

o Before the first day of class, write out a set of learning objectives (see Section 2.1) that specifies what the students should be able to do if they have the prerequisite knowledge and skills you plan to build on. Put the objectives in the form of a study guide for an exam ("To do well on this exam, you should be able to . . .").

o On the first day of class, announce that the first midterm exam will be given on _____ (about a week from that day) and will cover only prerequisite material. Hand out the study guide and briefly review it, assuring the students that every question and problem on the exam will be based on items on the study guide.

o (Optional) Hold a review session before the test date at which students can ask questions about anything on the study guide. Alternatively, tell the students that they are free to raise questions about the study guide in class or during your office hours.

o Give and grade the test. Count the grade at least a small amount toward the final course grade. (If you don't count the test, many students won't take it seriously.)

o (Optional) Allow students to take a take-home retest to regain up to, say, half the points they lost the first time.

When you adopt this strategy, most students will do whatever it takes to relearn the required material, and you won't have to spend a lot of class time on content they should already know. The few students who do poorly on the test will be on notice that unless they do something dramatic to get that material back in their heads, they are likely to struggle throughout your course. If many students have problems with a particular topic on the test, think about giving additional review of that material.

3.6.5 Start using formative evaluation

Chapter 2 talked about the importance of defining learning objectives— the tasks you expect your students to be able to complete if they have learned what you want them to learn. An equally important component of teaching is determining how well each student has mastered your objectives. The terms *assessment* and *evaluation* are commonly used to denote this teaching function. Sometimes they are used interchangeably, but often—as in this book—they have the following meanings:

Assessment: Identifying the data that will be collected to measure knowledge and skills; selecting or creating the instruments that will be used to gather the data; and administering the instruments.

Evaluation: Analyzing assessment data and drawing conclusions from the results. Evaluation may be used to improve the quality of the students' learning and the instructor's teaching (formative evaluation), to assign grades or make pass-fail decisions (summative evaluation), or both.

We describe one common formative evaluation technique below, offer some additional suggestions in each of Chapters 4 through 7, and say a great deal about summative evaluation in Chapter 8—how to conduct it effectively, mistakes teachers often make when conducting it, and how to avoid those mistakes.

The formative technique we recommend using early in your course is a powerful and easy-to-use device called a *minute paper* (Angelo & Cross, 1993; Wilson, 1986; Zeilik, n.d.).

Minute Paper

Stop your class with one or two minutes to go in the period and have the students—working individually or in pairs—anonymously answer two questions on a sheet of paper: (1) *What was the main point of today's class?* (2) *What was the muddiest point (or most confusing point or your most pressing question)?* Stand at the door and collect their papers as they leave.

After class, skim through the papers, look for common responses to both questions, and use them as the basis for how you begin the next class session. If most of the students got the main point, compliment them and briefly restate it; if many didn't, go over it again. Then note two or three common points of confusion and clarify them.

When you use this technique you are communicating a vitally important coaching message to the students: "I am concerned enough about your learning to take time from my planned instruction to find out what's causing problems for you and to come back and try to help." Giving them that message can compensate for a multitude of teaching sins you might commit.

Some instructors collect minute papers in every class, but doing that can easily become tiresome to you and the students. We recommend collecting them every two or three weeks, focusing on class sessions that cover material many students are likely to find difficult.

3.7 Ideas to Take Away

○ The tasks of preparing a new course and redesigning an existing one can be made easier and faster by starting with colleagues' course materials and drawing on digital resource libraries, as opposed to creating everything from scratch.

○ Course preparation time should be limited to an average of two to three hours per hour of lecture. Spending much more time than that may lead to excessive course content, lower course quality and student evaluations, and leave insufficient time to spend on other important activities. The primary focus in course planning should be placed on need-to-know material (which directly addresses the instructor's learning objectives) rather than on nice-to-know material (which doesn't).

○ Course policies should be spelled out in detail in the syllabus or in separate handouts, including how course grades will be determined and rules regarding attendance, late assignments, unacceptable behaviors in class, and what constitutes cheating.

○ *Curving course grades should be strictly avoided.* Letter grades in courses should be determined entirely by how well the students meet the instructor's learning objectives and the evaluation criteria specified in the syllabus, not by the students' relative position in the class.

○ What happens in the first week of a course plays a critical role in the students' subsequent performance and attitudes. The first-week strategies suggested in the chapter can help instructors establish rapport with the students, set expectations of them, and motivate them to study and learn the course content.

3.8 Try This in Your Course

○ Create a graphic organizer for your course to help you overview the course on the first day of class.

○ Give a test on course prerequisites in the second week of your course. On the first day of class, hand out a study guide with your learning objectives for the test. Hold a single review session during the first week. Administer the test, and count the grades by a small amount toward the final course grade.

○ Use one or more of the techniques suggested in this chapter to learn all of your students' names within the first week of class (or longer for larger classes).

○ Create a first-day exercise in which you pose a substantial real-world problem that will require a considerable fraction of the course content to solve, and give groups of students several minutes to outline how they would approach the solution. Bring the problem back whenever you begin a new topic and show how what you are about to teach will enable making progress toward the solution.

○ Try one additional suggestion for how to get a course off to a good start in the first week.

○ Conduct a minute-paper exercise early in the course after a lecture containing material likely to confuse students.

INTERLUDE. HOW TO WRITE CLASS SESSION PLANS (OR ANYTHING ELSE)

Here's the situation. You're preparing to teach a new class next semester, and you've worked up the syllabus and have a rough idea of the learning objectives you want to address. Now you're trying to get a head start on the class session plans, because you know it will be hard to stay ahead of the class once the course begins. It's not going well—in the last week, all you've managed to get done is one measly page.

We have two suggestions for getting your class sessions planned in this lifetime: (1) commit to working on them regularly and (2) keep the creating and revising functions separate. (We didn't invent either strategy—you can find variations of both in many references on writing, such as Boice [1990] and Elbow [1998].)

Do your course session planning in short and frequent intervals.

See if this little monologue sounds familiar. "I don't have time to work on planning next semester's course now—I've got to meet with a student and get Wednesday's class ready and answer a ton of e-mail and go to a faculty meeting and pick the kids up after school and ... BUT, as soon as fall break (or Christmas or summer or my sabbatical) comes, I'll get to it."

It's natural to give top priority to tasks that can be done quickly or are due soon, whether they're urgent (preparing Wednesday's lecture) or not (answering most e-mails), and so the important long-range projects keep getting put off as the weeks and months go by. A much more effective strategy is to make a commitment to devote short and frequent periods of time to major writing projects. For thirty minutes a day or maybe an hour four times a week, close your door, ignore your phone and all your in-boxes, and work on the project. When the time is up, stop and go back to the rest of your life. You'll be astounded when you look back after a week or two and see how much you've written.

Keep creating and revising separate.

Here's another common scenario. You sit down to write something and come up with the first sentence. You look at it, grimace, delete it, try again, change some words, add a phrase, delete a comma, and continue to beat on the sentence for five minutes until you get it where you want it. Then you draft the second sentence, and the first one is instantly obsolete. You rewrite those two sentences following the same procedure, work on them for ten minutes until they satisfy you and then go on to Sentence 3 and repeat the process. An hour or two later you may have a paragraph to show for your efforts.

If that sounds like your writing process, it's little wonder that you can't seem to get those class sessions planned. When you spend hours writing and revising, one sentence and diagram and equation and graph at a time, the plans can take forever to finish. When the course begins you don't have much of a stockpile, and you end up cranking out every session plan the night before the session. What happens then is not a good experience for either you or the students.

You're now ready for our second tip, which is to keep the creating and revising processes separate. Use *freewriting* for your first drafts (Elbow, 1998), writing whatever comes into your head without looking back. If you have trouble getting started, write anything—random words, if necessary—and after a minute or two things will start flowing. If you're still having trouble with the beginning, start in the middle and fill in the beginning later.

Throughout this process, you will of course hear the usual voice in your head telling you that what you're writing is sloppy, confusing, trivial, and so on. Ignore it! Write the first paragraph, then the next, and keep going until you get as much written as your budgeted time allows. Then, when you come back to the project the next day (remember, you committed to it), either continue writing or go back and edit what you've written—and at that point you can worry (if you must) about polishing the prose and making the diagrams look good.

Here's what will almost certainly happen if you do all that. What you write in the first few minutes of a session may be as worthless as you told yourself it was, but the rest will be significantly better than you thought. You'll crank out a lot of material in a short time, and you'll find that it's much easier and faster to revise and edit it all at once rather than in tiny increments. The course will be dramatically improved, and you'll have much more time for the rest of your life.

P.S. Once you've successfully used this two-step approach for class session planning, consider also using it for proposals, articles, and books, and tell your graduate students to use it for their theses and dissertations. It always works.

4

PLANNING CLASS SESSIONS

4.0 Introduction

You're starting on a new topic next week, and you estimate that it will take you at least four class periods to cover it. You now need to figure out what's going to happen during those periods—which is to say, you need *class session plans*. The more thorough you are about constructing your session plans, the more likely you will be to effectively address all your learning objectives.

Here are the principal questions this chapter will address:

o What are common class session planning errors, and how can I avoid making them?
o When I introduce new material in class, how can I maximize the chances that students will store it in their long-term memories (i.e., that they will learn it) and later be able to retrieve it and transfer it to new contexts?
o Why should I try to engage students during class? How can I do it without compromising my ability to cover the syllabus?
o What questions can I ask in class that will promote meaningful learning more effectively than "Is that clear?" and "Do you have any questions?"
o How can I maximize the effectiveness of my laboratory course?

Before we start, a quick note about terminology. The term *lesson plan* is often used to denote what we are referring to as a *class session plan,* and many professors refer to their plans as *lecture notes.* We won't use either term in this book. *Lesson* sounds like something teachers give students

Table 4.1-1. Common Planning Errors and How to Avoid Them

	Error	Consequence	Suggestion
1	Trying to cover too much content.	Instructors have to race to cover everything. The students have few opportunities for practice and feedback in class.	Link content tightly to learning objectives, focusing on need-to-know material and minimizing nice-to-know material.
2	Overestimating what students know and can do.	Course content and assessments are too advanced, and qualified students do poorly or drop the class.	Give an early test on course prerequisites (Section 3.6.4). Review prerequisite content when the test results show widespread deficiencies.
3	Filling most class sessions with Bloom Level 1 content students can only memorize and repeat.	Students acquire few high-level skills and little deep conceptual understanding.	Give students handouts with material you want them to memorize, and focus class time on higher-level objectives.
4	Putting theory and derivations before applications and providing insufficient examples.	Most students can't relate the material to their prior knowledge, needs, and interests, and do poorly on tests.	Provide examples and applications for every important concept and method. Introduce applications before theory.
5	Showing long procedures without focusing on the reasoning behind difficult steps.	Everything looks logical in class, but students can't carry out similar procedures on their own.	Make complex procedures the subject of in-class activities or omit them if they don't directly address learning objectives.
6	Failing to include enough questions and activities in class sessions.	Students get insufficient practice and feedback, and the instructor can't tell where they need help.	Build good questions and activities into every session plan.

in elementary school, and we'll be encouraging you to use more effective class formats than straight lecturing.

4.1 Avoid Common Planning Errors

Most new teachers—and many experienced ones—make certain mistakes when planning instruction. Table 4.1–1 lists several common ones.

Instructors who commit the errors listed in Table 4.1–1 and give tests that call for more than rote memorization are almost invariably disappointed in the results, and they tend to conclude that the students must be either incompetent or too lazy to study. Although that conclusion may be true for some students, more often the problem results from the way the students are being taught. If you avoid the errors, your courses will be more effective and more students will meet your higher-level learning objectives.

4.2 What's in a Class Session Plan?

A session plan might include the following elements:

o **Session learning objectives.** Statements of what the students should be able to do after they have gone through the session and studied and absorbed the material presented in it.

o **Preliminary messages to the class.** Reading assignments, possibly the session learning objectives (*Today's class will prepare you to …*), and anything else you want to communicate up front.

o **Outline of session content.** Material to be covered in lectures and activities (text, mathematical formulas and equations, tables, diagrams, plots, etc.), questions you will ask and their answers, problems you will pose and their solutions, and activity prompts you will give and the desired responses. (Try to start the session with an interest-provoking activity.) Include enough detail so that you can teach the same session again without having to do a lot of re-creating. Don't go overboard with detail, however—use abbreviations instead of full sentences and paragraphs, and underline or boldface key items to reduce the chances that you'll forget to cover them in class.

You may be able to think of questions and activities spontaneously during class but they are likely to be fairly low level, and you'll have to think of new ones when you teach the course again. If you take time to formulate them in advance and include them in the plan, you will usually come up with as many as you want at whatever levels you want to make them.

○ **Wrap-up.** A summary of the major points made during the session (you might make the construction of a summary the focus of a student activity) and a list of assignments to be completed before the next class.

4.3 Promote Long-Term Memory Storage, Retrieval, and Transfer

When you present new material in class, it must be stored in the students' long-term memories before it can be subsequently retrieved and applied. As we saw in Chapter 1, the conditions that favor long-term storage are, in decreasing order of priority, that the material (1) involves a threat to the students' survival or well-being, (2) has strong emotional associations for them, (3) has *meaning* for them (relates to their interests and past experiences), and (4) makes *sense* to them at their current level of knowledge. Linking lesson content to threats generally wouldn't work out well even if you could find a way to do it—what the students store is unlikely to be what you are trying to teach. If you can link your content to something likely to have positive emotional associations for your students, however, go for it, and always think about providing meaning and making sense when planning class sessions.

For example, suppose you are preparing a lesson on angular motion in a physics class. All students have had experiences with angular motion that can be used to give meaning to the upcoming course content. You could mention a sharp turn in a car or roller coaster, a heavy object being swung at the end of a rope, a washing machine in its spin cycle, or an orbiting satellite, or you can get the students to come up with their own examples. Consider beginning the session by bringing up one or more of those phenomena and reinforcing the connections with strong visual images, and then teach the content in the context of understanding the phenomena. What you teach is then likely to have meaning and sense for the students, and so it has a much better chance of being learned than when you jump directly into torque and angular momentum and moments of inertia without making explicit connections to prior knowledge.

Storing information in long-term memory is a necessary first step toward meaningful learning, but it's not the end of the story. There are an uncountable number of facts and procedures you once knew and memories you once had that you can no longer recall. In principle, everything stored in long-term memory remains there as long there is no brain damage; to be useful, however, stored material must be *retrievable* when a need for it arises. If you can't retrieve it, it's as if you never knew it in the first place.

And even retrievability is not enough for learning to be considered complete. If you are like most teachers, you've probably complained about students who can solve a specific problem in your course but can't handle problems that are only slightly different, and if they encounter the same problem in a subsequent course they act as if they've never seen it before. The students can retrieve the solution procedure for that particular problem in the exact context in which they learned it, but are unable to *transfer* it to other contexts.

4.3.1 What conditions promote retrieval and transfer?

Brainwave: Retrieval and Transfer of Stored Knowledge

A body of related information in long-term memory is known as a *schema*. It may be a memory of an incident or a face or a poem or a procedure for completing a mental or physical task. A schema is stored in clusters of neurons distributed through different regions of the brain. When it is initially stored, the connections between the neurons in each cluster and the linkages among the clusters are relatively weak, so the brain may have difficulty when it tries to retrieve the contents of the clusters and reassemble them into the original schema. However, if the schema is reinforced through *rehearsal* (e.g., repeated recollection of the memory, exposure to the face, repetition of the poem, or practicing the procedure), the connections within and among clusters are strengthened. Retrieval of the schema then becomes faster, less effortful, and more automatic (Mastascusa et al., 2011, pp. 23–25, 84–89).

To be truly useful, a schema for a problem-solving procedure should be retrievable in a broad range of situations and transferable to new settings. Similar to retrievability, transferability is enhanced by rehearsal. It is also increased by presenting a broad range of examples of how the procedure can be applied, exercises that call on the students to find applications themselves, assignments that call for applying the procedure in different contexts, and explicit statements of conditions that make one procedure more appropriate than another for a particular type of problem (Bransford et al., 2000, pp. 62, 65; Sousa, 2011, Ch. 3).

These observations suggest several ways to increase the chances that what you teach will be learned and subsequently retrieved and transferred.

Broaden the context of what you teach.

When students form a schema, anything might become part of it, including the specific examples the instructor uses, features of the classroom, even what the instructor is wearing. Teaching the same material in a variety of contexts increases the chances that the students will be able to transfer it to new situations without needing irrelevant cues, such as having to be in the room in which the material was initially taught. For example, you might introduce new material using in-class lecturing and online screencasts or videos, show how a method can be applied to several widely different types of problems or applications in several different fields or disciplines or have the students come up with their own applications, and occasionally wear different clothes to class. (No joke!)

Provide as much opportunity in class as you can for students to reflect on and practice what you are teaching.

The traditional teaching model presumes that showing information to a class of passive students should get the information into their brains, and they should then be able to retrieve it and use it to complete assignments and understand new material that builds on it. We hope you are convinced by now that the human brain simply doesn't work that way. Information fire-hosed at students nonstop is unlikely to make it into long-term memory and less likely to be subsequently retrieved and transferred. To increase the chances that your students will absorb important session content, give it to them in relatively small digestible chunks, followed by opportunities for them to retrieve and reflect on it and practice applying it. The remaining sections in this chapter, much of Chapter 5, and all of Chapter 6 suggest ways to do that.

When you introduce new material, try to give it meaning by making connections to the students' interests, goals, prior knowledge, and past experiences. Consider teaching *inductively*—applications before theory—as a strategy for showing connections.

One of the most common complaints you will hear about STEM courses is that the students don't see what the course content has to do with the "real world," by which they mean the world of their experience, interests, and goals. Part of the reason they don't see it is that the conventional approach to teaching STEM subjects is deductive, starting with the instructor showing basic principles and methods and gradually progressing to applications. Because applications provide the meaning that can facilitate storage and retrieval of the principles and methods, the students' learning consequently suffers and their complaints are justified.

In *inductive teaching and learning*, when a new topic is introduced, students are first confronted with challenges—questions to be answered, problems to be solved, or observations to be analyzed and interpreted— and then acquire the desired knowledge and skills in the context of addressing the challenges. Common inductive teaching methods include inquiry-based learning, case-based instruction, problem-based learning, and project-based learning (Prince & Felder, 2006, 2007). In the next subsection we briefly examine two of these methods. The two others are described in Chapters 9 and 10, respectively, and a number of inductive methods are surveyed and compared in Section 12.2.

4.3.2 Inquiry-based Learning and Case-based Instruction

To use *inquiry-based learning,* begin your coverage of each course topic with a question or problem you would usually introduce after you have covered basic course material, and give the students—working individually or in small groups—a short time to think about how they would approach it. (*What do we know? What do we need to find out? Where would we start?*) Then teach them. When you reach content that can no longer be taught in the context of a challenge, bring up a new challenge.

Many instructors have a reasonable concern about asking students to wrestle with problems before teaching them the strategies and tools they need to solve the problems. It turns out that doing so creates *desirable difficulties* that deepen learning and promote subsequent retrieval of the learned information (Brown et al., 2014, p. 86). We gave an example of an inductive approach in Chapter 3 when we suggested beginning the course with an open-ended real-world problem and using the problem to provide context for the entire course. The idea of inquiry is to do something similar but on a smaller scale, using challenges to set the stage for individual topics. Examples of inquiry-based instruction in different STEM disciplines are given by Douglas and Chiu (2013),

Lee (2004, 2012), and Process Oriented Guided Inquiry Learning (POGIL, n.d.).

Case-based instruction is a powerful method that has been used extensively in the biological and medical sciences and to a lesser extent in other STEM disciplines. Students are given a case study of a real or invented scenario in which a problem or situation is outlined, a decision is made about how to proceed, and the outcome is described. The complete study might be handed out and the students asked to summarize, explain, interpret, and discuss it; alternatively, the students might be presented with the problem or situation and asked to propose what should happen and justify their proposal before being given the rest of the study to analyze. The method might be deductive, with the analysis being performed after the required course material has been taught, or inductive, in which case the case study would be introduced first and the course material taught in the context of the study. An extensive library of case studies in a variety of STEM disciplines and suggestions on how to use them effectively can be found in the archives of the National Center for Case Study Teaching in Science (n.d.).

Thought Question

Most curricula have courses or topics within courses that students commonly consider pointless or boring and have trouble motivating themselves to study. Do you teach any of those courses or topics? What might you do to persuade the students that what you will be teaching is relevant to their interests and goals and likely to be needed in their careers? (If you can't make a good case for its relevance and importance, why are you teaching it?)

4.4 Two Cornerstones of Effective Class Sessions

Of all instructional methods, nonstop lecturing is the most common, the easiest, and the least effective. Studies show that most students cannot stay focused throughout a lecture: after about six minutes their attention begins to drift, first for brief moments and then for longer intervals. They find it increasingly hard to catch up on what they missed while their minds were wandering, and eventually they switch the lecture off altogether like a bad TV show (Bunce et al., 2010). When information is presented in a class and students are paying no attention to it, the chances of their learning it (storing it in long-term memory) range from slim to none.

Classes that consistently hold students' attention have two primary features: *activity* and *variety*. Actively engaging students instead of simply lecturing to them (*active learning*) has been shown by extensive research to lead to greater student interest in the subject, improved attendance, deeper questioning, and most important, increased learning (Felder & Brent, 2009; Freeman et al., 2014; Prince, 2004). As we have seen, cognitive science suggests an explanation for those impressive results: having students actively recall information, reflect on it, and apply it increases the likelihood that the information will be stored in long-term memory, retrieved when it is needed, and transferred to other contexts when it applies.

But as effective as active learning is, you can't—and shouldn't—make every class a total activity marathon. If you do that, the repetitiveness of the approach could lead to a decline in its effectiveness, plus you won't be able to do other things that capture students' interest, motivate them to learn, identify and fill in gaps in their knowledge, and clear up their misunderstandings.

That's where variety comes in. The more of it you have in your class, the more likely you'll be to hold the students' attention, and there are many ways to get it. You don't have to use all of them, but if you select a good assortment and the students never know what you'll do next, the session will probably be effective. Following are some possibilities.

Vary the format and frequency of activities.

Have students formulate responses to your questions, get problem solutions and derivations started or take the next step, vote on responses to multiple-choice questions (possibly using *clickers*, which we will discuss in Chapter 6), or brainstorm responses to open-ended questions. Sometimes have the students work individually; sometimes in groups of two, three, or four; and sometimes individually followed by pairing to select the best response or construct a better one. Give them as little as ten seconds and as much as three minutes for an activity. They may work at their seats or (in small classes) come to the board and work there. The time between two consecutive activities may be one minute or twenty minutes or anything in between.

Vary what you do besides activities.

Lecture for brief intervals, trying not to go much beyond most students' attention span (roughly six minutes). Show and discuss screencasts, videos and photos of course-related phenomena, and physical or simulated experiments. Tell course-related stories from your experience. Respond to questions students ask spontaneously or generate in an activity. Occasionally bring in practicing professionals who do interesting work and have them briefly describe their jobs and respond to students' questions, a few of which you might plant in advance.

4.5 Plan Good Questions and Activities

If questions and activities are essential components of effective class sessions (which they are), two logical questions for instructors are, what can I ask students, and what can I have them do?

Most questions asked in STEM classes follow one of two models:

○ A patient's blood glucose level is measured daily over a two-week period, and the measurements are repeated three months later after a change is made in the administered dose of a medicine undergoing clinical trials. The mean and standard deviation of both sets of data are .... Did the average glucose level decrease significantly at the 5 percent significance level after the change was made?
○ Do you have any questions?

Although these questions are important, they don't exactly stimulate deep thought. "Can we say with 95% confidence that the glucose level decreased significantly?" can be answered correctly by following a prescribed statistical test without understanding what it really means and where it came from. "Do you have any questions?" is even less productive: the leaden silence that usually follows makes it clear that the answer for most students is always "no," whether or not they understood the material just presented.

Questions can have a dramatic impact on learning. A good question in class can provoke curiosity, stimulate thought, and trigger a discussion or serve as the basis of an activity that leads to new or deeper understanding. As you outline your plan for a class session, consider inserting some questions and activities that require the students to think deeply about the material you're presenting, practice complex skills, and monitor their own understanding.

A few types of questions (selected from countless possibilities) are illustrated in the following list (Felder, 1994). Any of them can be asked during lectures, used as bases for class activities, or included in assignments and tests.

○ **Define a term or concept in your own words.** *Examples:* Using terms a bright high school senior [a student just beginning this class, your nonscientist grandparents] could understand, briefly define covalent bond [viscosity, derivative, plate tectonics, Young's modulus, leukocyte]. *Warning:* Don't ask your students to give a comprehensible definition of something such as entropy, moment of inertia, temperature, or mass unless you're sure *you* can do it.

○ **Begin a problem solution or derivation, or take the next step in one.** When you work through a complex derivation or problem solution in class, if you're a good lecturer everything may seem clear and logical to the students, including the parts that are actually quite difficult or tricky and took you a long time to learn. When the students then go home and try to do something similar, they discover that they didn't understand much of what you did at all. If you first make them struggle briefly with the hard parts in class activities and give them feedback minutes later, they are much more likely to leave the class with the understanding they need to do the homework.

○ **Explain familiar phenomena in terms of course concepts.** *Examples:*
  ❑ Why is there a stable foam on top of espresso but not drip coffee?
  ❑ Why do your leg muscles tremble after a long, hard run?
  ❑ Why do you feel comfortable in 65°F still air, cool when a 65°F wind is blowing, freezing in 65°F water, and even colder when you step out of the water?

○ **Predict system behavior.** *Examples:*
  ❑ Sketch the dynamic system response you expect to see if you increase the integral action on the controller.
  ❑ How would you expect the crop yield to change if you increase the ratio of phosphorus to potassium in the soil?
  ❑ The values and formulas shown below are entered into the specified cells of an Excel spreadsheet. What numerical values will appear in place of the formulas?
  ❑ Estimate the time it will take for all the water in the teakettle to boil off [for the capacitor to reach 99% of its full charge, for the I-beam to collapse under the applied central load].

  When possible, follow these exercises with physical or simulated demonstrations that test the predictions.

○ **Think about what was just calculated.** *Examples:*
  ❑ Why would an intermediate operating temperature be optimal for this system? (Put another way, what are the drawbacks of very low and very high temperature operation?)

▫ The computer output says that we need a storage tank volume of 3.657924×10^6 m^3. Any problems with this solution?

▫ How can we verify that the problem solution we just obtained is correct [the device or design or code we just created should work as intended]?

○ **Brainstorm a list.** *Examples:*

▫ Make the longest list you can of possible ways the process [product, procedure, experiment] we just designed might fail. The student with the longest list gets a two-point bonus on the next test. You have two minutes—go!

▫ How many ways can you think of to measure the relative humidity of the ambient air [flow rate of a river, pH of a soil sample, depth of an oil well]? You get double credit for any method that involves the use of a stuffed bear.

▫ Suppose we construct the amplifier [JAVA code, hemodialyzer, stack gas scrubber] exactly as we designed it, and the output signal [screen display, rate of uric acid removal, sulfur dioxide emission rate] is not what we predicted. List possible reasons.

▫ What might you do differently to raise your score on the next midterm exam?

○ **Formulate questions.** *Examples:*

▫ Create three good questions about what we covered today.

▫ A problem on the next test will begin like this: [Set the stage for a nontrivial multipart problem that might show up on your next test.] Generate a set of questions that might follow. Your questions should be qualitative and quantitative and should involve every relevant topic the test covers.

This exercise is an excellent one for a pre-exam review session. Have the students work in small groups to generate possible questions related to the system or process or whatever your setup paragraph describes, and then have them outline answers.

4.6 Don't Turn Classes into Slide Shows and Verbal Avalanches

Professor Fulano comes into her class three times a week and delivers a 50-minute slide show, mostly reciting the bulleted lists and derivations on the screen and occasionally adding a few comments. She posts the complete PowerPoint file on the course website for the students to print out and bring to class if they choose to do so. In class she periodically asks if everything is clear or if anyone has questions, and she usually hears only from the same two or three students. Few students ever take notes. Attendance in the 70-student class drops dramatically after the first week and continues to drop after that, so by mid-semester the average attendance is about 15, with another 20 to 30 showing up at the session before each exam hoping for some useful tips. Fulano attributes the low attendance to student laziness and apathy.

Fulano is wrong. The students are not being lazy or apathetic—they're being rational. Watching Fulano go over the content of slides that they have finished reading long before she finishes reciting is a waste of their time. They know they can cut class, download the complete lecture notes, and miss nothing, so why should they bother attending? The point is not that slides don't add value to a course—they usually do—but they should only be used to present information that cannot be better presented in other ways (Felder & Brent, 2004a; Garber, 2001).

The deadliness of classes that consist entirely of slide shows is compounded if the slides are almost exclusively verbal—sentences, bulleted lists, and equations. The same caution applies to lectures delivered in ways other than slides. If class sessions consist entirely of 50- or 75-minute avalanches of spoken and written words and equations occasionally punctuated with diagrams, very little learning is likely to take place. To most students, a picture really is worth a thousand words.

Cognitive science gives us a clue about why visual presentation of information facilitates students' learning.

Brainwave: Two Channels Are Better Than One

Only a small fraction of the information perceived by our senses is passed on to working memory, after which, if certain conditions are satisfied, it is stored in long-term memory. Two separate components of the brain are responsible for coding sensory input into working memory: the *visuospatial sketchpad,* which processes visual images, and the *phonological loop,* which repeats (rehearses) words. Presenting information visually and verbally improves the likelihood that it will be encoded and stored (Baars & Gage, 2007, p. 284).

Except for courses in art and architecture and sometimes life sciences, lectures tend to be overwhelmingly verbal. Our challenge is therefore to increase the visual content of our classes. There are good and ineffective ways to do that. A common ineffective approach is to put heavily verbal lecture notes into slides with multicolored backgrounds and flashy transitions and builds. You may capture a class's attention for a short time that way, but presentations like that quickly become tiresome and—if they go on too long—irritating. Here are several better approaches.

Use diagrams, schematics, photographs, videos, animations, and demonstrations that illustrate points you are trying to make.

Constructing visuals yourself can take considerable time and skill, but you usually can find good ones for anything you want to illustrate. One obvious source is a DVD or CD that comes bundled with the course text. Other sources that enable you to enter a keyword and find downloadable visual images and videos are suggested in Section 3.2.

In slides, let visuals and brief headlines make your main points. Put the details in narrative and handouts.

Research has shown that the more words and equations you put on a slide, the less likely the students are to absorb and remember the slide's content. In a related vein, cognitive scientists have demonstrated that seeing written words on slides may interfere with processing of visual images in working memory (Clark & Mayer, 2003; Mayer, 2003). These observations suggest limiting most slides to visual images and brief headlines that summarize major points (Alley, 2013). Verbal and mathematical details that clarify and expand on the slides should be provided orally and in handouts.

Show *graphic organizers*—visual depictions of the structure of a topic, reading, course, or program—or *concept maps*—visual depictions of important concepts with connecting lines that show the interrelations among them.

Even though graphic organizers and concept maps consist primarily of words, the placement of the words in boxes connected by lines conveys the structure of the information much more effectively than a purely verbal list or outline can. Chapter 1 and the introductions to Parts I through III of this book contain graphic organizers that show the content of the included chapters, and illustrative organizers and concept maps for different subjects are shown in Kiewra (2012) and Nilson (2007). Getting students to construct their own concept maps in class activities or assignments is a powerful way to deepen their understanding (Ellis et al., 2004; Kiewra, 2012; Nilson, 2007; Novak & Cañas, 2008).

4.7 Use Handouts with Gaps

The title of this section is our response to two questions that frequently arise in teaching workshops:

- If I start incorporating activities into my classes, how can I still cover my complete syllabus in the course?
- What can I do to catch up with my class schedule when I fall a week or more behind?

Here's how: *use handouts with gaps.* Put your lecture notes in class handouts or (if you have the complete set of notes) a course pack, but not the complete notes. Show straightforward parts of the lecture material—definitions, facts, simple math, diagrams, and plots—with interspersed blank spaces (gaps) for students to insert answers to questions, missing parts of problem solutions and derivations, and visuals such as molecular, physical, and biological structures, free-body and circuit diagrams, and process and algorithm flow charts. In class, give students brief periods of time to read the straightforward parts themselves, and use lecturing or active learning to fill in the gaps.

Exhibit 4.7–1 shows an excerpt from a handout for a fluid dynamics course in physics, biophysics, mechanical, civil, or chemical engineering. It was prepared by taking a word-processed session plan and adding blank spaces or pasting blank rectangles over parts of the handout to insert gaps. If you were conducting this particular class session, you would begin by asking the students to open their handout or course pack to Page 35 and read the top half of the page, which contains a simple description of fluid flowing in a pipe. You would stop them when you think they've had enough time and ask if they have any questions (they generally won't). You've just saved a chunk of time relative to a traditional lecture, because the students can read much faster than you can speak and write.

Next comes a problem statement (*"Derive an expression for the mass flow rate ... "*) and a gap for the solution. There are three different things you can do at that point:

Option 1. Lecture on the material that goes in the gap.

Tell the students that what they just read is straightforward but that derivation is tricky, and students often have trouble with it. Then go through the derivation as you would in a traditional lecture, and the students can copy it into the gap. The general idea is to focus most of the class time on material the students really need help with, as opposed to

---

Steady-state laminar flow: Incompressible Newtonian fluid in a horizontal circular pipe

Read text, Sect. 2.9B, pp. 78–80.

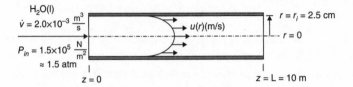

Water enters a 5.0-cm ID × 10.0 m long pipe at a volumetric flow rate $\dot{v}$ =2.0×10⁻³m³/s and a pressure P = 1.5×10⁵ N/m² (150 kPa ~ 1.5 atm). Our goal is to find out as much as we can about relations among system variables at steady state.

$u(r,z)$ – local velocity profile
$\dot{v}(z)$ – volumetric flow rate
$P(r,z)$ – local fluid pressure

- Derive an expression for the mass flow rate, $\dot{m}$ (kg/s), at the inlet, in terms of the velocity profile, $u(r)$. (Hint: first derive an expression for the volumetric flow rate.)

- Does $\dot{m}$ vary with z? Explain.

- Does $\dot{v}$ vary with z? Explain.

Exhibit 4.7–1: Excerpt from a Handout with Gaps

---

spending a lot of it on definitions and simple calculations that the students can quickly read through on their own.

Option 2. Use active learning (Section 4.4) to get students to fill in the gap.

A more effective strategy is to tell the students to get into groups of two or three and give them a short time to go as far as they can with the derivation, then stop them and call randomly on several to report on the steps they carried out. Write correct responses on the board so everyone in the class gets them. Some students will work out the derivation themselves and so will own it because they did it rather than just watching you do it and imagining that they understood all of it. (Few students understand complex material when they just listen passively to a lecture on it.) Others will try but won't get the solution in the allotted time. As it goes up on the board, though, most of those students will pay careful attention, ask questions if necessary, and understand it by the end of that class session.

Option 3. Leave filling in the gap as an exercise for the students to complete outside of class.

Tell the students that you don't plan on going over a particular gap in class, but they should make sure to find out what goes in it before the next test. They can work with each other and ask about it in class or in your office if they can't figure it out themselves. If you fall behind your lecture schedule, increase your use of this option for easier or less important material.

Rich used handouts with gaps for the last 20 years of his active teaching career. Even though he also used active learning extensively, his syllabi actually got longer than they were when he felt it necessary to say every word and draw every diagram and work through every step of every derivation and problem solution in class. The brief struggles his students had in class followed by immediate feedback saved many of them hours of wrestling with similar exercises in the homework.

Research has confirmed that handouts with gaps have a powerful impact on learning and performance on assignments and tests. In several studies, students who got incomplete notes on course material earned higher exam grades, higher course grades, and higher marks on conceptual questions than students who had complete notes (Cornelius & Owen-DeSchryver, 2008; Hartley & Davies, 1978; Kiewra, 1989).

Faculty members sometimes raise objections to the concept of handouts with gaps.

Objection 1: Students learn a lot by taking notes in class. If I give them most of the lecture notes in handouts, they won't bother taking their own notes and will learn less.
Response: The research says otherwise. When students are busy copying definitions, tables, figures, and equations, they can't simultaneously pay full attention to explanations in the lecture, and they consequently miss important material and their performance in the course suffers.

Objection 2: Putting my complete lecture notes into handouts with gaps will take much more of my time than I can afford to spend.
Response: What takes substantial amounts of time is preparing the notes in the first place. Once you have them, it doesn't take much additional time to add gaps by pasting physical or electronic blank rectangles over

calculations, drawings, and responses to questions you want students to fill in.

Objection 3: My students think I'm obliged to tell them everything they need to know. They'll complain if I leave gaps in the course handouts, and they may completely revolt if I make them fill the gaps in themselves. **Response:** Complete revolt over gaps is unlikely but you can count on some students complaining about them, just as you can count on complaints about active learning. Fortunately, you can take steps to defuse student resistance (see www.ncsu.edu/felder-public/Student-Centered.html# Publications-Resistance) long enough for most students to see that what you're doing is in their best interests. At that point the complaints generally stop.

4.8 Planning Undergraduate Laboratory Courses

In 2002, a group of about fifty educators attending a Sloan Foundation–sponsored colloquy formulated a set of functions of the engineering laboratory course (Feisel & Rosa, 2005). That work provides the basis for a list of skills students should develop in science and engineering labs and learning objectives that might be associated with the skills (Table 4.8–1). Every laboratory course cannot be expected to integrate all of the objectives in the table, but adopting a reasonable subset of them should lead to an excellent educational experience.

The traditional cookbook laboratory course—14 carefully scripted experiments in 14 weeks or the equivalent—is unsuitable for achieving any of the objectives in Table 4.8–1 in a meaningful way and does not in the least resemble the laboratories in which the students will work as scientists, engineers, or graduate students. In a real lab, you don't start off with a set of instructions that spell out everything you have to do, what data you should collect, and how you should analyze and interpret the data. Rather, you are given a challenging problem to solve and it is up to you to determine how to solve it. The problem is usually incompletely defined and open-ended, such as, *How does _____ vary with _____? Why isn't this product meeting design specifications? What is killing the cells in these cultures? Why did the reactor blow up? How did the hacker breach the system's security wall?* Because those are the types of problems our students will face in their future workplaces, shouldn't similar problems be the focus of our laboratory courses?

The obvious answer is "Yes, they should." To help your students develop the skills listed in Table 4.8–1 and prepare them for the problems many of them will face after graduation, consider assigning three or four

Table 4.8–1. Skills and Learning Objectives for Instructional Laboratories

1. **Experimentation.** Design an experiment to achieve a stated goal, run the experiment, analyze the data (including statistical error analysis), and interpret the outcomes in the light of relevant scientific principles.
2. **Instrumentation.** Select and use appropriate sensors, instruments, and software tools to make measurements of physical quantities and process variables.
3. **Troubleshooting.** Identify causes of deviations of experimental results from a prediction, and make corrections to either the experiment or the theory or model on which the prediction was based.
4. **Modeling.** Identify the strengths, limitations, and ranges of applicability of models as predictors of physical, chemical, and biological system behaviors.
5. **Self-directed and creative thinking.** Demonstrate independent thought and creativity in experimental system design and operation. (See Chapter 10.)
6. **Responsibility.** Identify health, safety, and environmental issues related to experimental systems and deal with them responsibly.
7. **Communication.** Communicate effectively about laboratory work, orally and in writing, at levels ranging from brief summaries to comprehensive technical reports. (See Chapter 10.)
8. **Teamwork.** Work effectively in teams, including dividing responsibilities, monitoring progress, dealing with problems, and integrating individual contributions into a final report by a specified deadline. (See Chapter 11.)
9. **Ethical awareness.** Report all results, including those that fail to match expectations, and appropriately credit all sources of information in the experimental design and the data analysis and interpretation.

experiments in a semester-long course, each taking place over a three- to four-week period. For each experiment, give the goals and enough instruction so that the students don't destroy the equipment or endanger themselves, and require them to carry out with minimal guidance from you the experimental design, implementation, and data analysis and interpretation. As the final deliverable, require a laboratory report that includes an abstract; a background section with comprehensive and properly formatted literature citations; research hypotheses; a detailed plan of work; raw data and data analyses; a discussion of results and conclusions; a summary; and recommendations for future work. Other deliverables might include a preliminary draft of the background and plan of work, an executive summary of the final report, and an oral report.

Descriptions of lab courses taught using this approach can be found in Brownell et al. (2012) (biology); Etkina, Brooks, et al. (2006); Etkina, Murthy, et al. (2006) (physics); and Felder and Peretti (1998) (engineering). Such courses will cover fewer experimental procedures and types of equipment than the traditional cookbook lab covers, but the students will be far better equipped to deal with the problems they will face after they graduate. It's a good tradeoff.

4.9 Ideas to Take Away

- Class preparation time should be limited to two hours or less of preparation per hour of class. (That target won't often be reached in new course preparations but it should remain the target.) Instructors who spend much more time than that are probably jamming too much nice-to-know content (not directly related to their learning objectives) into their session plans, decreasing the effectiveness of the course and taking too much time away from the rest of their lives.

- Learning is enhanced if students can relate new topics to their interests, goals, and prior knowledge. They can be helped to see the connections by showing them applications of new material in different contexts before going into elaborate detail on theories and derivations.

- *Active learning*—periodically giving the students something to do individually or in small groups related to the session content— greatly increases the students' chances of storing new information in long-term memory and later being able to retrieve it and transfer it to other contexts. Activities should be included in session plans.

- Giving students handouts with gaps for the most important or difficult parts of the course content improves learning and enables coverage of more material, even when active learning is used extensively. The students can read the straightforward parts themselves, and gaps can be filled in by lecturing or active learning or out-of-class exercises.

- Cookbook laboratory courses don't promote development of high-level skills. A better alternative is to assign a few open-ended experiments in the course, give the experimental goals and minimal instruction, and require the students to carry out the experimental design and implementation, data analysis and interpretation, and full reporting.

4.10 Try This in Your Course

o Identify a topic that students commonly find irrelevant, boring, or difficult to learn. Next time you get ready to teach that topic, introduce it by giving several examples of why the students might need to know it once they start working in the field, and challenge them to come up with additional examples. See if you notice a difference in their subsequent interest level.

o Find a body of course material that you now teach primarily by showing slides that consist almost entirely of words or equations. Replace the slides with new ones that contain mainly visuals (pictures, diagrams, animations, plots, etc.) and brief headlines with your main points. Give the details in handouts and lectures.

o Look through your session plan before class starts and see if you've got several good questions that require deep thinking about the phenomena or methods being taught. If you don't, put some in (see Section 4.5). Use some of those questions as bases of small-group activities.

o Prepare a handout with gaps for a portion of your course that is particularly difficult or time-consuming or both. The handout should resemble Exhibit 4.7–1, with gaps for the hardest parts (answers to challenging questions, difficult parts of derivations and problem solutions, diagrams to be drawn, etc.). Work through the handout in class, letting students read the straightforward parts (such as definitions of terms and simple calculations) for themselves and either lecturing on the gaps or having students work in groups to fill them in.

PART TWO

TEACHING COURSES

Part I of the book—Chapters 2 through 4—outlined how to design a course, starting with the formulation of specific learning objectives and then selecting content and teaching strategies to address the objectives. This part—Chapters 5 through 8—deals with implementing the design and evaluating how well the learning objectives are being achieved. A graphic organizer is shown in Figure II-1.

Chapter 5 surveys techniques to make the class sessions planned in Chapter 4 as effective as possible, continually monitoring students' understanding of what you are teaching and making adjustments when necessary, and continuing to improve your teaching. Chapter 6 focuses on active learning (active engagement of students during class sessions)—ways to structure it, problems that may arise when you use it, how to minimize occurrence of the problems, and how to deal with them if they arise. Chapter 7 discusses technology-assisted instruction—effective and ineffective technology tools and methods, blending face-to-face and online instruction, flipped classrooms, and massive open online courses (MOOCs). Chapter 8 provides guidance on designing effective tests of content knowledge and analytical problem-solving skills, and evaluating conceptual understanding and writing and speaking assignments, such as lab and project reports and case study analyses.

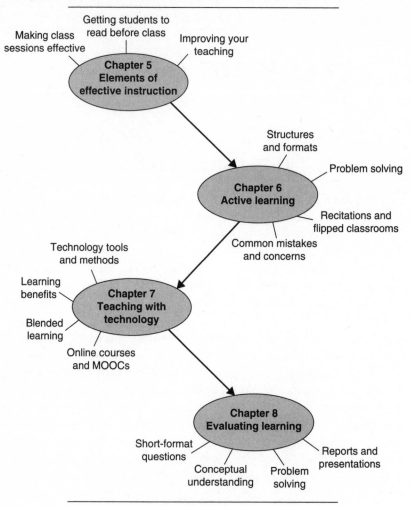

Figure II-1: Graphic Organizer of Part II

5

ELEMENTS OF EFFECTIVE INSTRUCTION

5.0 Introduction

So, you've figured out what knowledge and skills you want to help your students acquire in your course (Chapter 2), established your expectations and managed to get the course off to a good start in the first week (Chapter 3), and started creating or revising class session plans for the rest of the semester (Chapter 4). Now you have to show up one to five times a week, in a live classroom or online, and implement the plans. The question now is, how can you do that effectively—or more precisely, how can you help your students acquire the knowledge and master the skills you specified in your learning objectives and targeted in your session plans? That's what this chapter is about. Here are the questions it addresses:

- ○ What can I do in class to maximize my students' understanding of material I present? What can I do to maximize their long-term retention and subsequent retrieval and transfer of it?
- ○ What are good (and bad) ways to ask questions in class?
- ○ How can I motivate my students to complete pre-class assignments that I can build on in class? What can I do to promote their understanding of those assignments?
- ○ How can I use formative assessment to continually improve my teaching and my students' learning?

Most of our responses to these questions will work equally well for live and online instruction, and others may not apply online. In Chapter 7 we will offer additional ideas for effectively using technology in teaching, including teaching online courses.

5.1 Make Class Sessions Effective

If you have ever attended a seminar or workshop or course on effective lecturing, you were undoubtedly given many useful tips. *Speak slowly and clearly. Make eye contact with the students throughout the room and not just those in the front. Vary your tone, volume, and location to keep the audience attentive. Try to minimize verbal fillers ("um," "uh," "okay,"etc.). Don't ridicule wrong answers. Occasionally bring doughnuts.*

Okay, maybe the workshop leader didn't say the last one, but trust us, it's a good idea.

We're not discounting those suggestions—your classes will definitely be better if you follow them. There are others that are less regularly recommended but equally important, though, especially in STEM education. As usual, cognitive science provides the basis for many of them.

Brainwave: Chunking, Working Memory, and Cognitive Overload

A *chunk* is a collection of information that the mind can retain as a single unit. For example, *mzqifwun* is eight chunks of information. To remember it a short time after you read it, you would have to spend several seconds memorizing the letters and their sequence. To remember it after one or two minutes, you would have to *rehearse* it—go over it repeatedly either out loud or in your head, thereby keeping it active in working memory. However, *painting* would count as only one chunk—you would just need to memorize one word to be able to recite that sequence of eight letters on request.

Working memory is limited in the amount of information it can hold at any given time (roughly four separate chunks [Cowan, 2010]) and the number of operations it can perform on that information. The amount of work required to process the information currently in working memory is called *cognitive load.* When people's cognitive load at a given time exceeds the processing capacity of their working memory, their brain is in a state of *cognitive overload,* and they will be unable to process new incoming information without losing information already present in working memory. Cognitive overload occurs when information is transmitted to working memory at too high a rate or when most of working memory is taken up by a difficult or complex task, simultaneous multiple tasks, or distractions. If information is not adequately processed in working memory for any reason, it cannot be stored in long-term memory and so cannot be learned (Ambrose et al., 2010, pp. 103–107; Mastascusa et al., 2011, pp. 205–207).

There is no possible way students can absorb even a small fraction of the information that routinely bombards their senses during your class. You may be talking and showing images on a board or screen, and an uncountable number of other images, sounds, physical sensations, and thoughts are simultaneously competing for the students' conscious attention. Only a tiny fraction of all those inputs will ever make it into their limited working memories, and few of those that make it that far will be retained long enough to be stored in long-term memory. Your job is to do everything possible to ensure that the key parts of whatever you're trying to teach survive that stringent filtering process. Following are several ways to accomplish this.

Make your learning objectives and main points clear.

When you explicitly state your objectives and main points and repeat them during a session, you increase the likelihood that they will be stored in long-term memory and subsequently retrieved when they are needed. If the main points didn't make it into working memory and then into long-term memory when they were first stated, they will get another chance, and once they are stored, the repetition will strengthen the neural circuits that contain them. Consider the following steps to facilitate this process:

1. Come to class early and write or display your learning objectives for that session. Check off each objective on the list as soon as you have covered it.
2. Clearly state your main points during the session and reinforce them by writing them on the board. Use verbal markers such as "this is a crucial point" or "you will need this for the next assignment" or "there's a good chance this will be on the exam." (Don't overuse the last one—it loses its effectiveness with too much repetition.)
3. Summarize the main points at the end of class. Even better, get the students to do it. For example, you might ask them, "What should you have in your notes from today?"

Use active learning.

To keep students from being plunged into cognitive overload by a non-stop flow of information, occasionally turn off the flow. Pause the lecture and give the students—working individually or in small groups—a short time to do something related to what you were just discussing or demonstrating, which brings us back to active learning yet again. If Chapter 4 didn't convince you to try it, we'll take one more shot at it in Chapter 6. In that chapter, we'll suggest what you might ask students to do in activities, describe problems that might arise when you use active learning (including student pushback against it), outline strategies to overcome the problems, and summarize what the research says about the effectiveness of the method. If you're still not persuaded after all that, we'll applaud the strength of your conviction and move on to other topics.

Minimize distractions.

Just as too much information can put students into cognitive overload, distractions in class may knock important information out of their working memories before it can be processed and stored. For instance, when you are working through a problem solution, have the students put away their mobile phones and put down their laptop screens. (Research shows that today's students are not as good at multitasking as they think they are—in fact, there is probably no such thing as effective multitasking [Rosen, 2008].) If you have anecdotes to tell, don't put them in the middle of a derivation. If you are making a point at the board, don't show a projected slide that contains different information. Once you've finished presenting a coherent body of material, then tell your story or do whatever else you want to do.

Periodically monitor your students' understanding of what you have just presented.

Even if you're a captivating lecturer, you will sometimes present material that confuses your students. Also, being human, they will experience occasional lapses of attention. If you charge through lecture notes without periodically checking on their understanding, you could end up wasting your time and theirs for a considerable portion of the class session.

So don't do that. Monitor their eyes while you're lecturing, and if you see most eyes looking around or down or closed, stop what you're doing and find out what's going on. The old favorite, "Do you have any questions?" is unreliable: if the students are totally bewildered or if they've been daydreaming, they won't know what to ask, and many will never volunteer a question even if they have one. Asking a question yourself and calling for volunteers to answer is not much better: you will hear only from the students who are following you, and you won't know how many of them are in that category. Here are some better alternatives.

- ❏ When you see clearly confused students, say something like "I'm seeing some confusion. What can I clarify?" Then look in the direction of the confused students and pause. Many students who would usually never volunteer questions will respond to such invitations.
- ❏ Ask one or more multiple-choice questions that test understanding of what you have just been teaching, and poll students to see whether or not most are on the right track. You might use clickers (personal response systems) or an online tool such as "Poll Everywhere" (www .polleverywhere.com), which enables students to submit responses using their smart phones.
- ❏ Put the students in groups and have them generate questions about the material covered that day. Call on several groups to share their questions and take additional questions from volunteers.
- ❏ Collect *minute papers* (Section 3.6.6) at the end of a class session, having the students write the main point of the session and the points that most confused them. In the next class, restate the main point if many students missed it and address common points of confusion.

Beware of asking challenging questions and always waiting for volunteers to respond or immediately calling on individual students.

In Section 4.5, we encouraged you to include high-level questions in your session plans and gave some examples. Here we'll say a few things about how and how not to ask them.

Students are often terrified of looking foolish in front of their classmates (Fassinger, 1995). They view questions in class as setups for them to say something wrong or stupid—and if the questions require real thought, the students' fear may be justified. When you ask a question, most students in the class are consequently likely to remain silent and avoid eye contact with you. If they know that all you will ever do after you ask a question is wait for someone to volunteer an answer, they have little incentive to think about what you have asked; they know that one of the same two or three students in the front will provide the answer, and if those students don't, you will. However, if you make a practice of firing questions at individual students before they have had time to think (*cold-calling*), you are likely to provoke as much fear as thought about the question—and as soon as you have chosen your target, most other students breathe a sigh of relief and stop thinking.

The way to get students to think about what you want them to think about is—yet again—active learning, at least for some of your questions. Ask the question, have the students reflect individually or work in small groups for a short time to generate answers, and then call on individual students or groups to share their responses. Even if you call on individuals, the threat level is relatively low because you are not asking them to respond without first giving them time to reflect, and if they were working in a group, they're speaking for the group and not just for themselves.

You don't have to use active learning for every question you ask—it's perfectly acceptable to sometimes call for volunteers to respond. One way to get most students to think about your question is to increase the wait time after you ask it. Rowe (1986) found that most teachers waited only one second before calling on someone or giving the answer themselves. If you wait up to five seconds, you are likely to get more and better responses. It's challenging to increase that wait time at first because five seconds of silence can feel like an eternity when you're in front of a class, but it won't take long for you and the students to get used to it.

Respond with respect to students' questions and their wrong answers to your questions.

If a student says something foolish or wrong, a respectful response helps to foster a better atmosphere for discussion. If there was a shred of rationality about what the student said, acknowledge it (*"Okay, you're probably thinking _____, which is good, but you also need to consider _____."*) and casually move on. If an answer to a question makes no sense at all, say something like "No, that's not it," and call on someone else. Sometimes call on several students for responses before you indicate the correct one. You'll get a wider range of responses and will be more likely to uncover misconceptions or incorrect reasoning than if you always stop when you get the answer you were looking for.

5.2 Make Pre-Class Assignments Effective

You assign a reading, planning to build on it in the next class. In that class, you ask questions about the reading and most of the students act as if they either never looked at it or didn't understand a word. You think ugly thoughts about your lazy or illiterate students, and then go over what they were supposed to read so you can proceed with your planned class session.

If we just described your experience, there are three questions you might consider. First, how important is it to get your students to read before a particular class? Second, if it *is* important, how can you get them to do it? And third, the students are all presumably literate to have gotten as far as they have—why are so many of them apparently incapable of understanding what you asked them to read?

We'll hold off on the first and second questions for a bit and consider the third one. There are several possible answers to the question of why students can't/don't/won't read. Some students may indeed be too lazy to go through assigned readings, or the text may be very poorly written. But the most likely answer is they can ignore the reading and there will be no consequences. It's worked for them in every other class they've taken, so why not do it in yours?

The value of pre-class assignments depends heavily on what they are. The most effective assignments call on students to work through interactive online tutorials, with multimedia presentations of information interspersed with questions and exercises. Less effective but still valuable are well-constructed screencasts with generous amounts of visual content, demonstrations, and examples. If your students complete assignments like those, you can build on the assignments in class and even flip the classroom, devoting the entire class session to problem-solving exercises based on the assignments. (See Chapter 7 for details.)

On the other hand, simply assigning textbook readings to introduce new material is generally unproductive. STEM texts are often dense, dry, and almost indecipherable to students who don't already understand much of what they are reading. To get anything but vague general ideas, the students would have to read the texts with painstaking care, making sure they understand definitions, explanations, steps in derivations, and meanings of diagrams and plots before moving on. Most of our students don't know how to read that way—it's not obvious and no one ever taught them to do it. Being rational people, once they find their text incomprehensible, they ignore it. Hobson (2004) cites studies showing that more than 70% of students in classes in all subjects ignore reading assignments, and the percentage may be even higher in STEM courses.

This is not to say, however, that we should give up on asking students to read. As professionals, they will have to get information from written documents, and they won't have classes or online tutorials to help them get started. Here are several ideas for getting students to read assignments and helping them learn how to do it:

Trim assignments down to essential material.

Your reading assignments should be clearly linked to your learning objectives. If you assign 50 pages of reading of which five directly relate to your objectives and the other 45 contain "useful things to know," don't be surprised if the students ignore the assignment. Instead, assign the five pages and suggest but don't require the rest.

Include online quizzes with reading assignments.

Quizzes that contain one or two questions for each important idea in the readings are particularly easy to administer and process using course management software. Two variants of this strategy have been used with great success:

- **Self-tests.** Students key in answers and immediately get affirmation or corrective feedback followed by prompts to try again. The assignment is not considered complete until a full set of correct answers has been submitted.
- **Just-in-time teaching** (Just-in-Time Teaching, n.d.). Students submit answers the evening before (or two hours before) the assignment is due. The instructor reviews their responses and adjusts the session plan to address common points of confusion. If course management software is not used, answers may be submitted via e-mail or an online survey tool.

Completing the quizzes should not count toward the course grade by a large amount, but it should count for something. That accountability significantly increases the chances that the students will actually do the readings and try to understand the main points.

Have students generate and submit questions about readings.

An alternative to preassignment quizzes is to have the students generate their own questions about upcoming reading assignments and use their questions as bases for in-class activities. An interesting variant of this approach for readings with substantial conceptual content is *guided reciprocal peer questioning* (King, 1993). The students make reading-relevant insertions in question stems such as "What is the main idea of _____?" "What's the difference between _____ and _____?" "What if_____?" "What assumptions were made in _____?" and "What is a real-world application of _____?" At the start of the next class session they try to answer each other's questions in small groups, and the whole class then discusses particularly interesting or controversial questions. You can either collect the questions and answers and grade them as part of the assignment or just use them to stimulate serious reading and discussion. This technique promotes critical thinking as well as reading skills.

Have students draw concept maps for assigned readings.

A *concept map* is a block diagram or flow chart that shows interrelations among the key ideas in a body of knowledge. Getting students to prepare concept maps either completely or from an instructor-created skeleton promotes a deep understanding of information structures

(Ellis et al., 2004). In Section 4.6 we provide a few details about using concept maps and cite references in a variety of disciplines.

Consider giving in-class quizzes on readings, and then consider not giving them.

A common strategy for getting students to read before class is to give short in-class quizzes on the readings at the beginning of class sessions. This technique may accomplish its objective, but it has drawbacks. The quizzes can take substantial class time to hand out, administer, and collect, and even more out-of-class time to prepare and mark, especially if the class is large. Because short quizzes generally test primarily low-level factual information, the additional learning they produce may not be worth their cost in time and effort. You should also bear in mind that your students have lots on their plates besides your course, and anything you do that pressures them to keep up with your readings on a daily basis may force them to neglect other equally important responsibilities in their lives. In short, the benefits of in-class quizzes are probably not enough to compensate for their disadvantages.

5.3 Don't Be a Slave to Your Session Plans

In a perfect world, each class session plan you write would be completely covered in one class period, so when you teach the next class you would simply move on to the next plan. In the world we live in, events frequently occur that slow you down. Following are some common situations that lead to falling behind schedule and how we recommend dealing with them. All but the last recommendation are likely to put you further behind your schedule but (we believe) you should do them anyway. The last one will help you catch up.

Event: A homework problem causes students a lot of confusion or difficulty, or their questions in class or responses to your questions make it clear that they're not grasping something important.
Response: When you have identified a source of major difficulty to a substantial fraction of your students, address it. If you just charge ahead, you could lose a large percentage of the class.

Event: Something unexpected and intriguing comes up in class. A student may ask a particularly good question, or an interesting discussion or debate may get started, or you may think of a clever example or story that makes a difficult concept clear.
Response: When anything happens that looks like it might move the class in a useful direction, go with it. Occasional spontaneous events make a

class more instructive to the students and more enjoyable to them and you than a class that runs like a Swiss clock.

However, if a student asks a tough question that you can't handle on the spot or would take more time to deal with than you want to spend, a perfectly acceptable response is "Good question. I don't have an answer right now, but I'll check on it and get back to you." Then either bring the solution to the next class session or post it on the course website.

Event: Five minutes are left in the period, and you still have a lot of material to cover.
Response: Whatever you do, don't go into overdrive at the end of class and rush through the planned material. Those last-minute blitzes rarely lead to much learning and they really annoy students, especially if you routinely run past the scheduled class ending time. You're much better off finishing the material in the next session.

Event: All those digressions in class have caused you to fall a week behind your planned schedule.
Response: In Section 4.7 we introduced the technique of using handouts with gaps to cover material in class, letting students read the straightforward parts themselves and covering the gaps using lectures and in-class activities. Even if you are not routinely using this approach, when you fall behind, prepare a handout with gaps for an upcoming body of material that would usually take you a week or more to cover. Working through the handout in class and leaving some of the easier gaps as out-of-class exercises instead of lecturing traditionally through all the material should enable you to catch up with your schedule fairly quickly.

5.4 Keep Improving Your Teaching

Even if your students have been rating your teaching at or near the top of the scale, you can always get better. Here are several ways to do it:

Post-class reflection

In your office immediately after a class session, spend a few minutes going through the session plan and reflecting on which lecture segments, questions, and activities went the way you had in mind, which ones didn't, and what changes you will make next time you teach the course. Jot the changes down on the session plan, and prepare revised plans for all sessions before you teach the course again. After you've taught the course two or three times following this procedure, the session plans should be close to where you would like them to be, and only minor tweakings should be needed after that unless there are major changes in the course learning objectives or in the backgrounds of the students.

End-of-course student ratings of teaching

At most universities and colleges, students complete evaluation forms at the end of every course. This practice is not universally valued by faculty members, some of whom argue that student ratings are worthless—they're just popularity contests, the highest evaluations go to the easy graders, and so on. Although those beliefs are common, thousands of research studies have discredited most of them (Benton & Cashin, n.d.; Felder & Brent, 2008; Hattie, 2009, pp. 115–118). The fact is that students are uniquely positioned to evaluate some aspects of a course, such as the instructor's approachability, ability to interest students, clarity, and availability outside class. Any summative or formative evaluation of teaching is incomplete without students' input.

Student ratings alone are insufficient for a comprehensive evaluation of teaching, however. They can be biased—for example, on average, required courses tend to get lower ratings than electives, STEM courses get lower ratings than non-STEM courses, and female STEM course instructors get lower ratings than male instructors (see references cited in Felder and Brent [2008]). Also, students are not qualified to evaluate certain aspects of course instruction, such as whether the course satisfies accreditation criteria and provides adequate preparation for subsequent required courses. In short, although student ratings provide essential information that can help you improve your teaching, they should be supplemented with other assessments.

Peer review of teaching

Unlike students, a faculty colleague can evaluate whether the content you are covering in your course is what you should be covering, and if the colleague is an excellent teacher, he or she can suggest improvements in your teaching that the students would be unlikely to identify. In many schools and individual departments, peer review is routinely used to supplement student ratings. One department uses a formal protocol for summative peer review of its faculty members prior to all reappointment, tenure, and promotion decisions, and also uses a formative version of the same protocol for all instructors in their first two years on the faculty (Felder & Brent, 2004d).

If your department doesn't usually conduct peer reviews—or even if it does—consider asking one or two of the best teachers among your colleagues if you can sit in on one of their class sessions (there's no higher compliment you can give them) and if they would be willing to observe one of your classes. Have debriefing sessions over coffee or lunch after each observation and exchange ideas about what went well and (in the case of your class sessions) what might have been improved. You may also exchange observations with a colleague who may not be an outstanding instructor but simply wants to work on his or her teaching (Sorcinelli & Yun, 2007).

Student ratings and peer review may be formative and summative. Minute papers (which we introduced in Chapter 3) and the methods that follow are purely formative.

Midterm evaluations

Four weeks or more into a course, hand out a short open-ended questionnaire toward the end of a class session and have the students complete it anonymously and turn it in before they leave the room. The questionnaire should contain variants of some or all of the following questions, with spaces below each question but the third one for students to insert responses:

1. What features of this course and its instruction are helping you learn?
2. What features of this course and its instruction are hindering your learning?
3. Is [name a specific feature of the course you want feedback on]
   _____helping you learn   _____hindering your learning
   _____neither helping nor hindering?
4. What can *you* do to improve your performance in the remainder of the course?
5. What other comments do you have about the course or instruction?

Notice that the first three questions are tied to learning. Structuring them in that way rather than just asking the students what they like and dislike won't completely eliminate requests for daily doughnuts and complaints about early classes and your taste in clothes, but it will maximize the amount of useful feedback you get.

The idea is not to read carefully through every comment you get and provide individual feedback, but rather to skim through the evaluations, note common responses, and reply to them in the next class. If students request something you consider appropriate and are willing to do (such as giving more examples in class), announce that you will do it, and if they ask for something you are unwilling or unable to do (such as giving less homework), acknowledge the request and explain why you won't be granting it. As long as the students know you care about their learning, are willing to listen to them, and give their requests serious consideration, most will accept your decisions uncomplainingly.

If you don't take any other suggestion we offer in this book, take this one. Don't wait until the end of the semester to uncover problems—identify them while there is still time to do something about them.

Classroom assessment techniques

Classroom assessment techniques (often referred to as CATs) are short in-class formative assessment exercises that quickly provide an indication of how well students have grasped material you have been presenting. The best known CAT is the minute paper (Section 3.6.6), and many others are described by Angelo and Cross (1993).

Expert consulting

Most campuses have centers for teaching and learning whose mission includes helping faculty members improve their teaching. Besides offering programs on different aspects of instruction, consultants from some of those centers will observe your class and possibly make a video of it, go over your student evaluations with you, and offer suggestions. If you have access to services like that, take advantage of them.

Watching yourself teach on a video can be a humbling experience ("Good grief—do I really do *that?*"), but after the initial shock you'll start to see things you're doing well and areas in which you could improve. It's relatively easy to set up a camera in a corner of the room, let it run during class, and later review the video with a consultant or by yourself.

Post-course reflection

After the course is over and the assignments and projects and exams have been given and graded and evaluations have been collected from students and faculty colleagues, spend an hour or so going over all of it and reflecting on how you think things went. Then make notes on your course materials about what you want to do differently next time, and carry out the changes when the time comes.

Self-education

Dozens of books and hundreds of journals and newsletters (Journals in Higher Education [JIHE], n.d.) are excellent sources of information about effective STEM teaching methods. Even if you don't have the time or the inclination to read them cover-to-cover, just opening one and reading a random section or article is sure to be worthwhile. Also consider attending education workshops on your campus and education-related sessions at professional society conferences.

Thought Questions

What do you currently do to learn about the following:

❑ What are students in your class confused about?
❑ What do they find effective and ineffective about your teaching?
❑ What new teaching techniques and resources have been developed in your discipline?

What more might you be willing to do?

5.5 Ideas to Take Away

○ Lecturing nonstop almost guarantees that most of the course content will not be retained in students' long-term memories. Providing repeated opportunities in and out of class for the students to recall important content, reflect on it, and work with it improves the chances that it will be stored in long-term memory and subsequently retrieved when it is needed.

○ Students' understanding should be monitored continually in class by asking questions. Cold-calling on students for responses (calling on individuals without first giving all students time to think about the question) and calling for volunteers after every question are generally less effective than providing time for individual reflection or small-group discussion and then calling on individuals.

○ Pre-class assignments should be made as interactive as possible. Use online multimedia tutorials, screencasts, short lecture clips, and short essential readings, with online quizzes on the content of the assignments and feedback on the responses. Avoid assigning long readings and complete videotaped lectures.

○ A combination of midterm and end-of-course evaluations, peer observation, minute papers and other classroom assessment techniques, consultation with experts, post-class and post-course reflections, and regular reading of education-related books and journals leads to continual improvement of teaching.

5.6 Try This in Your Course

○ Look over your plans for an upcoming class session and make sure they include a few good questions to ask during class. Look over the sample questions in Section 4.5 to get ideas.

○ Collect minute papers after one or two class sessions and conduct a midterm evaluation several weeks into the course. Respond to each of these formative assessments in subsequent class sessions. Before you give the midterm evaluation, speculate on how you think many of your students would answer the questions on it. Write your speculations and then compare them with the students' actual responses.

○ Ask a colleague with a reputation as an outstanding teacher if you may observe one of his or her classes. If the answer is "yes" (which it almost certainly will be), sit in the back and take notes on anything noteworthy you see.

○ Ask a departmental colleague or a consultant from your campus center for teaching and learning to watch you teach and make notes on what you do well and what needs improvement. After class buy him or her a cup of coffee and debrief the observation.

INTERLUDE. MEET YOUR STUDENTS:
AISHA AND RACHEL

The scene is a dormitory room, shared by two computer science students. Rachel is hunched over her computer, looking at an open manual next to the keyboard, as Aisha breezes in.

Aisha: Hey, Rachel—shut it down and let's go ... it's party time!

Rachel: (Silence)

A: Come on—everyone's going to be there before we even get out of this room.

R: Calm down, Aish, I'm trying to get this code to work. Why don't you go on ahead and I'll get there later.

A: Right—just like last week, when you were going to get there in 15 minutes and you never showed at all.

R: I told you I got involved with the AI homework and lost track of time ... anyway, you know I hate these parties.

A: Here, I'll bet I can figure that out ... a few line commands here, a couple of mouse clicks there, and we're off for the bright lights and the ...

R: Aisha, get your hands off my computer! Let me look at the manual again and do it right. Remember how you were going to help me program my DVR to record the Grammys last week, and you "didn't need no freaking instructions!" and we ended up with a two-hour PBS special on liver transplants?

A: That was only because I ...

R: And how about that hardware lab where you shorted out the whole building? "Let's just do it—lab manuals are for wimps," she says, just before the explosion.

A: Yeah, but don't forget whose crazy idea got a patent application on her summer job ... your problem is you spend so much time thinking about what you're planning to do and worrying about why it might not work that you never get around to doing it ... but it's OK, think all night if you can stand it, I'm out of here ... oh, and don't forget, I asked Jake and Marty and Amy and a couple of the others to get together here tomorrow to study with us for the AI test.

R: Aisha, why do you keep doing this to me? You know I study better alone—besides, you have an attention span of about 20 seconds, and if those jokers are over here you can forget studying or anything else but ...

A: No way—I'm really serious this time. I just like to have people around—keeps things from getting too dull.

R: Too dull? You ...

A: Later, Rache—I'll save some foam for you ...

Aisha and Rachel have been best friends since elementary school, and no one was surprised when they enrolled at the same university and became roommates. What was surprising was that they became friends in the first place, because their personalities are polar opposites. Aisha loves crowds for parties or studying, and Rachel dislikes them except for small quiet gatherings of people she knows well. "Let's try this out and see what happens," says Aisha, as she dives in to an unfamiliar task. "Hold on—let's think it through," responds Rachel, as she dips her toe in the water. Rachel likes to work in solitude, and Aisha surrounds herself with others at every opportunity.

Aisha is an *active learner* and Rachel is a *reflective learner*. The two categories represent *learning style preferences* (Felder & Brent, 2005), not mutually exclusive categories: the preferences may be strong or weak, and all people exhibit characteristics of both types to different degrees. Active learners are inclined to experience things in order to understand them; reflective learners want the understanding to come before the experiencing. STEM students and professionals benefit from the strengths of both types—the thoughtfulness, capacity for sustained concentration, and desire for understanding of the reflective learner, and the quick thinking, willingness to experiment, and comfort with teamwork of the active learner. Unfortunately, although both active and reflective learners can become excellent professionals, the usual way STEM subjects are taught—nonstop lectures, homework done individually, and minimal hands-on experience—stacks the deck against the actives.

Several instructional techniques make classes more effective and enjoyable for active learners or reflective learners or both. Introduce demonstrations of experiments—preferably hands-on—into traditional lecture classes (for the active learners), and mini-lectures on interpretation of experimental results into laboratory courses (for the reflective learners). Use interactive computer tutorials and simulations: active learners will enjoy the activity they provide and reflective learners will get practice in trial-and-error analysis in a relatively risk-free environment. Assign some homework to teams of three or four (active learners) rather than only to individuals (reflective learners). Use active learning (Chapters 4 and 6), which provides active learners with opportunities for interaction and reflective learners with opportunities to reflect (not everyone talks at once during activities).

Note: Learning styles have been used extensively to help design instruction in all disciplines (Felder & Brent, 2005). The point is not to teach each student in the way that he or she prefers; rather, it is to make sure instruction is balanced and not heavily biased in favor of one preference or its opposite. We discuss learning styles in greater detail—including some controversy about them in the academic psychology community—in Chapter 12.

6

ACTIVE LEARNING

6.0 Introduction

A point we have made frequently in this book (which won't stop us from making it again now) is that true learning results from doing things and reflecting on the outcomes, not from passively receiving information. To maximize students' learning, we should give them active practice and feedback, in and out of class, on the tasks listed in our objectives. Chapters 3 through 5 each offered a few suggestions for getting students actively engaged in class. This chapter looks more systematically at *active learning,* a teaching approach that encompasses anything students might be called on to do in class besides watching and listening to an instructor and taking notes. Hundreds of research studies and several meta-analyses of the research have shown that active learning outperforms traditional lecturing in promoting almost every learning outcome examined (Freeman et al., 2014; Prince, 2004; Wieman, 2014).

Active learning is not a difficult method but it is learner-centered, which means that it places more responsibility on students for their own learning than traditional teacher-centered methods do (Weimer, 2013). As we have also suggested several times in the book, not all students are overjoyed to have that added responsibility. The interlude preceding this chapter illustrates that some students (like Aisha) are perfectly happy and comfortable working with active learning groups, whereas others (like Rachel) may not be. Instructors who use active learning should anticipate pushback from a subset of their students and should be prepared to deal with it.

This chapter addresses these questions:

o What can I ask students to do in active learning exercises? What mistakes should I try to avoid?
o I'm concerned that if I use active learning, I will (a) have to spend lots of time thinking up activities, (b) sacrifice content coverage, and (c) lose control of my class. I also worry that students will (d) complain, (e) refuse to participate, and (f) give me low end-of-class ratings. How can I avoid each of those outcomes?
o How should I use active learning in recitations (tutorials, problem sessions) and flipped classrooms?

6.1 What Is Active Learning?

Thanks to some good research in recent decades, we know a lot about how learning happens—and how little of it happens in most traditional lectures (Ambrose et al., 2010; Bransford et al., 2000; Freeman et al., 2014; Mastascusa et al., 2011; Prince, 2004; Svinicki & McKeachie, 2014; Weimer, 2013). The ineffectiveness of boring and confusing lectures is obvious, but on every campus there are a few brilliant teachers—knowledgeable, articulate, charismatic, and sometimes funny. Their students give them top ratings year after year and line up to get into their classes. Can't traditional lectures given by *those* instructors be effective learning experiences?

It depends on what you mean by effective. A good traditional lecture can certainly serve several useful purposes, including sparking interest in the lecture topic, raising questions and provoking subsequent discussion, and filling in gaps in people's knowledge when they already understand most of the lecture content. However, even an excellent traditional lecture on complex and relatively unfamiliar content equips students to do what the instructor is describing as well as a lecture on diving would equip them to do three and a half somersaults off a ten-meter platform. The procedure could be meticulously laid out in the lecture, but the implementation would probably not end well.

The only way a skill is developed—diving, writing, critical thinking, deducing biochemical pathways, or solving dynamics problems—is through *practice*: trying something, seeing how it works, possibly getting feedback, reflecting on how to do it better, and trying again. Certainly that kind of thing happens (or should happen) in homework assignments, but you have roughly 40 contact hours with students in a typical one-semester course. Why not use at least part of that time to give the students some guided practice in the tasks they'll later be asked to perform on assignments and tests? In other words, why not use active learning?

Many different definitions of active learning are floating around the education world. This is the one we will use: *Active learning is anything course-related that students in a class session are called on to do other than simply watching and listening to a lecture and taking notes.* Some active learning tasks are listed in Table 6.1–1 and others are scattered throughout the rest of the book.

In the remainder of this chapter we will present different ways you can structure class activities, briefly survey the research that confirms the effectiveness of active learning, and discuss how to deal with problems that may arise when you use this method.

Table 6.1–1. Active Learning Tasks

---

o Recall prior material (e.g., what was covered in the previous class session).
o Answer a question.
o Start a [problem solution, derivation] or take the next step.
o Draw a [free-body diagram, circuit diagram, plot, flow chart, product life cycle].
o Think of a real-world application of [the material we just covered, the formula we just derived].
o Diagnose a [defective product, set of symptoms, computer error message].
o Predict [an experimental outcome, a system response to a change in input].
o Sketch the form of [a complex mathematical function, the solution of a differential equation] without doing any calculations.
o Critique a [writing sample, oral presentation, data interpretation, computer code, clinical procedure, process design, product design].
o Figure out why a calculated quantity may be wrong or different from a measured value of the quantity.
o Brainstorm a list of ways to do something.
o Think of a question about material just covered in class.
o Summarize a lecture or part of a lecture.

6.2 Structures and Formats of Activities

Once you have decided what you want the students to do (such as any of the tasks listed in Table 6.1–1), you can choose from three basic active learning formats:

Individual exercises.

Assign a task and give the students a brief period of time—generally between five seconds and three minutes—to work on the task individually. They all may not have enough time to complete the task, which is fine: collective closure will be reached before the exercise is concluded. When the allotted time has elapsed, call on one or more students to share their responses, and call on volunteers for additional responses if the task is open-ended (that is, if there can be more than one acceptable response). Discuss the responses and then move on with your session plan.

Small-group exercises.

Similar to individual exercises, but have students get into small groups (generally two to four) to work on the assigned task. If the task requires writing, arbitrarily designate a single recorder for each group (e.g., the student farthest to your left, the student born in a location closest to the classroom, or any group member who has not yet recorded that day). When the allotted time has elapsed, get responses from one or more randomly chosen individuals or groups.

Think-pair-share (Lyman, 1981).

Have students work on a task individually and then get into pairs to compare and improve their responses. Call randomly on individuals to share their pairs' solutions. Think-pair-share may take longer than jumping directly to groups, but the individual reflection can lead to more and deeper learning.

When faculty members first encounter the idea of active learning, many worry that they will have to spend a lot of time organizing and reorganizing groups. There is little value in doing that, so don't: just tell the class to form groups where they are sitting so that each student only has to lean over, turn around, or at worst move over a few seats to get into a group. Students will tend to work with the same people most of the time, but that's not a problem for the brief turn-to-your-neighbor sort of activities we are considering here. To expose students to a wider variety of thinking and problem-solving styles, you may occasionally ask the students at the beginning of class to sit with other people that day, but let it go at that.

(However, when students work in teams on major projects, group composition is extremely important and should not be left to chance. We discuss this issue in Chapter 11.)

Many types of structured activities have been developed to address specific learning outcomes and skills (Barkley, 2009; Felder & Brent, 2009; Johnson et al., 2006). Several particularly effective ones are described in this book (see Table 6.2–1).

Table 6.2–1. Active Learning Structures That Address Specific Outcomes and Skills

---

○ **Getting courses off to a good start.** Several exercises are given in Chapter 3.

○ **Technical problem solving and mathematical analysis skills.** *Handouts with gaps* (Chapter 4). *Chunked analysis:* Break problem solutions and derivations into relatively small parts and have students work through the parts in activities (this chapter, Chapter 9). *Thinking-aloud pair problem solving (TAPPS):* Students work through analyses in pairs, alternately explaining steps (one pair member) and questioning explanations and giving hints when necessary (the other pair member) (this chapter, Chapter 9).

○ **Computing and programming skills.** *Pair programming:* Students work at computers in pairs alternating roles of pilot (keyboarding, tactical thinking) and navigator (checking, strategic thinking) (this chapter).

○ **Communication skills.** *Writing, speaking, and critiquing exercises* (Chapter 10).

○ **Conceptual understanding.** *ConcepTests* (Chapter 8).

○ **Reading for comprehension.** *Guided reciprocal peer questioning:* Students formulate questions about assigned readings, using question stems that promote high-level thinking, and quiz one another in class (Chapter 5).

○ **Creative thinking skills.** *Brainstorming, problem formulation exercises* (Chapter 10).

○ **Critical thinking skills.** *Decision-making, critiquing exercises* (Chapter 10).

○ **High-performance teamwork skills.** *Crisis clinics:* Evaluating and addressing hypothetical team member behaviors and team dysfunctionalities (Chapter 11).

6.3 How Well Does Active Learning Work? Why Does It Work?

Prince (2004) reviewed a large volume of research on active learning and concluded that activities in class sessions consistently increased short-term and long-term retention of information presented. A more recent meta-analysis specifically for STEM courses showed that using active learning led to an average increase in examination scores of about 6%, an even greater increase in scores on tests of conceptual understanding, and a whopping 33% reduction in the incidence of failure (Freeman et al., 2014).

Why do in-class activities have such significant effects on learning, retention, and conceptual understanding of information? We will suggest several reasons, including a key one having to do with cognitive retrieval (recalling information from long-term memory).

Brainwave: Retrieval Practice Promotes Learning

Students can take several different approaches to studying course material. They can reread their textbooks and assigned readings, perhaps highlighting parts that they think are important, and look over their old homework assignments. They can prepare outlines, concept maps, or study guides of course material, or they can try to recall the material without looking it up.

An impressive body of recent research has clearly shown that the last approach (recalling from memory), which has been called *retrieval practice* and *test-enhanced learning,* leads to greater, longer-lasting, and more transferable learning of previously learned information than other common studying techniques do. The effect increases when the recall activities are challenging, rapid feedback on the responses is provided, and the retrievals are spaced over relatively long intervals rather than taking place in short concentrated bursts (Brown et al., 2014; Karpicke & Blunt, 2011; Pyc et al., 2014; Roediger & Butler, 2011).

This *retrieval practice effect* has important implications for teaching and studying, and we'll bring it back at several points in the rest of the book. For now, though, we'll just note that it accounts in part for the research-proven effectiveness of active learning relative to traditional lecturing. In a lecture you might outline a problem-solving method and give an example, and if you're a decent lecturer it might all seem clear to the students. Only later when they spend hour after frustrating hour on assignments do they discover that they didn't get critical parts of the lecture. In active learning, you teach the method in small steps, followed by activities that require the students to retrieve what was just taught and—ideally—integrate it with previously learned material, which they also have to retrieve. Their chances of being able to subsequently use the method on their own are then significantly higher than they would have been without the retrieval practice.

There are many other reasons active learning works as well as it does. Two notable ones follow.

Active learning reduces the cognitive load on working memory, making retention and storage of new information more likely.

It takes time for the brain to examine new information in working memory; evaluate its relevance to the individual's interests, goals, and prior knowledge; and decide whether or not to store it in long-term memory. Since working memory has a severely limited capacity for information, if you subject your students to a nonstop content-heavy lecture, you flood them with new information at a rate faster than their working memories can process. The consequence is that relatively little of what you present has a chance of being absorbed. However, when you periodically give your students something to do that requires using recently presented information, their working memories have a chance to rehearse the information, increasing its chances of being stored in long-term memory.

Learning requires attentiveness. It is difficult or impossible for students to pay attention to anything for very long while they are passive.

Several researchers have measured the percentage of students paying attention to a lecturer at different times during the lecture (Bligh, 1998, Ch. 2; Bunce et al., 2010; Middendorf & Kalish, 1996; Penner, 1984; Stuart & Rutherford, 1978). The plot for a typical lecture with no activities looks like Figure 6.3–1. The scale on the y-axis can vary considerably from one class and instructor to another, but in a number of studies the maximum of the curve was somewhere around 70% and the minimum around 20%.

We don't know precisely what leads to the response pattern shown in Figure 6.3–1, but we can guess. In the beginning of class, many students are occupied with a variety of activities, such as getting their course notes and textbooks out and ready, copying an assignment from the board or a slide, and chatting with their neighbors. As they settle in, their average

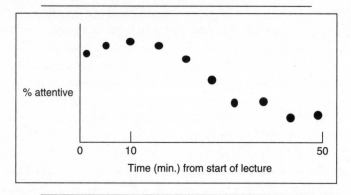

Figure 6.3–1: Attentiveness versus Time in Lecture—No Activities

attentiveness to the instructor goes up and reaches a maximum about ten minutes into the class. Then the curve plummets as the students give in to the natural human inability to keep attention focused on anything for very long while being passive. (If you doubt it, try to sit still and keep your attention fixed on something for, say, a minute, and see how long it takes before your mind drifts off to something else.) Because information that never makes it into the students' brains in the first place can't possibly be retained there, the last part of the lecture is pretty much a waste of time for them and the instructor. However, when students are periodically given something course-related to do during a class, the attentiveness data look more like Figure 6.3–2 (Middendorf & Kalish, 1996).

Granted, even when you incorporate activities into a class session, some students may still be disengaged. There is much less disengagement than

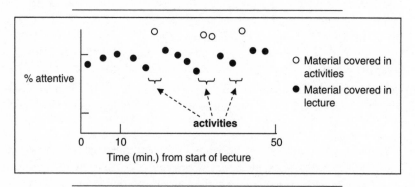

Figure 6.3–2: Attentiveness versus Time in
Lecture—Activities Interspersed

in conventional lectures, though, and—as the research clearly shows—the amount of learning that occurs is correspondingly greater.

Other reasons to use active learning are that it generates much more energy in a classroom than traditional lectures can—sometimes literally waking students up—and it actively engages most or all students, not just a select few sitting near the front. In addition, when small-group active learning is done correctly (we'll soon say what that means), academically weak students get the benefit of being tutored by stronger classmates, and stronger students get the deep understanding that comes from teaching someone else. Students who successfully complete a task understand it in a way they never could from just watching a lecturer do it, and students who are unsuccessful are put on notice that they don't know something they may need to know. When the answer is provided shortly afterwards, the latter students are likely to pay attention to an extent seldom seen in traditional lectures.

Before we get into details of how to do active learning, we want to make one point clear. *We are not telling you to abandon lecturing and make every class you teach a nonstop festival of activities.* The key concept is balance—some lecturing and some activity. As Maryellen Weimer (2013) suggests, "Teachers need to stop doing so many of the learning tasks for students. Teachers should not always be organizing the content, generating the examples, asking the questions, answering the questions, summarizing the discussion, solving the problems, and constructing the diagrams. The key word here is 'always.' On occasion (and in some classes there may be lots of occasions) teachers need to do all of these things for students. The principle is about gradually doing them less" (p. 72).

6.4 Active Learning for Problem Solving

When STEM instructors unfamiliar with active learning hear about it, many quickly reject the idea. Take Professor Schmendrick, for example. A colleague somehow talked him into going to a workshop on active learning. After a few minutes, he got up and walked out. When asked about it later, he snorted and said, *"Oh, that stuff is fine for liberal arts, but I teach science! The law of conservation of mass is what it is, period. My job is to tell my students what it is, not to have a discussion or debate or share my feelings about it."*

Very shortly after that rant, Schmendrick could be heard reciting another familiar speech. *"These students are nothing like the ones I went to school with. I solved a simple boundary value problem in class last*

Wednesday and gave them an identical homework problem due Friday, and only two students in the whole class had the slightest clue how to do it. If I didn't curve grades I'd end up failing this whole class, which is probably what should happen."

One thing you can say about Schmendrick is that at least he's consistent: everything he's saying is wrong. The law of conservation of mass has been a subject of discussion and interpretation since the early twentieth century, and if you want to hear arguments as intense as anything you'll ever hear in a philosophy class, go to any scientific conference and sit in on a few sessions. Schmendrick is equally wrong about the students. Almost all of them will go on to do fine in their courses, graduate, and have successful careers—and if they need to solve boundary value problems in their jobs (which very few ever will), they will learn to do it.

Active learning works as well for teaching STEM courses and topics as it does for teaching anything else. One of the best-known active learning formats is *peer instruction*, the clicker-based strategy developed and popularized by the physicist Eric Mazur (1997) of Harvard University and now widely used in physics and every other STEM discipline. We will say more about peer instruction and clickers in Chapter 7 on teaching with technology, and discuss their application to the identification and correction of student misconceptions in Chapter 8. The rest of this section describes other active learning strategies that are particularly effective for teaching technical problem solving.

Chunked problem analysis

Instead of simply presenting a fully worked-out solution or derivation in one continuous block, break it up into small chunks. (This use of the term *chunk* to denote breaking down a complex structure or process into relatively simple parts is common and should not be confused with the neurocognitive use of *chunk* to denote a coded unit of information in working or long-term memory.) Some of the chunks will be straightforward algebraic and numerical calculations, and others will be conceptually difficult or tricky—the kind of work students might think they understand in a lecture but completely baffles them when they try to do it on their own. Quickly lecture through the straightforward parts (or let the students read through them on handouts) and then have the students work through the hard parts in active learning exercises. If a part is too long for most students to complete in three minutes or less, break it into smaller chunks. Details on how and why this technique works are given in Section 4.7 ("Use Handouts with Gaps") and in a video illustrating its use in an engineering class (Active Learning, 1998).

Working through worked-out examples

Most STEM instructors follow a pattern of teaching a problem-solving method, showing an example of its use, and then having the students solve similar problems in assignments. If the assigned problems are almost identical to the example, the students may be able to solve them by copying what they saw in class, but if the problems are slightly different the students are likely to flounder helplessly. The flaw in this teaching approach is that it quickly shows students a complex method and an example of its application without giving them an opportunity to reflect on the individual steps of the method. Their working memories are consequently likely to be in cognitive overload, incapable of doing all the perceiving and processing necessary to integrate the new information into their long-term memories.

As an alternative, when first introducing a method, consider handing out worked-out derivations and problem solutions and having the students explain them step-by-step, first to one another and then to you. Studying worked-out examples reduces cognitive load considerably. Instead of having to absorb the *hows* of every step, the students can focus on the *whys*. Especially in the initial stages of learning a new problem-solving method, this approach has been shown to reduce learning time, improve learning outcomes, and promote transfer of methods to other problems and contexts (Ambrose et al., 2010, p. 106; Renkl, 2014; Sweller, 2006; Sweller et al., 2011).

The next active learning structure is ideal for taking students through worked-out solutions.

Thinking-aloud pair problem solving

Thinking-aloud pair problem solving (TAPPS) is a powerful technique for facilitating deep understanding of something complex—a difficult problem solution or derivation, for example, or an analysis of an article or case study (Lochhead & Whimbey, 1987). The students work in pairs, alternating in roles of *explainer* (if they will be going through a worked-out problem solution or analysis) or *problem-solver* (if they will be solving the problem or performing the analysis themselves) and *questioner*. The explainer explains a small portion of the solution or article or case analysis, line-by-line, to the questioner. The questioner asks questions if the explainer says something that isn't completely clear, gives hints if the explainer is stuck on something and the questioner can help, and prompts the explainer to keep talking if he or she falls silent for too long. The instructor stops the pairs after one to three minutes, calls randomly on several students to summarize the analysis they just carried out, discusses the analysis, answers questions from the class, and then has the pairs reverse roles and move on to the next part of the problem or text. The process continues until the complete analysis has been worked out.

During this exercise, the instructor intersperses questions about the solution method *(Why was this equation used? How could you verify this result? What would have happened if instead of _____ you had used _____? Why_____? What if _____?)* and has the students address the questions using the same explainer-questioner alternation. By the end of the class session, most students are likely to understand the solution method, derivation, or analysis to a depth rarely achieved with any other teaching technique.

Pair programming

Pair programming, a variation of TAPPS, works very well for assignments that involve writing code or using software or simulations (Williams & Kessler, 2002). Students work in pairs at computers. One student in each pair—the pilot—does the keyboarding, and the other one—the navigator—watches what the pilot is doing, suggests strategies for approaching the task, and watches for errors. Periodically the students switch roles. In a computer lab setting, the instructor circulates to offer help when students are stuck and may intersperse mini-lectures or questions about the assignment. It may take a bit longer for students working this way to complete tasks than if they were working individually, but they generally make fewer mistakes.

6.5 Common Active Learning Mistakes

Active learning is an easy and remarkably robust teaching method that functions well in every conceivable academic setting—a claim supported by a mountain of literature. Instructors who start using it often limit its effectiveness by making certain mistakes, however, and many drop the method when the results disappoint them or they experience vigorous student resistance. Table 6.5–1 lists six mistakes to avoid when you use active learning and strategies to avoid making them, and the paragraphs that follow elaborate on the strategies.

Set the stage before you start using active learning.

Many of your students may have experienced only traditional lecturing before they show up in your class. If you suddenly plunge them into active learning with no preparation, their assumption may be that you're either playing some kind of game with them or conducting an experiment with them as the guinea pigs, neither of which they appreciate, and you may experience some vigorous pushback.

Table 6.5–1. Six Common Active Learning Mistakes

Mistake	How to Avoid the Mistake
1. Plunge into active learning with no explanation.	First explain what you're going to do and why it is in the students' best interests.
2. Expect all students to eagerly get into groups the first time you ask them to.	Be proactive with reluctant students in the first few group activities you conduct.
3. Make activities trivial.	Make active learning tasks challenging enough to justify the time it takes to do them.
4. Make activities too long, such as assigning an entire problem in a single activity.	Keep activities short and focused (five seconds to three minutes). Break large problems into small chunks.
5. Call for volunteers after every activity.	After some activities, call randomly on individuals or groups to report their results.
6. Fall into a predictable routine.	Vary the formats and lengths of activities and the intervals between them.

You can minimize and possibly even eliminate student resistance to active learning by taking a little time on the first day of class to explain what you'll be doing, why you'll be doing it, and what's in it for the students. An illustrative explanation in the interlude "Sermons for Grumpy Campers" preceding Chapter 11 may be helpful. Felder and Brent (1996), Felder (2011a), and Seidel and Tanner (2013) discuss student resistance to learner-centered teaching methods—why it occurs, what forms it may take, and how instructors can deal with it when it arises.

Be proactive in the first few group activities.

When you first ask students to get into small groups in class and do something, if they are active learners (see preceding interlude) or accustomed to group work they are likely to jump right into it. However, if they are reflective learners or novices or veterans of bad experiences with groups, they may ignore your request and start to work alone. Instructors who encounter that behavior tend to be discouraged by it, and when they encounter it they may be tempted to give up on active learning.

If you find yourself in that situation, don't give up. When you assign your first activity, give the instructions calmly and confidently, as though fully expecting all of the students to do what you ask. If some start working individually, casually move toward them and tell them to work with each other. With rare exceptions, they will. The second time you call for an activity, most of the class will engage immediately, and by the third time you should see at most one or two students remaining isolated. Don't worry about them—it's their loss. (We'll explain that statement later in the chapter.)

Make group activities challenging.

Students expect to be treated like adults and are likely to resent being asked to do anything they consider trivial. A common active learning mistake is to put students in groups to address questions with obvious answers. You are wasting their time, and they don't appreciate it. Make the questions and problems hard enough to justify the time it takes to get into groups and figure out answers.

Keep activities short.

Two problems commonly arise when students are given, say, ten minutes to solve a problem. Some finish in two minutes and spend the next eight on their smartphones or talking to their neighbors about the football game, which is a waste of valuable class time. Other students struggle for the full ten minutes and fail to complete the task, which is intensely frustrating and also generally a waste of time after the first few minutes. If you keep the activities short and focused—anywhere between five seconds and three minutes—you avoid both problems.

Most technical problems take more than three minutes to solve, so rather than allowing enough time for most students to get complete solutions, break the problems into chunks. The students may struggle with something but only for a short time before they get feedback and clarification, and they can then proceed to the next step.

Sometimes call on individuals after activities.

Probably the most common active learning mistake is to call on volunteers for responses after every activity. When you do that, many students won't even bother to think about what they were asked to do, knowing that someone else will eventually provide the answer. The benefits of active learning will then be realized by only a small fraction of the class.

However, most students don't want to be in the embarrassing position of having had time to work on something, individually or with others, and then being called on and having nothing to say. If they know that after any given activity you might call on them, most or all of them will make a serious effort to do whatever you asked them to do. You don't have to call on individuals after every activity—as long as you do it often enough for the students to be aware that it *could* happen, it will have the desired effect.

Don't be predictable.

Active learning has the potential to create a lively and instructive classroom environment. If you conduct it with the monotonous regularity of a cuckoo clock, however (lecture ten minutes, one-minute pair activity, lecture ten minutes, one-minute pair activity, etc.), it can quickly become as monotonous as straight lecturing. The key is to mix things up. Vary the type of activity (answering questions, beginning problem solutions, taking the next step in a problem solution or derivation, brainstorming, etc.); the activity duration (five seconds to three minutes); the interval between activities (one to fifteen minutes); and the size of the groups (one to four students). If your students can never be sure what you're going to do next, you have a good chance of holding their attention for the entire class session.

Thought Question

If you are not experienced in active learning and you are like most instructors, you probably still have worries about it that could discourage you from trying it. What are they? Make a list before reading the next section, which reviews and addresses the concerns we hear most often. See how many of your worries show up on our list, and then see if you find our reassurances convincing.

6.6 Common Active Learning Concerns

Faculty members who have never tried active learning—and some who have tried it—commonly express concerns about it. Table 6.6-1 shows the five we hear most often. Here are our responses to them.

I'll never be able to cover my syllabus if I have to spend all that time on activities.

Yes, you will. First, remember that we are talking about incorporating some brief activities into lectures, not completely replacing lecturing with active learning. In a typical class session, you may spend only a few minutes on activities and the remaining time may be business as usual. If you want to do more, put your lecture notes into handouts with gaps (Section 4.7), and then instead of lecturing on everything, have the

Table 6.6–1. Five Common Concerns about Active Learning

1. I'll never be able to cover my syllabus.
2. I'll have to spend lots of time designing activities.
3. The noise level will become excessive, and I'll waste a lot of time getting the students' attention back.
4. Some students will refuse to get into groups.
5. The students will complain that I'm not doing my job, and my student ratings will plummet.

students quickly read through the straightforward parts themselves and fill in some or all of the gaps in activities. You'll be able to do as much active learning as you want and still cover the entire syllabus, possibly even extending it.

If I use active learning, I'll have to spend lots of time designing activities.

You can spend as little time designing activities as you want to, all the way down to none. You probably already ask some questions during your class sessions to see if students are following you. Instead of always directing those questions to the whole class, occasionally ask a question, tell the students to turn to one or two neighbors and try to answer it, and then process the responses as usual. No preparation time is required.

You can do a much better job with active learning, however, if you build some activities into your session plans, spend a few minutes after each session reviewing how the activities went, and modify them if necessary. After one or two repetitions of the course, the activities will be in place and no additional preparation time will be required.

The noise level will get out of hand, and I'll waste a lot of time getting the students' attention back.

All you need is a signal (such as a loud handclap or bell or timer on your phone) that tells the students to finish their sentences and turn their attention back to you. After the first few activities, it shouldn't take you longer than five seconds to get them back with you, even if there are hundreds of them in the class.

Some students will refuse to get into groups.

As we observed previously in this chapter, the first time you tell a class of students who have never done active learning to get into groups, many are apt to stare straight ahead and start working alone. Our advice was to be proactive, casually and confidently directing neighboring resistant students to work with each other. After you've done that two or three times, either all of the students will get into groups when you ask them to or a small number will persist in working alone.

The sight of a few nonparticipants really bothers some instructors, tempting them to conclude that active learning isn't working and they should go back to straight lecturing. Here's a better way to look at it. Let's imagine that when you conduct active learning exercises, after the first few times you do it 90% of your students are actively engaged and 10% remain isolated. (It has never been remotely close to 10% in our classes after the first week, but we're doing a worst-case scenario.) Now think about what's happening when you're lecturing. Suppose, for example, that you've been going on for 20 minutes. If as many as 10% percent of your students *are* actively engaged with your lecture material at that point, you're doing very well.

The point is that no instructional technique comes with a guarantee that it will always work for all students at all times. The best we can do as teachers is to reach as many students as possible, and 90% engagement is obviously a lot better than 10%. Well-designed activities provide practice and rapid feedback in strategies and skills the students will need for assignments and exams. If a few choose not to take advantage of those opportunities despite your encouragement, don't lose sleep over it—it's their loss.

Students will complain that I'm not doing my job, and my student ratings will plummet.

Students are often uneasy about learner-centered teaching methods, which put more responsibility on them than traditional lecturing does. When you begin to use active learning in a class that isn't already accustomed to it, you can count on initially getting complaints from some of your students.

An effective way to deal with such complaints is to set the stage for active learning on Day 1 (see Section 6.5). You might also include a question about active learning in a midterm course evaluation, such as *"Do you think in-class activities are (1) helping your learning, (2) hindering your learning, or (3) neither helping nor hindering?"* Especially if you are avoiding the mistakes listed in Section 6.5, most of the students will probably be either positive or neutral and only a few will still be negative. If that outcome is indeed what you see, announce the response distribution in the next class session. Students in the negative category often imagine they are part of a mass movement. As soon as they find out that there are only a few of them in the class, their complaints are likely to stop and your end-of-course ratings won't suffer a bit (Felder, 1995; Koretsky & Brooks, 2012).

6.7 Active Learning in Recitations and Flipped Classrooms

STEM courses frequently involve a combination of class sessions conducted by the course instructor and other sessions known as *recitations* (the term we will use), *problem sessions,* or *tutorials,* which may be led by the course instructor or teaching assistants. At least in principle, recitations provide practice in the methods taught in the more formal class sessions and greater opportunities for interactions with an instructor.

A type of class that has elements in common with recitations is the *flipped* (or *inverted) classroom.* In this approach, students receive online instruction outside class and then come to class to work through activities that build on the online material, in much the way recitations build on class sessions. We provide more details about flipping—particularly the online part—in Chapter 7. In the remainder of this section, we will refer only to recitations, but everything we say will apply equally well to the in-class component of flipped classrooms.

Active learning should be the primary teaching method used in recitations. Most of the techniques and recommendations we have offered for active learning in regular class sessions apply perfectly to recitations, with the only substantive difference being the time allocated to the activities. For class sessions we recommended an upper limit of three minutes, but in recitations in which activities take up most of the period there is no need for that strict a limit. We recommend that you circulate among the students while they are working and observe what they are doing. When you see evidence that some are heading in wrong directions or not making satisfactory progress, offer hints to get them back on track. If several individuals or groups are having the same problem, stop the activity and either give a mini-lecture to clear up the issue, have a brief question-and-answer session, or ask a group that avoided or overcame the difficulty to explain how they did it. Then resume the activity.

6.8 Ideas to Take Away

- ○ Active learning is anything course-related that students are called on to do in class—individually or in small groups—other than simply observing a lecture and taking notes. Research has demonstrated conclusively that a combination of lecturing and activity promotes learning much more effectively than lecturing alone.
- ○ The longer students sit passively in a class, the more their attention drifts from the presentation and the longer the drifts last. If you go for more than about 15 minutes without an activity, you may have lost more than half of your students.

o Showing students how to solve a technical problem or derive a complex formula by lecturing through an example in class has very limited instructional value. A much better approach is to break the problem or derivation into small chunks, lecture on the simple parts or have the students read those parts themselves in a handout and guide the students through the hard parts in active learning exercises.

o Students often learn more by explaining a worked-out example step-by-step than by working out the complete solution themselves, especially when they are first learning a problem-solving method.

o The effectiveness of active learning is maximized if the instructor (1) explains how it will work and why it is in the students' best interests, (2) proactively encourages students to get into groups the first one or two times they are asked to do it, (3) avoids trivial activities, (4) keeps the activities short (generally less than three minutes), (5) doesn't always call on volunteers after activities, and (6) varies the formats and lengths of activities and the intervals between them.

6.9 Try This in Your Course

o At the beginning of a class session, do an active review of the preceding session. Give the students one minute to individually list from memory the main points made in the previous class (perhaps reminding them of the topics covered). Stop them and give them another minute to get into pairs and expand their lists, and then call on some of them to state one or two points they remembered.

o When working through a problem solution or derivation in class, stop when you get to a difficult step, tell the students to get into groups of two and three, and give them a short time to see how far they can get on the solution. Stop the groups after the allotted time and call on several to report on what they did (writing the correct solution on the board as it is reported). When the step has been completed satisfactorily, either discuss it or proceed to the next step.

o After you have covered some complex or difficult material, instead of asking if anyone has questions, put the students in pairs and give them thirty seconds to think of one or two good questions, and then call randomly on students to share their questions. You will get as many questions as you want.

o Give the students a handout containing a partially completed problem solution or derivation, and have them work through it using TAPPS.

INTERLUDE. IS TECHNOLOGY A FRIEND OR FOE OF LEARNING?

A popular debate topic in education circles is whether or not the rise of instructional technology (blended learning, distance education, flipped classrooms, MOOCs, and all that) signals the end of higher education as we know it. As it happens, we believe it might, but we regard this as good news, not bad. Consider the following three scenarios.

Scenario 1

Noriko goes to her 8 a.m. intro biology class, drops her homework on the front desk, takes her seat, yawns, and wonders if she'll be able to stay awake until 9:15. About a quarter of the students enrolled in the class are there. Dr. Maxwell greets them and asks if they have any questions. They don't. To review the previous lesson, she asks a question about Mendel's experiments on the crossbreeding of peas. Eventually a student in the front row volunteers a response. Dr. Maxwell fills in the rest of the review and goes on to show a long series of slides describing and differentiating between mitosis and meiosis and outlining how those processes relate to Mendel's principles of inheritance. Noriko glances frequently at her watch, and when she sees it is 9:13 she closes her notebook. The instant Dr. Maxwell stops lecturing, Noriko wakes her neighbor and heads for the door with the rest of the class.

Scenario 2

Angela boots up her computer, logs in to a website managed by Noriko's university, and watches a screen capture of the same lecture Noriko attended. Afterwards she downloads the next assignment and heads off to her job. She will complete the assignment in the next few days and upload it to be graded.

Scenario 3

Almost every day, Josh boots up his computer, connects to his course website, reviews the assignment schedule, and works for one to two hours. This week, he does the following:

○ Quickly reads through last week's posted handout on Mendel's experiments and reviews a seven-minute screencast of the course instructor lecturing on that topic.
○ Works through a virtual genetics lab session that enables him to simulate and replicate Mendel's experiments.
○ Takes a short quiz about the lab. If he misses a question he is given a hint and asked to try again. If he misses again, he is given the answer.
○ Logs in to a threaded discussion on the course website to review a thread dealing with a confusing homework problem, and posts a question about the problem that had not been addressed.
○ Views another screencast in which cell mitosis and meiosis are illustrated with animations and linked with Mendel's inheritance principles. He is confused by one step in meiosis and replays that part of the screencast, which clears up his confusion. He then takes and submits a quiz about the screencast and gets instant feedback.
○ Begins an assignment that requires him to make predictions about fruit fly experiments and then simulates the experiments and tests his predictions using the virtual genetics lab.
○ Checks his messages and finds one from his instructor answering a question he had sent late the previous night. Sends a message to the other members of his class project group reminding them of their scheduled virtual meeting and logs off.

Scenario 1 describes the traditional classroom, which dominates higher education as this book is being written and may still dominate it when you read it. The students are passive recipients of information, except for the few who ask questions if they don't understand something. Scenario 2 is an online equivalent of Scenario 1, except that technology is used to broadcast the class via the Internet and Angela has no opportunity to ask questions. The lesson in Scenario 3 uses the full power of technology to actively engage students. All of the instructional tools used in the lesson—screencasts, visualizations, virtual labs, online discussion forums, virtual project group sessions, and online quizzes with corrective feedback—are increasingly available for many STEM topics.

The scenarios raise an important question. If Noriko, Angela, and Josh are roughly equivalent in intelligence and background, which of them will learn more—the one attending a traditional live lecture, the one passively receiving an online lecture, or the one taught with interactive technology? There's no way to know for sure, of course—how much a student learns in a course depends on many factors—but interactive technology is unquestionably the way to bet. The rich mixture of visual and verbal presentation and knowledge retrieval practice provided by the technology in Scenario 3 and described in greater detail in Chapter 7 is far more likely than traditional live and online lectures to promote significant learning. The fact that Josh lives 750 miles away from the institution where his course originates and has never seen his instructor in person doesn't change that likelihood.

7

TEACHING WITH TECHNOLOGY

7.0 Introduction

Most of the teaching and learning principles discussed in Chapters 1 through 6 apply to any learning environment, including the three described in the preceding interlude—face-to-face classes, purely online courses, and a hybrid of face-to-face and online instruction. Our objective in this chapter is to apply those principles explicitly to technology-assisted instruction and see what conclusions and suggestions emerge. Here are questions the chapter addresses:

o How can instructional technology enhance learning? How can it hinder learning? Which technology-based tools and methods are on the "enhance" and "hinder" lists?
o What is a *flipped classroom*? What are the potential benefits of flipping? What cautions should be exercised when doing it?
o How can active learning be done in online courses?
o What are massive open online courses (MOOCs)? How can instructors of face-to-face courses make use of MOOCs?

7.1 Instructional Technology Tools

Instructional technology encompasses a broad and constantly growing range of devices and methods (Hart, 2015), most of which can be used in both face-to-face and online teaching. Table 7.1–1 briefly surveys

Table 7.1–1. Instructional Technology Tools

Resource	Description	Uses	Sources
Course management system (e.g., Blackboard, Canvas, Moodle)	Online resources to carry out a variety of functions in a course	○ Archive class rolls, syllabi, study guides, handouts, assignments, exams, other course materials ○ Administer assignments, quizzes, and exams; record and grade submissions; compute averages	○ Most universities and colleges support one or more systems.
Presentation hardware and software	Slides, videos, screencasts	○ Deliver course content	○ Digital resource libraries
Personal response systems	Students respond to *polls* (multiple-choice questions) using clickers, smartphones, or tablet or laptop computers.	○ Provide retrieval practice, test conceptual understanding, identify common student misconceptions	○ Free or commercial polling software, course management systems
Simulations, virtual laboratories	Students interact with a computer model of a system or lab, changing inputs and system parameters and observing system responses.	○ Explore systems that cannot be directly, safely, or economically studied in physical labs ○ Enable further exploration of hands-on experiments	○ Free or commercial simulation software ○ Search "[topic] simulation" or "[topic] virtual lab"
Interactive multimedia tutorials	All of the above with interspersed quizzes and immediate feedback on responses	○ Alternate content delivery with assessment of student knowledge and skills ○ Provide affirmation, corrective feedback, and advanced or remedial instruction	○ Textbooks, digital resource libraries, media publishers ○ Search "[topic] tutorial"

Table 7.1–1. (*Continued*)

Resource	Description	Uses	Sources
Communi-cation tools	E-mail, chat rooms, discussion forums, video conferencing, social media	o Instructor-student and student-student communications about course content and logistics o Virtual office hours, project team conferencing	o Built-in and online software, course management systems

common instructional technology tools. Later in the chapter, we'll propose guidelines to help you identify appropriate tools for your classes and use them effectively.

7.2 Learning Benefits of Technology

Chapters 3 through 6 surveyed and discussed teaching strategies that repeatedly have been shown to promote learning. Instructional technology can be used effectively to implement many of those strategies. Table 7.2–1 lists several ways to do it; others are suggested by Svinicki and McKeachie (2014, Ch. 17); and descriptions of new ones constantly appear in the literature of technology-assisted and online education.

You may be wondering where you're supposed to find the time to implement all the techniques in Table 7.2–1 and create all those visual images, simulations, interactive tutorials, and online communication and assessment tools, not to mention managing all your other teaching and research responsibilities and trying to have a life. Fortunately, you don't have to do everything on the list; the things you decide to do don't all have to be done at once, and many of the resources are available at the click of a button from sources suggested in Table 7.1–1 and by Shank (2014).

Table 7.2–1. Applications of Instructional Technology That Promote Learning

Well-designed instructional technology can promote learning in several ways:

- ○ **Overview course content and applications.** Show an online graphic organizer or concept map that depicts the topics and organization of your course. Include hyperlinks to important applications of each topic that can stimulate students' interest in the course.
- ○ **Enable a wide variety of presentation formats.** Show screencasts, photos, videos, and animations of course-related phenomena and events [the crystals growing, the bacteria multiplying, the bridge collapsing, etc.].
- ○ **Facilitate active student engagement.** Use personal response systems to add active engagement to otherwise traditional lectures. Use system simulations that let students adjust system variables and observe and interpret responses. Use interactive online tutorials that provide students with information about methods, practice in applying them, and feedback on their efforts.
- ○ **Enhance student-faculty and student-student interactions.** Create interactive message boards and threaded discussions. Communicate with students via posted messages, virtual office hours, and teleconferencing. In online courses, form virtual student groups and learning communities and involve them in active learning exercises and collaborative assignments and projects.
- ○ **Assess knowledge and skills.** Give and grade quizzes online. These assessments may be *formative* (providing students with feedback on what they know and what they need to work on), *summative* (counting toward the course grade), or both. Conduct peer assessment, in which students provide formative feedback on each other's products and on their performance as team members.
- ○ **Provide adaptive, individualized, self-paced instruction.** Different students have different backgrounds, interests, strengths, and weaknesses, and therefore different learning needs. An emerging industry has begun to develop instructional modules that assess students' needs and adjust instruction to accommodate those needs (Kolowich, 2013).

7.3 Setting Up Communications

In his massive study of higher education, *What Matters in College,* Astin (1993) found that the quality of students' interactions with faculty members correlates with the students' grade-point average, degree attainment, enrollment in graduate or professional school, every self-reported area of intellectual and personal growth, satisfaction with quality of instruction, and likelihood of choosing a career in college teaching. These findings are based on studies of predominantly face-to-face courses taught at traditional brick-and-mortar universities, which begs the question of whether they also apply to online education. Recent reviews of the literature on online courses suggest that they do. Boettcher and Conrad (2010, p. 75) found that student satisfaction with online courses is directly related to the virtual presence of the instructor, and Croxton (2014, p. 318) concluded that "one of the greatest predictors of student satisfaction is the prevalence, quality, and timeliness of student-instructor interaction." This conclusion holds for all student populations studied—undergraduates, graduate students, and professional trainees. Although greater student satisfaction does not automatically translate to greater student learning, it seems likely that students having a good online experience are less likely to drop out and more likely to meet the instructor's learning objectives than students having a less satisfying experience.

Astin (1993) also notes that as important as the student-faculty relationship may be, "the student's peer group is the single most potent source of influence on growth and development during the undergraduate years" (p. 398). The quality of student-student interactions correlates with GPA, graduating with honors, analytical and problem-solving skills, leadership ability, public speaking skills, interpersonal skills, preparation for graduate and professional school, and general knowledge, and correlates negatively with feeling depressed. Croxton (2014) found that online interactivity is a crucial element of undergraduate student satisfaction with their online courses and persistence in completing them. (It is less essential for graduate students and professional trainees.).

Technology facilitates faculty-student and student-interactions in face-to-face and hybrid classes and it enables virtually all communications in online courses. Here are several steps you can take to establish good interactions with and among your students:

Write a "get acquainted" post or prepare a self-introductory video before the start of class.

In whichever of these electronic greetings you prepare, along with the usual background information consider including something about your research interests, personal interests, and family to help students sense a personal connection with you.

Hold virtual office hours.

Many students who are intimidated by the thought of going to a professor's office find it much more comfortable to communicate electronically. Designate several hours each week when you will be online to respond to texts, e-mails, and possibly video chats. You may choose to respond to messages from students whenever you are available or limit responses to specified time periods. If you are teaching an online course, virtual office hours are of course the only kind you can hold.

Use an announcement tool to regularly remind students of important assignments, activities, and resources.

Frequent short posts help give students a sense of your presence. Announcement tools are available in most common course management systems, as are tools to implement the next suggestion.

Set up a threaded forum.

In a threaded forum, students participate in discussions of various topics (threads) that are initiated by questions submitted by either students or the instructor. Such forums effectively promote communications between students and instructors and among students. They motivate students to reflect critically about course content and increase the frequency and effectiveness of formative feedback from instructors and classmates. Croxton (2014) and Gikandi et al. (2011) offer suggestions for making forums work smoothly and effectively.

Give timely feedback.

A vitally important function of communication in course instruction is giving feedback to students on how well they have mastered the instructor's learning objectives. A chronic complaint of students in traditional courses is that their instructors don't return graded assignments and tests for weeks. Online instruction is no different. In several of the studies cited by Croxton (2014), students' satisfaction and—in at least one study, their grades—correlated significantly with how quickly they got feedback on their work.

Technology can be used to provide formative and summative feedback in several ways. When students are polled on multiple-choice questions in a face-to-face class and submit their responses using clickers, as soon as the poll is closed they can see a histogram of all the responses. If they then consult in pairs and revote, they can see movement of student opinion either toward or away from what is subsequently revealed to be the correct answer. Students raising questions in online discussion forums or virtual office hours can get responses in real time or close to it. Online quizzes can be used to test students on material presented in readings, screencasts, and online tutorials, affirm correct responses, and correct errors. In purely online courses, students' grades on assignments and tests can (and should) be communicated to them as soon as the grading has been completed.

Get students actively engaged with one another in face-to-face, hybrid, and online courses.

Active learning is arguably the teaching strategy least common, most needed, and hardest to achieve in online courses. We have already proposed using discussion forums as a vehicle for promoting student interactivity online. A broader recommendation is to integrate active learning as it is described in Chapter 6 into online instruction. We discuss how to do that in Section 7.6.

7.4 Integrating Technology into Instruction

Whether you plan to use technology in face-to-face classes, online classes, or hybrid classes that include face-to-face and online instruction, the suggestions that follow are worth considering.

Let your learning objectives be your guide.

Look for technology tools that give students practice in skills targeted in your learning objectives, and tools that provide feedback on the students' mastery of the objectives to both them and you.

See if suitable technology-based resources for your course are available online before setting out to create your own.

Section 3.2, Table 7.1–1, and Shank (2014) offer suggestions for finding resources online. In addition, you might search education journals and conference proceedings in your discipline for articles on flipped and online versions of your course, and see what resources they cite.

Keep online presentation segments short and focused.

Let's review three important facts about the process of learning: (1) the longer students remain passive, the more likely their attention is to wander and the less information they absorb; (2) subjecting students to a long unbroken presentation puts them in cognitive overload, making them incapable of absorbing most of the presentation content;

(3) presenting material in small chunks with interspersed rehearsal (practice) opportunities maximizes the probability of long-term storage and subsequent retrieval and transfer of the material. These observations support a well-established guideline: *lecture clips and screencasts in hybrid and online courses should be no more than ten minutes long, and some research suggests six minutes or less for maximum effectiveness* (Guo et al., 2014). If you have a presentation segment outside that time range, break it up into smaller segments with activities or assessments inserted between them. If you can't do that, give students a list of questions they can use to test themselves on the segment content.

Use videos and simulations (including virtual labs) in active learning exercises.

Videos and simulations of phenomena and experiments provide excellent opportunities for activities. Before you show a video, you might describe it and have students—working individually or in small groups—predict what they will see. In blended or synchronous online instruction, collect individual responses or use personal response systems to collect predictions. Then show the video and have the students compare their predictions with the actual outcome. If many of their predictions were wrong, it gives you a fine opportunity to correct common student misconceptions. Tucker (2013) has developed a good online guide to using videos effectively in class.

If you are using a dynamic simulation of a system, have students predict the system response to changes in selected variables and then compare their predictions with the simulated outcomes, or have them optimize the system performance by adjusting variables and observing the simulated responses. Excellent examples are provided by Koretsky et al. (2011a, 2011b), who describe virtual labs in which students optimize production in chemical and biological processes, clean up hazardous waste sites, and study the responses of multistory structures to earthquakes.

7.5 Blended Learning and Flipped Classrooms

Given the different strengths of face-to-face and online instruction, you might guess that greater learning would result from a well-designed blending of the two forms than from either form by itself, and on average you would be right (Means et al., 2010; Singh, 2003; Velegol et al., 2015). The key qualifier is *well designed,* however. The face-to-face instruction should include a mixture of lecturing, demonstrations, and individual and group activities, and the online instruction should include multimedia resources such as lecture clips, screencasts, and videos, and resources that provide active student engagement such as simulations, interactive tutorials, and (especially) online assessments. If many of those elements are present in a course, the learning benefits of blended instruction demonstrated in numerous studies cited by Means et al. (2010) are likely to be realized.

A *flipped* (or *inverted*) *classroom* is a form of blended learning that has attracted a lot of faculty attention in recent years. In traditional teaching, students first encounter new course material in class and then use it to solve problems in out-of-class assignments. In a flipped classroom, the opposite approach is taken—new material outside class, followed by problem solving in class.

As with every other teaching method, there are good and bad ways to implement flipping. Here are two common bad ones:

How not to flip a classroom

1. Before students come to class, assign them to read some of the course text or watch slides or a video of a complete lecture.
2. Assign new material before class, and then present more new material in a lecture.

What's wrong with those strategies? If you have ever assigned students a technical reading and expected them to use the content to solve problems in the next class session, you have known disappointment. Getting students to sit through an entire recorded lecture is no better—they have little chance of understanding the content without being able to ask questions about it or get feedback on their initial attempts to apply it. And assigning readings or online lectures before class and then giving more lectures in class is not flipping anything—it's just doubling the rate of fire-hosing the students with information.

So if those strategies don't work, what does? Effective classroom flipping has two components: *interactive online presentation of information before class* and *well-implemented active learning in class* (Means et al., 2010). The online materials might include short videos, lecture clips, and screencasts; hands-on experiences with virtual labs, control rooms, and plants; and quizzes on presented material. Again, to accommodate students' attention spans while they are passive observers, presentation segments should not last much more than six minutes (Guo et al., 2014).

The in-class sessions should consist almost entirely of activities designed to build on and reinforce the concepts and methods introduced in the on-line lessons and should incorporate the active learning guidelines and avoid the pitfalls described in Chapter 6.

Many individual studies of flipped classrooms have shown positive impacts of the method on students' attitudes, and a smaller number have shown positive effects on their learning (e.g., Deslauriers et al., 2011). A probable explanation for the lack of stronger research support is that the flipping in many of the studies did not meet both specified conditions (high-quality interactive online materials and well-implemented active learning in the face-to-face class sessions). In addition, most studies probably did not include assessment of high-level thinking and problem solving, the skills most likely to be affected by learner-centered methods. We anticipate that as the design, implementation, and assessment of flipped classrooms all continue to improve, studies will show increasingly positive impacts of flipping on learning.

Here are several suggestions to consider before flipping your class:

Don't try flipping until you're comfortable with active learning and know how to deal with student resistance to it.

Flipping gives students the responsibility for their own learning that active learning always imposes, and it also forces them to learn material on their own before they come to class. Many students are not thrilled about either feature of this teaching method, and some aren't shy about letting their instructors know about it. If you're not prepared for push-back, your first flipped classroom experience could be grim for you and the students. If possible, teach for several semesters using active learning before you flip a course, and if student resistance starts becoming uncomfortable, take the steps to defuse it that we outlined in Chapter 6. When you are confident that you can handle active learning effectively, if you still want to flip (not every teacher has to), go for it.

When you decide to flip, get help if you can, and start gradually.

If you have colleagues who have successfully flipped their classrooms or a campus center for teaching and learning that provides consulting assistance, call on them for guidance. Instead of trying to flip an entire course, identify a small portion of the course that you feel enthusiastic about teaching and for which good online materials are available, and try flipping only that portion. Learn from that experience and continue expanding your use of the method in subsequent course offerings.

Have good online lessons with integrated assessments in place for every class session you plan to flip.

If slide shows and complete recorded lectures are the only online resources you have, hold off on flipping until you can assemble interactive materials of the kinds we've mentioned. Screencasts, simulations, and interactive tutorials suitable for most core STEM courses can be found at sources cited in Table 7.1–1 and in Shank (2014). Koretsky (2015), Silverthorn (2006), and Velegol et al. (2015) offer excellent examples of online materials and assignments.

A powerful component of online instruction is quizzes during and following online lessons, with immediate affirmative or corrective feedback on the students' responses (Gikandi et al., 2011; Szpunar et al., 2013). The quizzes should not just be simple tests of factual information but should include assessments of deep understanding of the online material. We say more about assessing conceptual understanding in Chapter 8.

If quizzes are integrated into online instruction, another good practice is for instructors to access students' responses to them and begin subsequent face-to-face sessions with mini-lectures and activities that address areas of common misunderstanding. This technique is the basis of an instructional method known as *just-in-time-teaching (JiTT)* (Simkins & Maier, 2009). The record of quiz submissions also provides a measure of individual accountability for completing the online assignments.

Make face-to-face class sessions mainly activities that build on previous online lessons.

Focus on active learning exercises, including *thinking-aloud pair problem solving* (see Section 6.4) for working through complex problem solutions (Brent & Felder, 2012; Felder & Brent, 2009). Section 6.7 includes other suggestions for making effective use of active learning in flipped classrooms.

Consider flipped flipping.

In a flipped class, the basic material is presented in online modules and some or all of the application is done in a subsequent class. Another approach is to introduce new material via active exploration in class, *then* send the students out to view the screencasts and work through the tutorials online. Researchers at Stanford University refer to this approach as the "flipped flipped classroom" and have found it superior to flipping in many respects (Schneider et al., 2013).

Jensen et al. (2015) carried out a study in which student performance and attitudes in a flipped classroom and a flipped flipped classroom were compared. No significant between-section differences were found in the students' learning gains or in their attitudes about their instruction. The authors concluded that the key to the effectiveness of both approaches is the extensive use of active student engagement in the online and in-class instruction.

In short, flip your class if you want to, observing the precautions we suggested—and if you don't want to flip, don't flip. As long as you keep students actively engaged in both flipped classrooms (new material out of class, problem solving in class) and nonflipped classrooms (vice versa), you should see the learning you're looking for.

Thought Questions

Which of the classes you teach would you consider the best candidate for flipping? What would the advantages of flipping be? What would your concerns be, and how would you address them? Which topic in that course would be a good one to start with?

7.6 Online Courses

7.6.1 Active learning in online courses

Many instructors—including some who use active learning in face-to-face classes—don't believe that active student engagement is possible in online instruction. In fact, it is possible, fairly easy to attain, and as effective at promoting learning as it is in traditional classes. Students in online courses can engage asynchronously in discussion forums and synchronously in homework, project, and exam study teams, using a conferencing and screen-sharing program to work together on problems and projects.

But what about those live in-class active learning exercises we've been talking about since Chapter 3? Can you give students in an online class session something to do, allow them time to do it, and stop them and gather and process responses if you're not right there in the room with them?

The answer is yes (except in some circumstances for the gathering responses part). Go ahead and assign activities exactly as you would in a face-to-face classroom. At that point, what you do depends on whether the instruction is synchronous (the online students view the class while you're teaching) or asynchronous (the students view the class at a later time on streaming media), and whether or not some students are in the room with you as you are presenting. The activities may proceed as follows.

Face-to-face instruction of some students, with other students watching online.

Keep the camera running during the activity, showing a slide with the instruction for the activity and a video of the students working in the room. Stop the activity after an allotted period of time has elapsed. Collect and process responses from one or more students in the room, either individually or (for multiple-choice questions) using personal response systems and polling software. If the online instruction is synchronous and the technology permits off-site students to communicate with you, collect responses from them as well. When you process the responses, make sure correct responses are clearly stated and discuss why common mistakes are incorrect.

Synchronous online instruction only.

Conduct the activity as with face-to-face instruction, only just show the instruction slide during the allotted time. If the technology permits it, poll all students for responses to multiple-choice questions and collect and process individual responses to other questions via two-way communication; if neither is possible, just state the correct response and discuss mistakes students are likely to have made.

Asynchronous online instruction.

After assigning the activity, tell students to pause the transmission and resume it after a specified period of time or when they have done as much as they can. Pause, then state the correct response, and discuss common mistakes.

In online instruction as in face-to-face instruction, always tell students from the outset that you plan to use active learning and explain why, and then encourage the online students to attempt the activities. In the first class session, after you give the motivational sermonette described in Chapter 6, tell the online students that when you initiate an activity, they have a choice. They can either (1) attempt to do what you asked them to do, (2) stare at a screen with nothing happening on it for a minute or two (synchronous), or (3) skip the activity and jump immediately to the answer (asynchronous). Strongly recommend Option (1), noting that it leads to greater learning and makes the class more interesting. After the first test has been graded and returned, remind the students about that advice, suggesting that if they were disappointed in their grade they might help themselves by attempting the activities in future lessons.

7.6.2 Massive open online courses (MOOCs)

Massive open online courses are courses that may be taken at little or no cost by an unlimited number of people. The courses consist of a series of online lessons that may include full lectures, lecture clips, screencasts, slides, videos, discussion forums, and quizzes. Students who finish MOOCS may choose to receive certificates of completion for which they pay a fee. (In the latter case the courses are technically no longer "open" to everyone who takes them, and some refer to them as MOCs.)

The benefits of MOOCs are undeniable. They are either free or cost far less than courses at traditional brick-and-mortar institutions; they can be accessed by anyone with connectivity to the Internet, including people living where there is no easy access to conventional campuses; they often are given by some of the finest instructors in the world making full use of multimedia tools; students can attend classes at their convenience rather than having to arrange their schedules around fixed course times, and the students can review lessons as many times as they wish. In 2014, Georgia Tech initiated a MOOC-based Master of Science degree program in computer science, and in the following year Arizona State University announced that students would be able to complete their first year entirely with online courses. It is clearly just a matter of time until students can use MOOCs to complete most of their degree requirements for much less than they would pay for traditional courses, and many will choose to do so.

So, what can MOOCs do for you, besides enabling you to supplement your own education? Keep your eyes open for MOOCs that cover topics you cover in your course. Check those courses out (it's free), sample their lessons on those topics, and consider assigning excerpts from the lessons instead of textbook readings, possibly as part of the online component of flipped classrooms. (Find out what's legally required to do that—the ground on this issue will be shifting rapidly in the coming years.) Use the time you gain by not having to give those lessons yourself to set up the kind of individual interactions with your students that online instruction will probably never be able to provide.

7.7 Ideas to Take Away

o Online instruction enables interactive multimedia presentation of information and gives students practice and feedback and opportunities to repeat lessons as often as they wish. Face-to-face instructors can serve as role models and mentors to their students in ways that technology is unlikely to ever provide, and face-to-face class environments maximize the learning benefits of student interactions in and out of class. The best education is provided by blended instruction that capitalizes on the strengths of each approach.

o Instructional technology resources that actively engage students, such as personal response systems, interactive multimedia tutorials, simulations, online quizzes with immediate feedback on responses, and communication tools, including discussion forums, enhance learning. Applications that make students passive observers for long periods of time, such as extended slide shows and complete recorded lectures—not so much. Lecture clips and other presentation segments can be instructive, but to be fully effective they should be less than six minutes long and should rarely if ever exceed ten minutes.

o Creating technology-based tools and presentations can be exceptionally time-consuming. Seek existing materials before setting out to create your own.

o Flipped classes that introduce new material with online instruction and then provide follow-up face-to-face instruction can be effective if the online instruction is interactive and the follow-up consists primarily (but not exclusively) of active learning. Assigning students to read texts or watch complete lectures outside class is generally ineffective, as is following online lessons with traditional face-to-face lecturing.

o Explore incorporating material from massive open online courses (MOOCs) into your courses, whether the courses are face-to-face, online, or hybrid.

7.8 Try This in Your Course

o As part of a homework assignment, ask the students to each go online and find a video, screencast, or tutorial that illustrates what you are teaching about a specified topic. Offer a few points on the next test to students who find good resources. Incorporate the best ones they find into your course materials and use them in future course offerings.

○ Try holding some virtual office hours using an online conferencing tool (such as Google Hangouts or a similar tool in your course management system). Monitor the frequency of student visits to see if the virtual sessions draw more or different students than you generally see in your office.

○ Set up a discussion forum for your class using course management software.

○ Try flipping a small segment of your course. Find and assign good online instructional materials for a course topic, and in the next class session conduct active learning exercises that require using the information and methods taught in the online lessons. Do that several times during the course until you and the students become accustomed to it. If it seems to be having the effects on your students' motivation and performance that you're looking for, consider extending the approach to additional parts of the course.

INTERLUDE. MEET YOUR STUDENTS: MICHELLE, RYAN, AND ALEX

The scene is the student lounge at a large university. Three juniors—Michelle, Ryan, and Alex—are studying for the second test in their biofluid mechanics course. Alex got the high grade in the class on the first test, Michelle was close behind him, and Ryan was fifteen points below class average. They've been at it for over an hour.

Michelle: What about this stuff on non-Newtonian flow—I don't think I really get it.

Alex: I think we can forget it—I've got copies of Snavely's tests for the last five years, and he's never asked about it this early in the course.

M: Maybe, but it's the real stuff ... you want to analyze blood flow, for instance, Newtonian won't work.

A: So what ... the only blood flow we're going to have to worry about is ours on this test if we don't stick to the stuff Snavely IS going to ask.

M: Yeah, but if we don't ...

Ryan: Hey, Alex, is there going to be any of that Navier-Stokes junk on the quiz?

A: Yeah, there usually is, but no derivations—you just have to know how to simplify the equation.

M: I've been looking through the text ... there are all sorts of Navier-Stokes problems in there—we could try to set some of them up.

R: Nah, way too much work—I just need to get my C, my degree, and my eighty-inch TV ... let's haul out those old tests and memorize the solutions.

A: Okay, but that may not ... hey, look at this question—he's used it three years in a row ... Parts (a) and (b) are just plug-and-chug, but he throws a real curve ball here in Part (c)—I don't know how to do it.

M: Let me see it ... okay, he's asking about velocity profile development—you just need to use the correlation for entrance length.

A: What are you talking about—I never heard of that stuff.

M: He never talked about it in class, but it's in the book—you need to calculate the Reynolds number and then substitute it in this dimensionless correlation, and that gives you ...

A: So it's just this correlation—do I need to dig into where it comes from?

M: Probably not for the test, but I was trying to think why you would want to know the entrance length, and it seems to me that if you're analyzing blood flow again, in capillaries, or flow of dialyzing fluid in an artificial kidney, or ...

A: Forget it—that stuff's not going to be on this test ... even Snavely wouldn't be that tricky ... now look at this problem here ...

These three students illustrate three different *approaches to learning* (Felder & Brent, 2005; Ramsden, 2003).

1. Michelle tends to take a *deep approach* to studying material that interests her, meaning that she tries not just to learn facts but to understand what they mean, how they are connected, and how they might relate to her experience. A deep approach has been found to correlate with attainment of most learning outcomes other than memorizing factual information and implementing routine procedures.

2. Ryan usually takes a *surface approach*, memorizing facts but not trying to fit them into a coherent body of knowledge and following routine solution procedures but not trying to understand where they come from.

3. Alex's primary goal is to get an A in the course, whatever it takes. He uses a *strategic approach,* which involves finding out what the instructor wants and delivering it—staying superficial when he can get away with it, digging deep when he has to.

Faculty members often complain that many of their students are Ryans and very few are Michelles. You can motivate your students to adopt a deep approach to learning using the following by now familiar strategies (Ramsden, 2003):

Establish the relevance of course content to the students' interests and goals.

Neither Michelle nor Ryan will struggle to achieve a deep understanding of material that seems useless to them. Interest in material may be sufficient for Michelle to take a deep approach, and if the interest is strong enough, even Ryan may be motivated to do it.

Clearly state high-level learning objectives and conduct assessments that address them.

If all assessments require only memorization and routine calculations, Alex and Ryan will take a surface approach to studying. If a few high-level challenges are certain to be on the assessments, Alex and possibly Ryan will be motivated to adopt a deep approach.

Previous chapters observed that students are more likely to store new information in long-term memory if they perceive it to be relevant to them. The fact that perceived relevance motivates the adoption of a deep approach is another reason to take the first of those recommendations. The second recommendation calls for designing assignments and tests that effectively assess mastery of high-level objectives. We discuss how to do that in the next chapter.

8

EVALUATING KNOWLEDGE, SKILLS, AND UNDERSTANDING

8.0 Introduction

The interlude preceding this chapter introduced three students who tend to adopt different *approaches to learning*. Michelle typically takes a deep approach to subjects she considers interesting and important, motivated by a desire to truly understand what she is being taught rather than by grades. Ryan is more likely to take a surface approach, doing as little work as possible to get a minimal passing grade and relying mostly on rote memorization when he studies. Alex uses a strategic approach to getting the top grade, digging deep if he has to and staying superficial if he can. Extensive research has shown that certain teaching practices correlate with students' adoption of a deep approach to learning (Biggs & Tang, 2011; Case & Marshall, 2009; Felder & Brent, 2005; Marton et al., 1997; Ramsden, 2003; Trigwell et al., 1999). They include writing and sharing learning objectives that require a deep approach, and creating and grading assignments and tests that assess mastery of those objectives.

In Chapter 3 we defined and differentiated two terms that are often used interchangeably:

Assessment = identifying the data that will be collected to measure knowledge, skills, attitudes, and learning; selecting or creating the instruments that will be used to gather the data; and administering the instruments.

Evaluation = analyzing assessment data and drawing conclusions from the results. Evaluation may be used to improve the quality of the students' learning and the instructor's teaching (formative), to assign grades or make pass-fail decisions (summative), or both.

This chapter describes and discusses assessment and evaluation strategies that serve formative and summative functions, with the formative ones including motivating a deep approach to learning. We'll start by reviewing methods for evaluating students' content knowledge and move on to the evaluation of conceptual understanding, problem-solving skills, and professional ("soft") skills. Here are the some of the questions the chapter addresses:

o How can I assess high-level thinking and problem-solving skills with multiple-choice and short-answer questions?
o How can I evaluate and promote conceptual understanding?
o How can I design, administer, and grade problem-solving assignments and tests to maximize their formative benefits?
o How can I tell if a problem-solving test is too long before I give it?
o What should I do if grades on a test are abnormally low?
o How can I help students prepare for and take problem-solving tests?
o How can I evaluate written student products (e.g., lab and project reports) and oral presentations objectively and efficiently? How can I help students develop the skills needed to do well on the evaluations?

8.1 Multiple-Choice and Short-Answer Questions

Students' ability to recall and explain factual material is usually assessed with closed-book tests containing multiple-choice or short-answer questions, but those formats can also be used to assess higher-level material.

8.1.1 Multiple-choice questions

Their ease of grading makes multiple-choice tests the assessment instrument of choice for large classes with few or no teaching assistants. Faculty members often report that many of their multiple-choice questions test high-level thinking, but analyses of test questions show that most of the questions are low level (Momsen et al., 2010). Following are examples of multiple-choice questions at five of the six different Bloom levels (see Section 2.2).

Level 1—remembering.

Ask a factual question that has a unique answer. The bonds that hold together the two strands of a DNA molecule are (a) weak covalent bonds (b) weak hydrogen bonds (c) strong hydrogen bonds (d) strong covalent bonds (e) strong ionic bonds.

Level 2—understanding.

Present several alternative statements of the meaning of a term, alternative interpretations of an observation or experimental outcome, or alternative illustrations of a concept or theory, and ask the respondent to choose the best one. You enter a two-story house and feel comfortable, and then go upstairs and feel uncomfortably warm. The most likely cause is (a) heat conduction (b) heat convection (c) equal amounts of a and b (d) sunspots.

Level 3—applying.

State a problem and ask the respondent to identify the correct solution or best solution method or best first step in obtaining the solution. A plot of the velocity of a vehicle versus time is a straight line going through 12 ft/s two seconds after startup and 18 ft/s one second later. The distance traveled by the vehicle between five seconds and ten seconds after startup is (a) 45 ft (b) 75 ft (c) 150 ft (d) 225 ft (d) 300 ft.

Level 4—analyzing.

Describe a system and ask the respondent to choose the best prediction of its behavior, or describe a system behavior and ask the respondent to choose the best diagnosis, interpretation, inference, or conclusion. Which of the following outputs or error messages would be returned by this C++ code [show code]? (a) ....

Level 5—evaluating.

Describe a situation that calls for decision making and ask the respondent to choose the best decision or best justification for a specified decision. A patient enters a hospital emergency room with the following symptoms [list symptoms]. (1) Which of the following ailments is the most likely possibility? (a) .... (2) What is the first treatment or test you would order? (a) ....

Level 6—creating.

You can't truly assess creativity using multiple-choice questions.

Multiple-choice questions may also be designed specifically to assess students' conceptual understanding (Section 8.2). *Caution:* Only include high-level questions on tests if you have given the students practice on similar questions in class activities and assignments.

Following are several ideas for making multiple-choice questions and tests as effective as possible, in general and for assessing objectives above Bloom Level 1. Some of the ideas are variants of suggestions in several references (University of Oregon, 2014; Zimarro, 2004). In presenting them, we will use the traditional terminology of multiple-choice exams, wherein the test questions are *items*; each item consists of a *stem* followed by several numbered or lettered *options*; and the options include one correct answer (sometimes called the *key*) and two to four *distractors* (incorrect answers).

Good Practices for Multiple-Choice Questions

- Keep both the stems and the options as brief as possible (especially the options). If options take more than two or three words to state, list them on separate lines.
- Distribute the correct response randomly among option positions, make sure that the correct option is not always the longest one, and make most distractors plausible and equivalent in structure and length.
- Beware of "all of the above" as an option, be even more cautious about "none of the above," and shun "always" and "never." Those common options frequently cause confusion, particularly among the better students in a class, who often think of possibilities that hadn't occurred to the author of the items.
- Try to avoid negatives in the stem, especially double negatives. A guaranteed way to give a large number of students splitting headaches is to use a stem such as "Which of the following is not an inappropriate definition of entropy?" You can finish off any students who survive that stem by making one of the options "none of the above."
- Consider presenting a short paragraph, chart, or data table followed by several test items related to it. This structure lends itself to assessments of higher-level skills.
- Get one or more colleagues and/or graduate students to take and critique the test before you administer it in class. Get feedback from them about any items they missed or found ambiguous.
- If you plan to include the same or similar questions on tests when you give the course again, apply item analysis to the results (see following).

Constructing and validating high-level multiple-choice questions is not trivial (validating them means verifying that they really assess the knowledge or skills they are intended to assess), and the required effort is generally worthwhile only if you plan to build an archive of test items and use them in subsequent course offerings. If you do, consider using *item analysis* (DeMars, 2010) to evaluate and strengthen the questions. A common item analysis procedure is to compare the average performance on a test of the top quarter of the class with the average performance of the bottom quarter, and identify test items and distractors that should be eliminated or modified. Questionable items include those that are too easy (almost no one misses them), too hard (almost everyone misses them, including many of the top scorers in the class), or have poor discrimination (the high scorers are more likely than the low scorers to miss them, suggesting that there may be something misleading about them). Questionable distractors include those hardly ever selected by anyone and those selected by more high-scoring than low-scoring students. Item analysis routines are included in common course management programs and many statistical analysis packages and are also available as add-ins to spreadsheet programs such as Excel.

8.1.2 Short-answer questions

Similar to multiple-choice questions, questions that call for brief written responses are usually used to assess low-level content knowledge, but they can also be designed to address higher levels of knowledge and understanding. All of the examples of high-level multiple-choice questions in the preceding section can be converted to short-answer questions. Here are some additional examples:

o The vapor pressure of benzene at 48°C is 251 mm Hg. Explain in one or two sentences the physical significance of that value in terms that a nonscientist could understand.

o The following mathematical proof leads to an incorrect conclusion [show proof]. Identify the flaw in the proof.

o The following design of a bridge across a river gorge has been submitted for your review [show design]. Briefly outline three calculations you would perform, and for each one, state your criterion for acceptability.

o You have been given the following prescription to fill [show prescription]. What recommendations and warnings would you give the patient in a consult?

o An advertisement claimed "80% of survey respondents reported headache relief after taking Zanoblyx and only 70% reported relief after taking aspirin." List up to ten statistics-related reasons for not immediately buying a box of Zanoblyx.

o Examine the attached picture of a fungus and the descriptive material below it [show picture and description]. Classify the fungus as either *Hymenomycetes* or *Gasteromycetes,* and state your reasoning.
o The following abstract was submitted last year for a project report in this course [show abstract]. Using the criteria we have discussed in class, assign a grade to it, and in a few brief sentences state your reasoning.

Here are several ways to make high-level short-answer questions objective and fair.

Good Practices for Short-Answer Questions

o Test no more than one or two objectives per question.
o Have a colleague or teaching assistant read each question for clarity.
o Indicate the point value of each question and suggest an expected response length.
o Allow about two minutes for a question requiring more than a sentence to answer.
o Keep student identities anonymous while grading.
o Calibrate your grading by glancing through all responses to a question before grading any of them.
o Before including discussion questions on a test, clearly state your grading criteria and show the class illustrative questions, typical good and bad responses to them, and how you would grade those responses.

Sources: Jacobs (2002); Svinicki and McKeachie (2014, pp. 102–104).

8.2 Evaluating and Promoting Conceptual Understanding

Traditional STEM instruction does not generally lead to much improvement in conceptual understanding (Ambrose et al., 2010; Taylor & Kowalski, 2014). In a widely cited example (Lightman & Sadler, 1993), roughly 30% of students beginning an astronomy course passed a pre-test of their understanding of the concept of gravity, and only 15% passed the same test at the end of the course. A more typical result was obtained when understanding of several heat transfer concepts was assessed for 344 students at the beginning and end of a traditional lecture-based chemical engineering course (Prince et al., 2012). Modest gains in scores were recorded for the four concepts examined (53% to 55% for temperature versus energy, 61% to 69% for temperature versus perceptions of hot or cold, 37% to 43% for rate versus amount, and 44% to 49% for thermal radiation), but they were well below what any instructor would hope for after a full semester of instruction.

There are three possible reasons why students can pass a course—perhaps with a high grade—and emerge without truly understanding important course concepts:

1. The course instruction did not effectively address the concepts.
2. The tests did not require understanding the concepts.
3. The students had misconceptions too firmly rooted to be overturned by the instruction.

There is an easy way to address the first two reasons, which we will briefly outline, after which we will tackle the more complex issue of robust misconceptions.

8.2.1 Teaching concepts

All STEM disciplines are grounded in important fundamental concepts. When courses and course topics are introduced, the instructors may mention and discuss the concepts and perhaps use them to derive formulas and problem-solving methods. Memorization of facts and applications of the formulas and methods then take center stage in lectures, assignments, and tests, and the concepts pretty much disappear. The students breathe a sigh of relief to be back in familiar territory and don't give concepts another thought until a new topic is introduced, at which point the process repeats. If the students happen to participate in a study of conceptual understanding, their scores at the end of the course are not much different from their scores coming in. The instructors are mystified but they shouldn't be, because they never really taught the concepts.

Understanding of complex concepts at a truly deep level can take years and considerable effort to attain, but one easy strategy you can use to move your students fairly far along that path is to embed questions that call for conceptual understanding in class activities, homework assignments, and tests. Here are several types of questions that do so:

o Define _____ in your own words in a way that [someone who has never taken this course, your nonscientist grandparents, a ten-year-old child] could understand.

○ Predict the behavior of the following [system, device, patient] under the following circumstances: _____.
○ Brainstorm possible reasons why the following [system, device, patient] might fail to behave in a predicted way: _____.
○ Explain the following [familiar phenomenon, experimental outcome] in terms of concepts taught in the course: _____.

Challenging your students to answer such questions in class activities and assignments and giving them feedback on their responses will deepen their conceptual understanding, especially if you make it clear that you plan to include similar questions on the tests. (Then include them!)

8.2.2 Misconceptions and ConcepTests

Students often have mistaken ideas about the world, such as that it is colder in the winter than in the summer because in the winter the earth is farther away from the sun. Some of those misconceptions are particularly robust, persisting in the students' minds no matter how hard instructors try to correct them. The students can sit through a lecture and hear that the cause of the seasons is the tilt of the earth's polar axis, and they may memorize that fact and repeat it on an exam if asked about it directly; however, if they are later asked a question that requires understanding of why there are seasons, they are likely to go back to their original belief.

Similarly, physics students can be told that when a force on an object is zero the object cannot accelerate, and they can repeat that corollary of Newton's second law on a test. However, when they are asked to sketch the trajectory of an object at the end of a horizontal rope that is swung around several times and then released, many will draw a horizontal curve. Misconceptions are particularly robust if the corrections involve abstract phenomena that students cannot experience directly, such as nuclear and atomic forces and electromagnetic and gravitational fields (Chi, 2005).

The keys to overturning a robust misconception are (1) identifying the misconception, (2) getting students to commit themselves to it, (3) confronting the students with a clear demonstration that it is wrong, and (4) giving the correct conception and demonstrating its validity (Taylor & Kowalski, 2014). A *ConcepTest* (Mazur, 1997) is a multiple-choice question that can be used to carry out all four steps. The ideal question has at least one distractor that reflects a common student misconception. Following is an example of a ConcepTest that could be used in an evolutionary biology course or almost any other biology or bioengineering course (Rutledge & Warden, 2000).

Which of the Following Phrases Best Describes the Process of Evolution?

(a) The development of man from monkey-like ancestors
(b) The change of simple to complex organisms
(c) The development of characteristics in response to need
(d) Change of populations through time
(e) The change of populations solely in response to natural selection

---

If most of the students get the correct response to a ConcepTest, there is no need to spend much time on it in class, but if many responses are incorrect, then more instruction is clearly called for.

A well-tested and validated approach to helping students identify and correct their misconceptions is *peer instruction* (Mazur, 1997). The instructor poses ConcepTests in class and students choose from among the options, generally using clickers or their smartphones (see Section 5.1). Their responses are automatically logged in and tabulated, and the final response distribution is displayed as a histogram. If the students are not almost unanimous in selecting the correct option, they are put into groups of two or three to compare their responses and try to reach consensus on the correct one, and then vote individually again. The instructor then gives the correct response and guides the students in a discussion of why it is correct and why the distractors are wrong. Extensive research has shown that the systematic use of this technique is far more effective than traditional lecturing at promoting conceptual understanding (Lasry et al., 2008).

Designing good ConcepTests is not trivial. Fortunately, some STEM instructors have developed and published archives of them for single disciplines, such as the AIChE Concept Warehouse (American Institute of Chemical Engineers, n.d.) for all courses in the core chemical engineering curriculum, and others have compiled lists of such archives, such as the Carl Wieman Science Education Initiative (n.d.) at the University of British Columbia. To find ConcepTests in a particular subject, enter "concept tests _____" [fill in subject] in a search engine.

Another effective approach to promoting conceptual understanding is to have students run physical or simulated experiments with outcomes that refute common misconceptions. The students first predict the outcomes, then run the experiments, and if their predictions were wrong, figure out why and draw conclusions about the concept in question. The instructor then states the concept to make sure that most of the students get it right.

8.2.3 Concept inventories

A *concept inventory* is a collection of ConcepTests that address important concepts and common misconceptions in a subject. If you administer an inventory at the beginning of your course (the pre-test) and then again at the end (the post-test), you can use the average pre-post gain in the score as a measure of how successful the course was at improving the students' understanding of the targeted concepts. If the inventory is widely used and data obtained with it have been compiled and published, you can also see where your students rank compared with others at a comparable educational level.

Designing and validating a concept inventory is an exceptionally long and challenging undertaking (Streveler et al., 2011). Unless you have a few years to devote to the effort, we advise you to look for an existing inventory. In recent years inventories have been developed and validated in most STEM fields, and their development continues at a far brisker pace than any archive can keep up with. To find one in a particular STEM subject, enter "concept inventory _____" [fill in subject] in a search engine. Especially if you use a concept inventory for work you plan to publish, be sure to select one that has been validated.

We have one request regarding concept inventories. Instructors looking for ConcepTests to use in their class may be tempted to find a published concept inventory and lift questions from it. Please don't! The validity of an inventory rests in part on students not being trained specifically on the inventory questions. If you take a question from a validated inventory and use it in a lecture, you may be compromising the inventory for yourself and possibly for other instructors if the question gets into widespread circulation.

8.3 Evaluating Problem-Solving Skills

This section offers suggestions for making problem-solving assignments and tests effective for summative and formative evaluation. Chapter 9 outlines methods of helping students develop problem-solving skills.

8.3.1 Designing problem-solving assignments

Most problem-solving skill development occurs when students work on well-constructed problems. Suggestions for creating and grading assignments follow.

Assign enough problems to provide adequate practice and feedback in targeted problem-solving methods, but don't overdo it.

For most courses that focus on problem solving, there should be at least one assignment per week. More widely spaced assignments are likely to omit important material, be too long, or delay feedback too much. Include some problems that bring back and reinforce material covered on previous tests (brainwaves in Chapters 4 and 9 discuss the importance of retrieval practice in learning), and some that look similar but require different solution methods to help equip students to transfer their learning to different contexts.

A common guideline for assignment length is an average of two hours of work outside class per hour of class. If you regularly go much above this limit, you will force some students to neglect other courses to keep up with yours and motivate others to copy solutions from classmates, student files of worked-out solutions, or online solution manuals.

Count performance on assignments toward the final grade, even if by a small amount.

STEM students are busy people—they may be taking five or six courses, engaging in extracurricular activities, and working part-time. If they get assignments that don't count toward the final course grade, many won't do them. If you believe that students learn through practice and feedback (which they do), and assignments and projects are the principal vehicles for providing both (which they are), and your goal is to help all of your students learn as much as they're capable of learning (which it should be), then assign homework, grade it, and count the results toward the final course grade.

What if you have a large class and few or no graders? Try not to eliminate graded assignments, but take steps to cut down on the grading load. You might select a subset of student papers to be graded, or randomly choose a portion of the assignment to be graded. Another option is to use peer grading, making sure to provide the students with clear and detailed grading guidelines, using practice tests to train the students in the use of the guidelines, and randomly checking the grading.

Beware of assigning problems directly from textbooks.

Solution manuals are readily available online for most common texts, and some of your students have them and are not above copying from them. If you assign problems from any widely-used text for your course, you are giving those students an unfair advantage. If you change at least one numerical value in a problem statement, you will force the students to go through the effort of reworking the solutions, which is better than nothing. Some textbooks come with supplementary online problems that specify different input variable values for each student, making it harder for students to copy solutions verbatim from one another or from downloaded solution manuals.

8.3.2 Designing problem-solving tests

To be effective, tests should be *comprehensive and rigorous* (covering a broad spectrum of the instructor's learning objectives, including those at high cognitive levels), *fair* (assessing only knowledge and skills that have been adequately taught and the skills adequately practiced in assignments), and *formative* (providing guidance to students on how to improve their performance on subsequent assessments). The next paragraphs offer strategies for designing problem-solving tests that meet these criteria.

Give study guides for midterm and final exams.

In the introduction to this chapter, we observed that making your expectations clear to students increases the chances that they will take a deep approach to learning, trying to really understand what you are teaching and not just relying on memorization. An excellent way to clarify your expectations is to give the students study guides for exams, as recommended and illustrated in Section 2.1.3. The students capable of meeting your objectives will be more likely to do so by the end of the course if you make the objectives explicit in the study guides, and you will never again have to deal with the dreaded "Are we responsible for _____ on the exam?" (*Answer:* "If it's in the study guide, you are; if it isn't, you're not.")

To make the positive effects of study guides on learning even stronger, assign students the task of creating their own guides the week before a midterm exam, letting them collaborate if they wish to. Then share your study guide. Finding items on yours that they hadn't thought of may motivate them to study important material that they might otherwise have neglected.

Include some high-level material on your tests, but only after you have taught it.

If you want your students to perform high-level mathematical analysis, solve incompletely-defined problems, or think critically or creatively, include those skills on your study guides, provide practice and feedback on them in class and on assignments, and then (and only then) include them on the tests. Consider the following guideline:

Undergraduate test design target: Design 10 to 20% of your tests to address high-level objectives—no more and no less.

Why maintain a minimum percentage of high-level material (10% in the guideline)? Remember Alex in the interlude before this chapter—the strategic learner who does the minimum work necessary to get a top grade? A lot of STEM students are like that. If they know that they can restrict their test preparation to the basics and still get a high grade, many who have the aptitude to perform high-level tasks will have little incentive to do the required preparation. Why a maximum (20%)? If much more than 20% of your test targets high-level objectives, the test loses some of its ability to distinguish between levels of mastery—more specifically, to separate A students from B students. The grade distribution will be bimodal, with a small narrow peak of high grades and a much larger and broader one of mainly low grades. The recommended 10 to 20% range helps avoid both of those problems.

Make tests cumulative, and don't exempt students from final exams.

The brainwave on retrieval practice in Chapter 6 made the point that greater, longer lasting, and more transferable learning occurs when retrieval practice and feedback are spaced over longer intervals. An implication is that midterm and final exams should call on students to recall and use material going back to the beginning of the course. This doesn't mean testing every single objective on every exam: it means testing a subset of the objectives and making sure students know that just because something was covered on a test, they shouldn't feel free to forget it for the rest of the semester.

Preparing for a comprehensive final exam is likely to be the only time the students review the entire course and come to understand the interconnections among the different course concepts and methods. Letting the students who did well on the midterms skip the final is not doing them any favors. Find better ways to reward them than depriving them of the most powerful learning experience they are likely to have in your course.

Closed book, open book, or a compromise?

Closed-book tests and open-book tests can be thought of as the extremes of an assessment continuum. At the first extreme, the student may not consult any reference, written or electronic; at the other extreme, the student may refer to anything—the course text, other books, graded assignments and tests, their smartphones and computers, and the entire content of the Internet if they have access. Between those extremes are many possibilities. For example, the students may be allowed to refer only to their textbook, or to a written or electronic handout prepared by the instructor, or to a single sheet of paper they prepare themselves containing anything they choose to write.

The kind of test you should give depends on the nature of the course content, your learning objectives, and your teaching philosophy. If it's important to you that your students have some information committed to memory, give them a closed-book test on it. If you don't care whether or not they have it memorized, let them look it up in the course text or a handout you prepare (which you should show them in advance of the test). If you are testing information of both types, give them a closed-book portion of the test, and when they hand it in, give them the open-book portion.

Be aware of one danger with open-book tests, especially if your students are unaccustomed to them. When you announce your first open-book test, many students will leap to the conclusion that it will be easy—if they need to know something, they can just look it up. They will study superficially and then spend a significant amount of time during the test frantically flipping pages, looking for worked-out examples similar to the test problems. Because you're not going to put duplicates of worked-out examples on an open-book test (right?), the students won't do well and some will fail. Do them a favor. About a week before your first exam, warn them against doing what we just described, and remind them about it when the graded tests are handed back. (Later in this chapter we offer other ideas for helping students prepare for and take problem-solving tests.)

Don't give tests that only the fastest problem solvers in class have time to finish.

Some of the most common complaints in student evaluations of teaching have to do with tests that are too long. If students have studied intently for a test, understand the concepts, and know how to solve the problems but fail because they can't work fast enough to finish and check their solutions before time runs out, they rightfully resent it.

Not a shred of evidence has shown that students who can finish a test in an hour are more likely to succeed in STEM careers than students who need 90 minutes or two hours to do it, whether the careers involve industrial plant work, research, software development, clinical practice, or any other professional activity. Engineers, scientists, and mathematicians who are methodical and careful but slow problem solvers are in fact likely to be *more* successful than their counterparts who are faster but make careless mistakes. When tests are too long, fast careless students may finish the test and lose some points for minor errors but still do well, while slow careful students may not be able to get to large portions of the test and fail. Overly long tests can therefore weed out students for reasons that have nothing to do with their potential for professional success.

Unless problems and questions are trivial, students need time to stop and think about how to solve them while the author of the problems does not. We endorse this widely accepted guideline:

Guideline for test length: You should be able to work through a problem-solving test in less than one-third of the time your students will have to do it, and less than one-fourth or one-fifth of the time if particularly complex and/or computation-heavy problems are included.

Take the test yourself before you administer it to your class.

Tests that look perfect when you make them up are usually far from perfect. Only when you subsequently take them as if you were a student do you discover that they are too long—and you are also likely to find that some problems are overspecified or underspecified, could easily be misinterpreted, or involve long calculations that don't address the skills you are trying to evaluate.

Following is the approach to test preparation we recommend.

Test Preparation Protocol
1. Draft the test several days before you're going to give it and edit it until you think it's perfect.
2. Let some time go by and then take the test as though you were a student, timing yourself. See if the test passes the one-third (or one-fourth or one-fifth) rule for length. If you have a teaching assistant, ask him or her to do the same.
3. Shorten the test if it failed the length rule (suggestions for how to do it follow), fix the glitches in the problem statements you are

guaranteed to find in Step 2, and take it again. Repeat this process until you are satisfied with the test.
4. Give the test.

If you're like most instructors, you won't want to go through all that effort, but you don't have much choice. Either you bite the bullet and do it, or you deal with the headaches that arise when a student discovers twenty minutes into the test that information is missing from the statement of Problem 2, and many students are confused by Problem 4 and solve a different problem than the one you intended to give, and a large percentage of the class is not even close to finishing when time runs out. Identifying and fixing these problems before you give the test will invariably lead to less pain for you and your students.

If a test draft is too long, shorten it.

Two ways to shorten a test draft are to eliminate questions or parts of questions and to give some formulas instead of requiring full derivations of all of them. Another particularly effective technique for problem-solving tests is to ask for solution outlines rather than requiring complete calculations. Quantitative problems can get quite long, requiring several hours to solve completely. You obviously can't put one of those problems on a fifty-minute test, but you still want to evaluate your students' ability to solve them. You can do it by using a version of the following generic problem:

Generic Quantitative Problem

Given [state a process or system to be analyzed and the values of known quantities], write the complete set of equations you would solve to calculate [state the quantities to be determined]. Do no algebra, calculus, or numerical calculations: just write the equations without attempting to simplify or solve them.

If students are capable of correctly writing n equations for n unknown variables in a problem, you can be fairly sure that they could solve the complete problem given enough time, either manually or with equation-solving software. It's usually the algebraic and arithmetic calculations that take hours, and unless you're teaching a basic mathematics course, those skills are probably not major components of your learning objectives. If they are, then put some short math problems on the test, and use the generic problem format for more complex problems.

Caution, however. If students have never worked on a problem framed this way, and one suddenly appears on a test, many will be confused and may do worse than they would have if they had to complete all the calculations. If you plan to use this technique, be sure you work similar problems in class and put some on homework, and *then* do it on the test.

8.3.3 Helping students learn how to prepare for and take problem-solving tests

"Professor, I know I failed the test we just got back, but I studied hard for it and really knew the material and I could do all the homework problems. I'm just no good at taking tests."

Most experienced STEM faculty members have listened to that little speech more times than they can count, and new instructors will not have to wait long before they get to hear it. Although some students have test anxiety and might benefit from several sessions with a trained counselor, the problem is much more likely to be that STEM students are rarely taught how to prepare for problem-solving tests and usually gravitate to remarkably ineffective strategies (Brown et al., 2014; Oakley, 2014). They reread and maybe insert underlines or highlights in their course notes and textbook, glance over solutions to past homework problems and old exams, and give themselves the "illusion of knowing," but it doesn't help them on the next exam. STEM students are also seldom taught how to take tests. Sooner or later they get stuck on a problem and continue to grind away at it while precious minutes tick by, end up ignoring other problems they might be able to solve, and crash and burn on the test.

Several test-preparation and test-taking strategies have been found effective, but unless instructors share them with students, the students may never discover them. Consider putting links to sources of helpful strategies in your syllabus or on your course website. Two sources that focus on problem-solving tests are "Tips on test-taking" (Felder & Stice, 2014) (hand out before the first test) and "Memo to students who are disappointed with their last test grade" (Felder, 1999) (distribute when the first graded tests are returned), and a web search yields many other possibilities. Another good support tool is an *exam wrapper*. When you hand back graded tests, attach a questionnaire asking the students to reflect on how they approached the test, how well their approach worked, and what they might do differently on the next test. Illustrative exam wrappers are found at Exam Wrappers (n.d.) and in Ambrose et al. (2010, pp. 253–254).

Also consider posting several of your tests from the last two to three years to give the students an idea of what they can expect to see on the tests they will be taking. If you do that, however, make it clear to the students that if they limit their studying to working through those old tests (which is what many of them tend to do), they will probably do poorly on the one they're getting ready to take because the problems will be different. Add that they will have a much better chance of doing well if they focus their studying on setting up as many problems as possible—in their text, in other texts, and on the study guide if you gave them one—without looking back at solutions they may have access to. (No number crunching—it takes too long.)

If students are still experiencing difficulty after you provide the help we have suggested, refer them to an academic support or counseling center on your campus that offers guidance on study skills and overcoming test anxiety.

8.3.4 Grading problem-solving tests

Even if you take all of the suggestions we have offered to make your test fair and prepare students to take it, you can still create a storm of discontent if you don't observe certain precautions when grading it. The students should be able to look at their graded papers and understand why they got the number of points they did for each problem, and if they don't, you should be able to give them a clear explanation. Two students should never be able to compare their graded tests and discover that different points were deducted for identical mistakes. (An exception to that rule is students who magically produce correct solutions without showing the work that led to them.) The following suggestions should help you meet those conditions:

Before you finalize and administer the test, create a detailed solution key that spells out how many points each part of each problem is worth.

Emphasize conceptual understanding and the correct solution process when allocating points, and don't deduct too heavily for algebra and arithmetic mistakes on time-limited tests. (Be stricter about careless errors in homework, where students have ample time to check their solutions.) Make sure each part of the test is graded by only one grader to avoid inconsistencies.

Get assignments and tests graded and returned as quickly as possible.

The longer the delay between the assessment and the feedback, the lower the formative benefits of the assessment will be. If it's possible to return graded papers at the next class session, try to do so, and try very hard not to go past the session after that one.

If test grades are much lower than you anticipated and you accept some of the responsibility, consider adjusting the grades.

Suppose you give a test expecting the average grade to be in the 70 to 75 range and instead it comes back 52, and some good students got abysmally low scores. If you don't curve course grades (in Chapter 3 we did our best to persuade you not to) and you don't want to put a large number of your students at risk of getting lower course grades than they deserve, what are your options?

You have several. The first thing you should ask yourself is, why were the test grades so low? Two likely possibilities are that there was something wrong with the test (e.g., it was too long, confusing, or unintentionally tricky) or you didn't provide enough practice and feedback on the kinds of problems most students did poorly on. If you are convinced that the students had ample instruction and practice and the test was fair, you may decide to let the grades stand. If you take some responsibility for the low grades, however, you can make any of these adjustments:

1. **Scale the grades** by adding enough points to make the top grade 100 or the class average 70 (or whatever target you choose). If you use the class average as your basis, it may be that someone gets 110 as their grade, which is fine. *This is not curving:* scaling test grades helps all students, whereas curving course grades can unfairly help some and hurt others.
2. **Give a retest,** counting the higher of the two scores for each student or adding a percentage of the grade improvement (if there was one) to the first score.
3. **Give a quiz and add the number of points students earn on it to their grade on the test.** If the test grades are low because almost everyone missed a specific problem, announce that the quiz will be a variant of that problem. By the time you give the quiz, most students will have learned with your help or without it how to solve the problem, and you will have turned a headache into a learning opportunity.

The second and third options have the drawbacks that they take additional class time and require additional preparation time from you and the students. However, they ensure that most students will end up learning course material that they had not learned prior to the original test, which we consider a good tradeoff.

Be reasonable about allowing grading appeals.

Some instructors tell their students that they may request regrading of a test if they think they deserve more points but the entire test will be reconsidered, not just the part they have a question about. We advise you not to adopt that policy. Students should have the right to ask for points they genuinely deserve without having to gamble that they won't lose a greater number of points somewhere else. Do your best to make sure the tests are graded fairly, and if a grader makes a mistake that benefits a student, let it stand. If you find that a number of students were penalized for what a grader incorrectly thought was a mistake, do whatever it takes to restore the points to all of those students.

Put a time limit on grading appeals, and require written explanations of why more points are deserved.

Here is a scenario that you have probably already faced, and if you haven't, you will. It's the last week of the semester, and students are standing in a long line outside your office door, clutching graded exams and assignments going back to the beginning of the semester, hoping to persuade you that they deserve more points. You are not happy right now—you have a lot of things to do in the final week of a course, including preparing your final exam, and it could take hours for you to process all those requests.

To keep from getting into this situation, announce in the course policies you hand out on Day 1 that students have one week after graded papers are handed back to request additional points. If the problem is that the points were incorrectly totaled, the students simply have to show you (or a teaching assistant) the graded paper, but if they think they deserve more points on one or more questions or problems, they must make their case in writing. Give such requests serious consideration, and make the grade adjustments you believe are justified. If you follow this policy, the volume of complaints you have to deal with in the last week is likely to drop dramatically.

Thought Question

This section offers several suggestions for making problem-solving tests fair and effective. Which of the proposed strategies do you think might improve your future tests? Can you identify one or two of them that you would be willing to try?

8.4 Evaluating Reports and Presentations

This chapter has so far dealt with knowledge and skills that could be assessed with multiple-choice and short-answer questions and quantitative problem-solving assignments and tests. Those assessments aren't trivial, as you've probably discovered for yourself, but at least it's not too hard to evaluate the data objectively and fairly. Students may argue about what you declare are the correct responses to some multiple-choice and short-answer questions, but once you've declared them, the grading is mechanical and all students get the same grades for the same responses. Grading quantitative problem-solving tests is trickier—you can get into some lively arguments over partial credit—but you can hit a reasonable level of objectivity if you prepare a complete solution key and specify point allocations in sufficient detail.

It's a different story when it comes to evaluating lab reports, written and oral project reports, analyses of case studies and ethical dilemmas, proposals, papers, and any other assignments that require written or oral communication. (From now on we will lump all such products together as *reports*.) No reports submitted by different students are identical, unless at least one was copied. Judgment calls can therefore dominate the evaluation process, and student complaints about unfair grading may reach avalanche proportions. Moreover, it can take many hours to read through written reports and provide detailed comments—and most of those hours are likely to be wasted, because students getting graded reports back tend to just look at the grade and ignore the comments (Crooks, 1988; Gibbs & Simpson, 2004–2005; Jackson, 1996). They may pay attention to feedback if they have a chance to revise and resubmit, but giving students that chance just makes the instructor's heavy grading load even heavier.

The challenge is to find an evaluation scheme that satisfies four criteria:

Validity.

The grades reflect only how well the students met the targeted objectives and are not affected by the students' prior grades, their personal attributes, or anything else but the quality of their work.

Reliability.

A given product would get almost identical grades from two or more independent expert raters and from the same rater at two different times (such as early and late in the grading of a submitted assignment).

Fairness.

The knowledge and skills being assessed were adequately taught, and the students knew in advance the criteria that would be used to rate their efforts.

Efficiency.

The instructor can grade all the work and give the students good constructive feedback without spending an inordinate amount of time.

The keys to meeting these four criteria are to formulate evaluation criteria explicitly (what counts and by how much?) and to make sure the students and graders understand the criteria before the evaluation is performed. Unfortunately, as obvious and reasonable as the first step (formulating criteria) may seem, it is often avoided by academics, who argue that the attributes that make an object or performance excellent are often intangible and hard to capture in words. (Some might add, *"but I know excellence when I see it!"*) Although that argument may have some merit, it has serious drawbacks when it comes to evaluating student products. How are students supposed to learn to communicate effectively, think creatively or critically, or make decisions ethically if their instructors can't clearly explain what those adverbs mean? Giving examples of good and bad reports can help, but it only goes so far toward enabling students to judge whether their work meets our expectations before they submit it and to figure out how they might improve it next time.

8.4.1 Grading forms: Checklists and rubrics

Two types of grading forms—*checklists* and *rubrics*—can help instructors make their expectations clear to the students and make the grading process valid, reliable, fair, and efficient (Felder & Brent, 2010). A grading checklist is a form that lists the evaluation criteria and the maximum points allocated to each criterion. Exhibit 8.4–1 shows an illustrative checklist for written reports. A grading rubric also lists the evaluation criteria, but now the instructor scores each criterion on a discrete scale, usually with either three points (e.g., 1—unacceptable, 2—acceptable, or 3—outstanding); four points (e.g., 1—poor, 2—below average, 3—above average, and 4—excellent); or five points (e.g., 1—poor, 2—marginal, 3—acceptable, 4—good, 5—excellent). For three-point and four-point scales, descriptions are given of performance attributes that characterize each rating, and for a five-point scale, descriptions are given either for each rating or every other rating (1, 3, 5). In the latter case, a product with characteristics of, say, both a 5 and a 3 for a particular criterion would be given a 4.

Exhibit 8.4–1. Grading Checklist for Written Reports

Team: Date:		Project phase: Evaluator:		
Criterion	**Max. Points**	**Score**	**Comments**	
Technical content (60%)				
Topic mastery, technical correctness	20			
All requested deliverables included	15			
Appropriate level of detail and thoroughness of documentation	15			
Completeness of analysis and interpretation of data	10			
Organization (15%)	15			
Clearly identified purpose and approach				
Well organized, supports purpose				
Good transition between topics				
Introduction and conclusion are tailored appropriately to the audience				
Presentation (15%)	15			
Easy to read				
Good grammar and style				
Uniform writing style				
Layout/Visuals (10%)	10			
Quality of graphics				
Uniform document design and layout				
Total Score	100			

Exhibit 8.4–1 created by and reprinted with permission of Dr. Lisa Bullard, Department of Chemical & Biomolecular Engineering, North Carolina State University.

Exhibit 8.4–2. Grading Rubric for Lab Reports

Team: _____ Experiment: _____ Evaluator: _____ Date: _____

Category	Score (S) = 4	S = 3	S = 2	S = 1	w	S	wS
Abstract	Clear, concise, accurate abstract of experiment and results	Clear and concise but incomplete abstract of experiment and results	Unclear or incomplete or too long	Inaccurate or illegible	5		
Background	Relevant background clearly summarized in students' own words; appropriate sources cited correctly	Background reasonably summarized in students' own words; appropriate sources mostly cited correctly	Inadequate but original background summary or questionable sources or incorrect citations	Illegible or directly copied background summary and/or few or no citations	10		
Experimental hypotheses	Hypotheses clearly stated and logically justified	Hypotheses clearly stated but inadequately justified	Hypotheses stated but not justified	No hypotheses stated	5		
Experimental setup and procedure	Setup and procedure clearly and accurately described	Setup and procedure adequately described	Setup and procedure poorly described	Inaccurate or unreadable description	10		
Data	Professional looking and accurate presentation of data in labeled tables and graphs	Accurate presentation of data in labeled tables and graphs	Accurate presentation of data in written form with no tables or graphs	Illegible presentation of data	10		
Data analysis	Data analysis (including error analysis) performed correctly	Data analysis with a few minor mistakes	Data analysis with many or substantial errors	Data analysis incorrect or illegible	20		

Data interpretation	All relevant scientific concepts correctly applied	Most relevant scientific concepts correctly applied	Limited application of relevant scientific concepts	No application of relevant concepts	15
Conclusions	Everything learned accurately stated; hypotheses convincingly supported or rejected	Everything learned accurately summarized; hypotheses inadequately addressed	Conclusions not clear from results	No conclusions included in report	5
Summary	Experiment, data analyses and interpretation, and conclusions completely and clearly described	Experiment, data analyses and interpretation, and conclusions described with minor omissions	Important information poorly described or omitted	No summary included in report	5
Writing	Correct grammar and syntax; clear and concise style	Correct grammar and syntax; awkward or unclear writing	Numerous mistakes in grammar and syntax	Almost unreadable	10
Appearance/ organization	Typed and well organized (headings and subheadings)	Neatly handwritten and well organized	Neatly written or typed but poorly organized	Sloppy	5
SUM					100

Report Grade : $20 + \frac{1}{5} \sum_{i} (w_i S_i) = $ (maximum = 100, minimum = 40)

If an overall quantitative rating (grade) is to be given, it is determined as a weighted sum of the points given for each criterion. Exhibit 8.4–2 shows an illustrative four-point rubric for grading lab reports.

Relative to checklists, rubrics make grading criteria more explicit to students and may give the students a better idea of what they need to do to improve their grades on subsequent assignments. Their disadvantage is that they take more time to create, because several descriptions must be written for each criterion. Completed checklists and rubrics may be augmented by brief comments on aspects of the work that were particularly good or poor, but exhaustively detailed feedback need not be provided. If students are unsure about why they got a low rating for a particular criterion, they can (and should) ask the instructor, who can then provide details orally.

8.4.2 Constructing a grading form for your course

Formulating explicit grading criteria can be challenging, but it is the only way to ensure that the grading is objective. You can make the task much easier by finding an existing rubric for the type of assignment you are planning to give and modifying it rather than starting from scratch. An Internet search for "rubric ____" [fill in the subject] is likely to bring up many links. At a particularly good website maintained by the Association for the Assessment of Learning in Higher Education (n.d.), you can find rubrics for evaluating case study analyses, critical thinking, essays of various types, lab reports, mathematical proofs, multimedia projects, written and oral project reports, and teamwork. You can use the rubrics verbatim, change or delete some of their criteria, change the descriptions under each rating, and add new criteria and descriptions. You can then convert the revised rubric to a checklist if that's your preference. Allen and Tanner (2006) give suggestions for designing and using rubrics in the biological sciences. The suggestions can be applied to other STEM disciplines with little effort.

8.4.3 Using grading forms to promote skill development

Once you have a grading form for your course, you can use it to help the students understand and meet your evaluation criteria. The process is shown in Table 8.4–1. After the students go through it, they will have a clear idea of your expectations and will also be aware of mistakes to avoid when writing their reports. The average quality of their first reports generally will be considerably higher than it would be without that training.

Table 8.4–1. Using Grading Forms to Teach Report-Writing Skills

1. Find or create one or (optionally) two short sample products, either complete reports or excerpts from longer reports. The first one should be poor, containing most of the mistakes you expect students to make in their first efforts (technical errors, sloppiness, poor visuals, inadequate citation of sources, etc.). The second one should be much better but still flawed.

2. In a class session before work starts on the first project or lab, put the students in pairs and give each pair copies of the first sample report and three grading forms. Briefly go over the evaluation criteria on the form.

3. Have the students individually read the sample and fill out a grading form. Then have them reconcile their ratings with their partners, filling in the results on another form. If they agree on a rating for a criterion, they move on; if they disagree, they briefly discuss their reasoning and try to reach consensus. If they can't, they average their ratings and move on.

4. Discuss the reconciled ratings with the class and then show your rating and explain your reasoning if any of your ratings differ substantially from most of the students' ratings. (Optional) Repeat the exercise with the second sample report.

Source: Felder and Brent (2010).

You can use a similar process to help students develop skill in oral reporting. Give the students a copy of your checklist or rubric, briefly go over it, and give a brief presentation or show a video of one that includes many of the mistakes students tend to make (e.g., reading their notes verbatim, not making eye contact, and showing garishly colored slides crammed with bulleted lists in small fonts). Have them complete the rubric or checklist individually and then reconcile their ratings in pairs, show them what your ratings would be for a talk like the one you just gave, or showed and discuss.

Chapter 10 provides more guidance on helping students develop communication skills as well as creative and critical thinking skills.

8.4.4 Peer review

In *peer review,* students critique one another's drafts of reports. The review may be summative but is more often used to help students improve their work before the instructor grades it. A rubric or checklist provides an excellent basis for peer review, especially if the students first receive training in its use.

To conduct the peer review, organize individual students or student teams into pairs. Have the members of each pair present their first drafts or presentations to their partners for mutual critiquing, then revise their assignments or presentations based on the critiques and submit the revisions to you for grading. Several studies have shown a high level of consistency between instructor ratings and peer ratings (Arnold et al., 1981; Orpen, 1982; Sadler & Good, 2006), and Cho and MacArthur (2010) found that receiving feedback from several peers led to higher quality revision than feedback from the instructor or a single peer. To sharpen your students' critical thinking skills, collect their first drafts and critiques and grade both.

Having your students critique each other's work before submitting it to you offers significant benefits to them and to you. When they critique their classmates' work, they learn different approaches to the tasks being evaluated and discover strengths and weaknesses in their own work. The revision they then submit to you will generally be much better than their first drafts, making grading much easier and more efficient for you.

8.5 Ideas to Take Away

o Sharing learning objectives—especially those that involve higher-level thinking and problem-solving skills—as study guides for tests maximizes the chances that the students capable of meeting the objectives will do so.

o Enough homework problems should be assigned in your course to provide adequate practice and feedback on skills that will be assessed on tests, but not so much that students have to neglect their other courses to keep up with the homework in yours. Performance on assignments should count toward the course grade.

o ConcepTests and validated concept inventories should be used to determine students' misconceptions about course content and to evaluate the effectiveness of attempts to correct them.

o Students should be given a guide to preparing for and taking problem-solving tests, either before their first exam in the course or shortly after it.

o Before giving a problem-solving test, instructors should take the test and time themselves. If they can't complete the test in less than one-third of the time the students will have to do it (or less than one-fourth or one-fifth of the time if the test is particularly complex or computation-heavy), the test is too long.

o Checklists or rubrics should be developed and used to evaluate written reports and oral presentations. Once the instructor has finalized the grading form, students should use it to rate sample reports—including a bad one—before they write and submit their first reports.

o We didn't discuss cheating on assignments and tests in this chapter, but we know it's on your mind. For suggestions on how to minimize it, detect it, and deal with it when it occurs, review Section 3.6.4.

8.6 Try This in Your Course

o Look back at the last few tests you gave and see if any of the suggestions in this chapter (especially those related to test length) might have improved them. If so, plan how you will incorporate the suggestions into your future test construction.

o When you design your next test, include one or more multiple-choice or short-discussion questions that address high-level thinking skills or conceptual understanding.

o Prepare an *exam wrapper* to give to students after the first test in your course to help them reflect on their preparation and think of ways to improve their performance. Alternatively, if the test focuses on quantitative problem solving, hand out copies of the questionnaire in Felder (1999) with the graded papers and encourage the students to complete it before starting to study for the next test.

o If you are teaching a course in which students write or present project reports, find a grading rubric (e.g., at Association for the Assessment of Learning in Higher Education [n.d.] or by entering "rubric [subject]" into a search engine), modify it to fit your evaluation criteria, and use it to grade the reports. Don't provide detailed individual feedback. Before the students prepare and submit their first reports, have them use your grading form to evaluate one or two sample reports and then show how you would evaluate those reports.

o Announce a course policy that students have one week to appeal grades on assignments and tests, and that appeals for anything but incorrect point totaling must be accompanied by written justifications. Enjoy the subsequent near-disappearance of frivolous appeals at the end of the term.

PART THREE

FACILITATING SKILL DEVELOPMENT

Part III of the book, which comprises Chapters 9 through 11, presents teaching strategies for equipping students with skills they are likely to need as STEM professionals, beginning in Chapter 9 with analytical problem-solving skills. The chapter surveys the attributes that have been found to characterize expert problem solvers, describes strategies for helping students develop those attributes, outlines a well-known problem-solving model, and discusses problem-based learning.

Past STEM graduates have always also needed nontechnical professional skills, but according to numerous surveys of their employers, recent graduates lack those skills—especially communication skills—and the need for them will continue to grow. Chapter 10 outlines techniques for facilitating development of communication, critical and creative thinking, and self-directed learning skills, and reviews project-based learning. Chapter 11 discusses cooperative learning, a powerful approach to equipping students with high-performance teamwork skills such as leadership, time and project management, and conflict resolution. Chapter 12 surveys aspects of student diversity, compares and contrasts several common inductive teaching methods, and summarizes how the different learner-centered teaching and assessment strategies discussed in the book combine to address the learning needs of diverse students. The structures of the chapters are shown in Figure III-1.

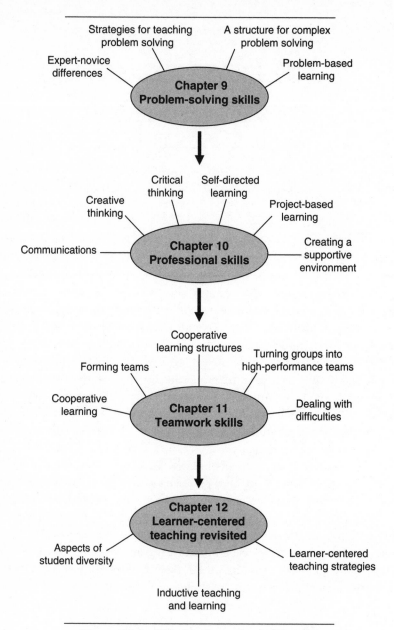

Figure III-1: Graphic Organizer of Part III

INTERLUDE. MEET YOUR STUDENTS:
STAN AND NATHAN

Stan and Nathan are juniors in chemical engineering and roommates at a large Midwestern university. They are similar in many ways. Both enjoy partying, video games, and midnight pizza runs. Both did well in science and math in high school, although Nathan's grades were consistently higher. Both found their mass and energy balance course tough (although they agreed the text was superb), thermodynamics incomprehensible, and most humanities courses useless. Both have nonengineer friends who occasionally accuse them of being "too logical."

For all their similarities, however, they are fundamentally different. Stan is an electronics wizard and is constantly sought after by friends with ailing computers, whereas changing a light bulb is at the outer limits of Nathan's mechanical ability. Stan notices his surroundings, always knows where his cell phone is, and remembers people he only met once; Nathan notices very little around him, misplaces things constantly, and may not recognize someone he has known for years. Stan often has trouble following lectures that Nathan follows easily, but when instructors spend a lot of class time going through derivations and problem solutions Nathan already understands, he gets bored and his attention wanders.

When Stan takes a test, he reads the first problem, reads it again, and carefully works through the solution. When he has gone as far as he can on the first problem, he checks all the calculations, moves on to the second problem, and repeats the process. Because of his painstaking approach, he often runs out of time and gets a test grade below class average. Nathan reads test problem statements only up to where he thinks he knows what to do and then plunges into solving them. He works quickly and usually finishes early and gets high grades, even though he doesn't like to check his calculations and often makes careless mistakes.

The one place where Stan outshines Nathan academically is the laboratory. Stan is sure-handed and meticulous and seems to have an instinct for setting up and running experiments, whereas Nathan rarely gets anything to work right. Nathan almost had a nervous breakdown in analytical chemistry: he would repeat a quantitative analysis five times, get five completely different results, and finally average the two closest estimates and hope for the best. Stan, however, would do the analysis twice, get almost perfect agreement between the results, and head for a victory soda while Nathan was still weighing out the reagents for his second attempt.

Stan is a sensing learner and Nathan is an intuitive learner (Felder & Silverman, 1988; Felder et al., 2002). Sensors tend to be practical, attentive to details, and uncomfortable with abstract theories and mathematical models; intuitors can handle abstraction but tend to be bored by details and repetition. Sensors like well-defined problems that can be solved by standard methods; intuitors prefer problems that require innovation. A student who complains about courses having nothing to do with the real world is almost certainly a sensor. Individuals of both types may be excellent STEM professionals: many observant and methodical sensors are good experimentalists, and insightful and innovative intuitors are often good theoreticians and designers.

A mismatch exists between the teaching styles of most STEM professors, who tend to emphasize basic principles and abstract analysis, and the preferences of many STEM undergraduates, who are sensing learners and prefer to focus on observable phenomena, facts, and hands-on experimentation. Intuitive students would consequently be expected to enjoy a clear advantage in most STEM curricula, and on average intuitors have indeed been found to get consistently higher grades except in courses that emphasize factual knowledge and experimentation (see studies cited in Felder et al., 2002).

Sensing and intuition are *learning style preferences* (Felder & Brent, 2005). The point is not to teach each student in the way that he or she prefers; rather, it is to make sure instruction is balanced and not heavily biased in favor of one preference or its opposite. In Chapters 9 and 12, we describe methods of achieving such instruction. Learning styles are the subject of some controversy in the academic psychology community, which we also discuss in Chapter 12.

9

PROBLEM-SOLVING SKILLS

9.0 Introduction

In the interlude preceding this chapter we looked at two hypothetical students who differ in several ways. Stan is practical, observant, and methodical; likes hands-on work; and is a relatively slow analytical problem solver. Nathan is creative, likes scientific theories and mathematical analysis, and is a fast analytical problem solver but is impatient with details and prone to make careless errors.

Unlike most problems that come up in STEM curricula, which fit neatly within single disciplines and can be solved with well-established methods, real science and engineering problems are multidisciplinary, often poorly defined, and require all of the positive attributes that Stan and Nathan have between them—creativity, attention to detail, experimentation, mathematical analysis and computation and design and troubleshooting, flashes of insight, and a tendency to check calculations and replicate data. Some gifted individuals have all of those traits, but there are not enough of them to meet the needs of industry, government, and academia for skilled applied scientists, technologists, engineers, and mathematicians. Both Stans and Nathans are therefore critically important in STEM professions.

Unfortunately, many STEM curricula—particularly the mathematical and physical sciences and most branches of engineering—stack the deck in favor of the Nathans. As soon as the students enter college, they plunge directly into the heavy-duty abstractions of first-year calculus, physics, and chemistry, and they stay mainly in those realms for the next four years. The mathematicians and scientists go on to a steady diet of increasingly abstract advanced math and science problems in assignments and tests, and the engineers move to "engineering science" that is almost as abstract—mechanics, circuits, fluid dynamics, thermodynamics, and quantum and statistical mechanics, with only occasional ventures into the laboratory.

As STEM instructors, we should be trying to equip all of our Stans and Nathans with the problem-solving skills required in STEM careers. The challenge is to teach in a way that balances the learning needs and preferences of both types rather than heavily favoring one over the other. This chapter is designed to help you achieve that balance. It addresses the following questions:

- What attributes distinguish problem-solving experts from novices? How can I help my students develop those attributes?
- Why is *metacognition* a critical component of expert problem solving? How can I motivate and prepare my students to practice it?
- What role does *self-efficacy* play in learning? What can I do to help my students develop it in problem solving?
- How can the *McMaster problem-solving strategy* help my students learn to solve the kinds of complex, open-ended, multidisciplinary, real-world problems they are likely to face as professionals?
- When and how should I use *problem-based learning*?

9.1 The Long, Steep Path from Novice to Expert

Remember your first time behind the wheel of a car in heavy traffic? Picture it for a few seconds, remembering what it looked and felt like. Now take another few seconds and picture yourself driving a car today.

Two completely different experiences, right? The first time you were frantically trying to keep track of all sorts of things at the same time. "Am I going too fast or too slow? Am I drifting into the next lane? Can I make the turn before that car coming at me gets to the intersection?" Nowadays (we hope) you deal with those situations with little conscious thought—in fact, while driving you might be thinking about other things. If something happens that requires your immediate attention—the driver in front of you suddenly slams on his brakes, for example—you instantly bring your conscious attention back to your driving.

Those contrasting behaviors illustrate differences between *novices* and *experts*. Novices think consciously about every step of what they are doing, whereas experts have a mental library of situations and reactions to them and so execute most steps automatically, devoting their conscious attention only to unfamiliar situations that call for decision making and action. To outside observers, experts appear smooth, comfortable, and confident, while novices may appear clumsy, tense, and uncertain.

Novice-expert differences follow that pattern in every sphere of human activity. The more challenging and complex the activity, the longer and more difficult the climb from novice to expert. Solving technical problems in any STEM discipline ranks high among human activities in challenge and complexity, but many experienced STEM instructors forget the long, steep path that led to their current fluency. They believe that if they simply show novice students an example problem in class and assign one or two similar homework problems, the students should be able to bypass all the repetitions that gave the instructors their mastery. They are wrong.

But the best instructors are able to bridge the gap between themselves and their students. They understand (often instinctively) which learning experiences will help students think like mathematicians, biochemists, computer scientists, or mechanical engineers, and they provide those experiences in their classes. This chapter describes experiences that promote expertise and discusses how they can be integrated into courses without sacrificing important content. To design the experiences effectively, it helps to know what experts do that novices don't and vice versa. The brainwave in Table 9.1–1 outlines four significant differences.

When novice students are faced with a complex and difficult problem on an assignment, many begin by searching for a similar problem in the lecture notes or course text, on the Internet, or in archives of worked-out problems from old assignments and tests. If they find one, they follow the steps of the solution without really understanding them until the assigned problem deviates from the one they found, at which point they either painstakingly figure out the necessary adjustments or abandon the effort. Some may get a solution that may or may not be correct, and others just flounder helplessly until they give up in frustration.

Compare that approach with that of experts presented with a problem. Their prior experience gives them confidence in their problem-solving ability (*self-efficacy*). They reflect on the problem and classify it— transient or stationary, linear or nonlinear, completely or incompletely defined, and so on (*problem classification*). Based on the classification, they identify and implement a solution approach but don't just breeze through it from beginning to end. After each step, they think of one or more ways to check their work, and only after satisfying themselves that it is correct do they go on to the next step (*metacognition*). They also continually reflect on their progress and ask themselves if the solution could be obtained more efficiently or accurately, adjusting their approach if

Table 9.1–1. Brainwave—Expert versus Novice Problem Solving

Attribute	Experts	Novices
Problem classification	Classify problem types based on their underlying principles and key attributes; place new problems into appropriate categories and quickly select corresponding solution strategies	Choose solution strategies based on superficial problem features (e.g., involves a chemical reaction, looks like Example 3.5–2)
Metacognition	Habitually monitor and reflect on their thinking before and during cognitive tasks, following successful pathways and quickly adjusting unsuccessful ones	Do relatively little thinking about their thinking; choose an approach and stay with it until forced to give up
Automaticity	Solve routine problems with little apparent effort	Have to think about each step consciously
Self-efficacy	Are confident in their ability to meet specific challenges or types of challenges (e.g., math problems or oral exams)	Lack confidence in their ability to meet specific challenges or types of challenges

Sources: Ambrose et al. (2010, Ch. 2); Bransford et al. (2000, Ch. 2).

necessary (*metacognition*). If they get stuck, they don't panic because they have been stuck many times before and always found a way around the obstacle (*self-efficacy*). They look for what makes this particular problem different and draw on their resources to find a new way to address it. Despite all of that metacognitive activity, to an outside observer their process appears quick, efficient, and effortless (*automaticity*).

Can we enable our students to develop those four attributes of expertise without the years of repetitive practice it takes most experts to develop them? For an occasional prodigy, possibly, but for most of the students, no. What we *can* do is help them get a good start on the process. Let's consider how.

9.2 Strategies for Teaching Expert Problem-Solving Skills

Instructional techniques surveyed in this section can help students develop the skills and traits associated with expertise in problem solving.

9.2.1 Teach students to classify problems

Ambrose et al. (2010, pp. 59–64) propose strategies for teaching students to do the kind of problem classification that experts learn to do through long years of experience. The following procedure is based on their proposal:

○ Identify attributes [underlying scientific principles, linear or nonlinear, closed-ended or open-ended, etc.] that distinguish different problems your students will confront. Classify the problems according to their attributes and identify solution strategies for problems in each category. Each time you go over a new problem in class, begin by having the students identify its category and outline the solution method, and have them do it again with homework problems.

○ Assign several problems that can be solved with one approach (such as using Newton's laws to solve mechanics problems), and then assign another problem that is difficult or impossible with that approach but easily solved with a different approach (such as using conservation of energy). Have students make necessary modifications in the problem classification system.

9.2.2 Show the full problem-solving process, including metacognition

A complex problem solution can look impossible to students when only the final result is presented. In Torrance's (1962) phrase, "Dispel the sense of awe of masterpieces." When working through example problems in class, don't always start with exactly the right principle or equation and proceed in a flawless progression from beginning to end. Novice students will get the idea that they should be able to do that, and when they try and fail, they are likely to get frustrated and give up. Instead, occasionally work through a new problem and say out loud what you are thinking as you decide how to begin, what to do next, how to monitor your progress metacognitively (*Is this working? Does that solution make sense? How can I check it? Might there be a better approach?*), and what to do if you get stuck or realize that you did something wrong. Occasionally modeling the expert process for students accelerates their progression toward being able to do it themselves (Weimer, 2013, p. 79).

Another technique to promote metacognition is the exam wrapper (introduced in Chapter 8), a post-test questionnaire on which students reflect on how they prepared for and took the test, why they missed what they missed, and what they could do to improve their performance on subsequent tests. The more students explicitly identify their mistakes and ineffective strategies on tests, the less likely they will be to repeat those mistakes and strategies in the future.

Thought Question

Are you currently doing anything to encourage your students to practice metacognition? What might you do next week?

9.2.3 Use problem chunking and TAPPS to promote metacognition

In Section 6.4 we introduced two active learning strategies that have a clear relevance to students' acquisition of problem-solving skills:

○ **Break derivations and problem solutions into parts.** Lecture quickly or let students read through straightforward parts, and use the analytical and conceptually challenging parts as bases for activities.
○ **Use thinking-aloud pair problem solving (TAPPS) to guide students through partially or fully worked-out examples.** Have student pairs go through derivations and problem solutions in a sequence of short activities. In each activity, one student explains the analysis, step-by-step, including the reasoning behind the steps, and the other student asks questions if the first one says anything unclear and gives the first one hints if necessary. The pairs reverse roles in successive activities.

(See Section 6.4 for full details on these strategies and the cognitive basis for their effectiveness.) When students work through the steps of an analytical procedure in either of these ways, they deepen their understanding of the procedure, increase the likelihood that they will be able to apply it to new problems, and develop their metacognitive skills.

9.2.4 Use repetition to promote automaticity

Most experts had to repeat actions again and again and again—practicing the swing, rehearsing the piece, making the soufflé, administering the injection, designing the process—before they developed the ability to do it in the seemingly effortless way experts do things. Cognitive science sheds light on the connection between repetition and learning.

Brainwave: Repetition and Learning

A stimulus of any sort triggers a pattern of signals transmitted from neurons to neighboring clusters of neurons. Afterwards, the activated neurons remain sensitized for hours or possibly days. If the stimulus is an isolated event and the pattern is not repeated *(rehearsed)* during that period, the event is likely to be lost from memory. If it is repeated, the neuronal group undergoes *long-term potentiation (LTP)*, developing greater sensitivity and a tendency to fire together rapidly. Enough repetition binds the neurons together so if one fires, they all do ("neurons that fire together, wire together"), forming a new memory trace. Learning a procedure—say, for solving a specific type of problem—involves forming a number of such traces. Repetition continues to strengthen the connections among the neurons, so that the procedure becomes more skillful and requires progressively less conscious effort, eventually reaching the automaticity that characterizes expert performance (Sousa, 2011, Ch. 3).

An implication of this brainwave is that just giving students a lecture on a problem-solving method and showing one or two examples is unlikely to lead to much learning, let alone expertise. If the students don't encounter the method again in that course, it should come as no surprise in a subsequent course when they act as if they never saw it before in their lives.

If you want your students to develop automaticity in a skill, build repetition into your instruction. Show a variety of applications of the skill in lectures, class activities, and assignments, and then put problems on the exams that require the skill. If the skill is important enough to be included on a list of learning outcomes or competencies that all graduates of your program should have, then make sure it is taught and exercised in at least one course in each year of the curriculum.

9.2.5 Use interleaving and overlearning to provide repetition

Two contrasting approaches to providing repetition are *interleaving* (alternating between two different methods of teaching a skill) and *overlearning* (repeating the same method again and again) (Brown et al., 2014; Dunlosky et al., 2013, Section 10; Rohrer et al., 2014; Taylor & Rohrer, 2010). In the context of problem solving, both approaches begin with the instructor outlining a method for solving a type of problem, giving several demonstrations and possibly in-class activities that illustrate the method, and assigning a few homework problems that require its use. What happens next depends on which strategy is being used.

In overlearning, the first problems would be followed by many more assigned problems that require applying the same method. The repetition helps accelerate student progress toward the apparently effortless execution of that method that characterizes expert automaticity. The downsides are that the effect fades over time relative to the effect of practice distributed over longer time periods (Rohrer et al., 2004), and if new problems differ from the original set in even minor ways, the students may be incapable of making the mental adjustments needed to deal with them (Rohrer & Pashler, 2007). Overlearning is consequently not the approach of choice for STEM problem solving.

Interleaving can have a variety of forms, each making its own contributions to expertise.

Illustrate a problem-solving method in a variety of different contexts.

For example, apply the diffusion equation to applications as diverse as the spreading of a drop of dye in a colorless liquid, separation of constituents of a mixture in a chromatographic column, dispersion of a pollutant in air or water, and transport of a gas or a drug through a membrane. We showed in Section 4.3 that presenting information in different contexts promotes the subsequent retrievability of the information from long-term memory. Illustrating a problem-solving method in different settings also improves students' ability to judge the suitability of the method for different types of problems (*problem classification*) and boosts their confidence in their ability to use the method (*self-efficacy*).

Apply different methods to a specific type of problem and evaluate their effectiveness.

For example, prove a conditional mathematical statement directly and then by contradiction, or compare and contrast several different bioseparation processes for blood analysis and identify the conditions under which each method would be most appropriate, taking cost into account. This form of interleaving also promotes the expert skill of problem classification.

Mix assignment and test problems on current course content with problems that bring back previously learned material.

It's not unusual for course concepts to be drilled extensively when they are first introduced (*overlearning*) and then to disappear until the final examination. Bringing a concept back later in the course in assignments and on tests (*spaced repetition*) reinforces its retrievability from long-term memory (Brown et al., 2014). The resulting ease of recall enables students to apply the original content more smoothly with less effort (*automaticity*), may require them to think about how previously learned methods relate to and differ from new ones (*metacognition, problem classification*), and raises their confidence in their ability to use the method (*self-efficacy*).

Caution, however. If you bring old material back on midterm exams, our advice in previous chapters to preview test content in study guides is doubly applicable. Making students guess what they are responsible for on a content-heavy test puts an unreasonable burden on them, even when tests are not cumulative. If you tell them that they are responsible for everything covered in the course up to the test, you are almost forcing them to rely on superficial memorization of facts and formulas rather than enabling them to focus on the principles, concepts, and methods you consider most important.

9.2.6 Promote your students' self-efficacy in the methods and skills you are teaching

Self-efficacy is a term coined by the psychologist Albert Bandura (1977) to denote a belief in one's ability to succeed in specific situations. Perhaps the most notable difference between novices and experts is the experts' self-efficacy in their area of expertise. When they face new challenges they know they've done similar things successfully in the past, and that knowledge equips them with the belief that they will be able to do it again.

Students' self-efficacy in a subject or skill plays an important role in their learning or failure to learn. Hutchison-Green et al. (2008) cite studies linking self-efficacy beliefs of STEM students to their achievement and persistence in their fields. Cognitive science once again provides insight into the reason for the connection.

Brainwave: Emotions Are Stored with Memories

The brain acts as a continuous information filter, coding sensory inputs it considers important into working memory and discarding other inputs, and either coding information in working memory into long-term memory or discarding it. An experience associated with joy, fear, anger, or any other strong emotion is relatively likely to be retained, in which case the amygdala (small organs in the temporal lobe) encode the emotions with the experience. When the experience is later recalled, the recollection brings back the emotion (Sousa, 2011, Ch. 1).

If a student has a negative experience in a certain type of course, such as getting a bad grade or being ridiculed or shamed by an instructor or classmates for poor performance or for asking a "dumb" question, the incident and the bad feelings it evokes are likely to be stored together in long-term memory. If similar incidents occur in the same type of course, the memories and associated negative feelings may reinforce each other and eventually coalesce into a low self-efficacy belief about the course subject ("I'm just no good in math."). Conversely, if students have a history of positive experiences with a type of course—getting good grades, earning the respect of the instructor and their classmates— their memories and associated good feelings may lead to high self-efficacy beliefs.

Similar to everyone else, students tend to pursue experiences they associate with good feelings and avoid experiences with negative associations. If they have high self-efficacy beliefs in the subject of a new challenge, their urge to re-experience the good feelings associated with that subject leads them to study hard and persist in the face of setbacks. Similarly, low self-efficacies prompt students to minimize the time they spend on the subject and to give up as soon as they experience setbacks, further reinforcing their sense of inadequacy.

The concept of self-efficacy is sometimes criticized based on misconceptions about what it is. Raising students' self-efficacy does not mean improving their self-esteem or self-importance; it simply means helping them gain confidence that they can succeed in meeting a particular type of challenge. If you take steps to raise your students' self-efficacy, you increase the chances that those capable of succeeding will end up doing so, and those who lack the necessary ability or work ethic will fail whether or not you take the steps (Dweck, 2006).

There are several ways to promote your students' self-efficacy in the subject you are teaching, all of which should sound familiar to you from suggestions we have previously offered.

Provide early successes.

A common teaching strategy is to make things really tough at the beginning of a course to send the message that it will take hard work to succeed, and then to ease off as the course proceeds. Although that idea has some logic behind it, it can easily backfire. If you start a course with seriously demanding assignments and exams on which most grades are low, many well-qualified students could incorrectly conclude that they can't succeed in the course, and they might either drop out or just stop trying. But if the early assignments and tests are reasonable and most grades are above the passing level, and competent students do well, most students should develop positive self-efficacy beliefs and be motivated to do the work necessary to succeed in the course. (Again, that doesn't mean they all will: students who either lack the ability to succeed or don't study enough will still fail.)

Provide balanced instruction.

Students differ in many ways—in strengths and weaknesses, likes and dislikes, work ethics, what motivates them and what turns them off, how they approach studying, and how they respond to different teaching strategies—and, of course, in race, gender identity and expression, sexual orientation, and socioeconomic status. One of the most significant challenges teachers face is determining how to teach a class full of students with that range of diversity.

It's not realistically possible to determine the optimal teaching strategy for each individual student and teach him or her that way. The key is to balance the learning needs and interests of diverse students: theory and practice, analysis and experimentation, lecturing and active learning, individual and group work, and so on. The value of balance in addressing student diversity and strategies for achieving that balance are discussed extensively in Chapter 12. For now, we will just note that a heavy curricular bias toward one facet of diversity over another—such as the almost exclusive early emphasis on theoretical and mathematical analysis over experimentation and real-world applications in many STEM curricula—can have a serious negative impact on the self-efficacy of the less-favored group. The consequence is that students are weeded out of STEM curricula for reasons having nothing to do with their potential for succeeding in STEM careers (Felder et al., 2002; Seymour & Hewitt,

1997; Tobias, 1994), representing a serious loss for them, STEM professions, and society.

Minimize speed as a factor in determining test grades.

In Chapter 8 we discussed the potentially disastrous impact on qualified students of tests that only the fastest problem-solvers in the class (such as Nathan in the interlude) can finish. Self-efficacy theory also provides an argument against long tests. Students frequently form their beliefs about their own competence by comparing themselves with their classmates. If they routinely run out of time on tests that many other students are able to finish, they could wrongly conclude that they lack the ability to succeed in the course. To minimize that problem, follow the guideline for quantitative problem-solving tests proposed in Chapter 8: *give the students at least three times as much time for the test as it takes you to work through the solution.*

Challenge negative self-efficacy beliefs.

On the first day of every undergraduate STEM course you ever teach, you are certain to be looking at some competent students whose educational experiences have led to low self-efficacies. You can do several things to counter those feelings. Here are a few:

- If you are teaching a course with an undeserved reputation for failing large percentages of students, announce on Day 1 that you've heard about that reputation, and then show the distribution of grades from the last time you taught the course.
- Share effective strategies for preparing and taking tests, such as those listed in Section 8.3.3.
- Compliment students, collectively or individually, on work that merits it. Make sure the compliment is directed at the work (that's a great paper) and not at the student (you're really good at this) and that it is really deserved, because insincere or overblown praise can backfire.

9.3 A Structure for Complex Problem Solving

In the last section we discussed the ineffectiveness of the traditional way to teach problem solving (show one or two worked examples in lectures and put a few similar problems on assignments). General problem-solving strategies have been developed as alternatives to that approach, many of which build on a four-step structure formulated by the mathematician George Pólya in *How to Solve It* (Pólya, 1945): *Define the problem, make a plan, carry out the plan, look back to validate and possibly extend the solution.* All of those strategies incorporate the principles of repetition

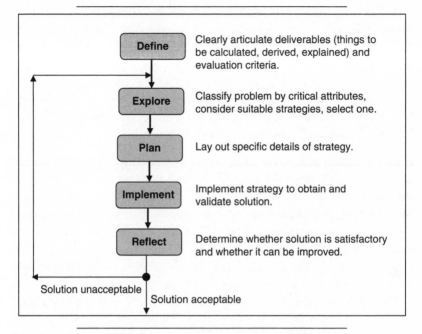

Figure 9.3–1: McMaster Problem-Solving Structure

(the more practice and feedback students have with a procedure, the more likely they will be to carry it out expertly) and metacognition (reflecting on one's own thinking leads to more rapid acquisition of expertise). A particularly robust variation of Pólya's model was developed by Donald Woods and his colleagues at McMaster University (Woods, 1985, 1994, 2000). A five-step version of the McMaster strategy is outlined in Figure 9.3–1. Fogler et al. (2014) use an essentially identical five-step model with different labels for the steps. In practice, the algorithm is usually not as linear as it might appear: there can be a fair amount of jumping around among the steps before the final solution is reached.

At this point, you might be worrying about how your students will react if you tell them they have to implement this multistep strategy on every problem you assign. Relax—telling them that would be serious overkill. The strategy is best suited to complex open-ended problems that require using one or more higher-level thinking skills on Bloom's Taxonomy (analyzing, evaluating, and creating) and don't have an obvious solution method. For example, if you are teaching an introductory calculus course and assign $\int (2x + x^2)dx$, you would not expect the students to apply the full McMaster strategy; they would simply evaluate the integral and check their solution.

In the remainder of this section, we will use the following industrial waste treatment problem to demonstrate the strategy. The problem might be assigned verbatim in courses in applied mathematics; calculus; differential equations; physical chemistry; chemical, civil, or environmental engineering. Equivalent problems can be readily created in other subjects by starting with a conventional word problem ("Given _____, determine _____") that might or might not be mathematical in nature and adding variations of Parts (b) and (c) of this problem.

Waste Treatment Problem

A toxic substance (S for short) is contained in the waste discharge from a pharmaceutical production plant. The waste contains S at a concentration $C_{SW} = 0.425$ g S/L (grams of S per liter). The company used to dump the waste directly into a nearby river, but a recently enacted environmental regulation says that discharges into the river must contain less than 0.01 g S/L. The chief science officer finds an article in a chemistry journal that states that in the presence of a small amount of a catalyst (B), S decomposes at a rate given by the following expression:

$$r_d \left(\frac{\text{g S decompose}}{\text{hr} \cdot \text{L reaction volume}} \right) = 2.05 C_S$$

where C_S(g S/L) is the concentration of S in the reaction mixture.

The scientist sends the following proposal to the Environmental Protection Agency:

> A collection of holding tanks equipped with stirrers is currently sitting idle in a lot adjacent to the river. The plant waste will be fed into an empty tank. When the tank is full, flow into it will be shut off and the waste discharge will be directed into another empty tank. A small amount of the catalyst B will be added to the full tank and the stirrer in the tank will be turned on. When the concentration of S in the tank falls to $C_{SF} = 0.005$ g S/L (well below the safe level of 0.01), the tank contents will be discharged into the river, and the tank will be prepared to receive a new batch of waste. There are just enough tanks in the lot to handle all the waste produced in the plant.

(a) Assume that the tank is perfectly mixed (so that the concentration of S is the same throughout the tank). Calculate the time it will take for C_S to reach 0.005 g S/L.

(b) The EPA responds that the company must test the proposed process using a single tank. The test is carried out, and after the time calculated in part (a) has elapsed, C_S is still well above 0.005 g S/L, so that the number of tanks on the lot would be inadequate to handle the volume of waste being produced in the plant. List three probable explanations for the difference between the predicted and measured decomposition times. Prioritize your list in order of likelihood and explain your reasoning.

(c) Suppose the predicted and measured decomposition times are almost the same. Brainstorm up to thirty possible ways the proposed system might still fail.

Part (a) of the problem requires converting a word problem into a differential equation and solving the equation. Depending on the mathematical sophistication of the students in the class, the solution involves either Level 3 (applying) or Level 4 (analyzing) thinking on Bloom's Taxonomy (Chapter 2). Part (b) calls for critical thinking (Bloom Level 5), and part (c) requires creative thinking (Bloom Level 6). (We discuss teaching critical and creative thinking skills in Chapter 10.)

The subsections that follow discuss each step of the McMaster strategy, and boxes outline how the steps might be applied to our example problem. You may go through the sections chronologically or skim through all the boxes first (those for Steps 4 and 5 are in the appendix at the end of the chapter) to get an overview of the entire solution procedure. Don't take the examples of the five steps as *The Correct Solution;* they are simply possible solutions selected from an infinite number of equally acceptable possibilities.

9.3.1 Define the problem

Students should articulate what they know and what they are being asked to determine if the problem definition is not obvious (as it is in "Given _____, calculate _____"). For certain types of problems, other steps may be recommended for the problem definition, such as summarizing known information in a visual representation (e.g., a free-body diagram, circuit diagram, or process flow chart). There is a chance that many of your students will not have been asked to produce an explicit problem definition before, so consider giving illustrations and practice exercises on doing it in class before they have to do it on homework.

Figure 9.3–2 shows the first of a series of illustrations the instructor prepared to serve as a model solution of the waste treatment problem.

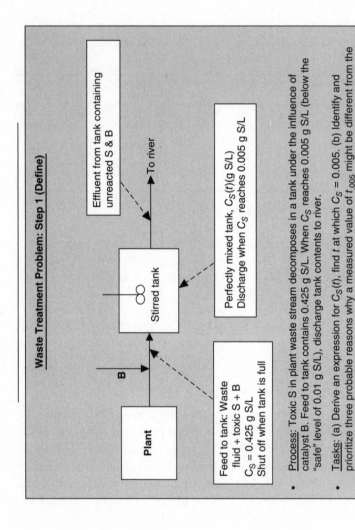

Waste Treatment Problem: Step 1 (Define)

Plant

B

Stirred tank

To river

Effluent from tank containing unreacted S & B

Feed to tank: Waste fluid + toxic S + B
C_S = 0.425 g S/L
Shut off when tank is full

Perfectly mixed tank, $C_S(t)$(g S/L)
Discharge when C_S reaches 0.005 g S/L

• Process: Toxic S in plant waste stream decomposes in a tank under the influence of catalyst B. Feed to tank contains 0.425 g S/L. When C_S reaches 0.005 g S/L (below the "safe" level of 0.01 g S/L), discharge tank contents to river.

• Tasks: (a) Derive an expression for $C_S(t)$, find t at which C_S = 0.005. (b) Identify and prioritize three probable reasons why a measured value of $t_{.005}$ might be different from the value calculated in Part (a). (c) Brainstorm up to 30 reasons the process might fail even if the values in (b) and (c) agree. List alternative approaches to waste disposal problem as part of "Reflect" step (not explicitly required in problem statement, but expected).

Figure 9.3–2: Definition Step of Waste Treatment Problem Solution

9.3.2 Explore the problem

Experts confronting a new problem try to match its important attributes to a known problem classification and identify a solution procedure for that classification. A possible exploration step for the waste treatment problem follows.

Waste Treatment Problem: Step 2 (Explore)

The system is governed by the law of conservation of mass applied to S. It is transient (a differential equation for $C_S(t)$ must be derived) and homogeneous in space (the differential equation will be ordinary). Part (a) has a unique solution; Parts (b) and (c) require multiple solutions and (b) requires prioritization.

If Part (a) were broader and open-ended, as problems calling for the McMaster strategy tend to be (e.g., *Design a process to keep from contaminating the river with S.*), the exploration step would involve looking in depth at a broader range of possible approaches well before the reflection step.

Similar to the define step, the process of problem exploration is likely to be new to many students and so should be demonstrated in lectures and class activities before it is included in an assignment. It can also be helpful to explain that classifying problems is something expert problem solvers routinely do and novices should learn to do sooner rather than later.

9.3.3 Plan a solution

Following is a possible solution plan for the waste treatment problem.

Waste Treatment Problem: Step 3 (Plan)

(a) Write the law of conservation of mass for species S in the tank (rate of change of amount of S = − rate of decomposition) to get a differential equation ($dC_S/dt = \ldots$, $C_S(0) = 0.425$ g S/L). Solve the equation to derive an expression for $C_S(t)$. Check the solution by first verifying that it satisfies the initial condition, then differentiating it to regenerate the original differential equation. Finally, calculate t at which $C_S = 0.005$ g S/L.

(b) Consider reasons the published decomposition rate correlation might not be correct or might not apply to the plant conditions, possible violations of assumptions made in the calculations, variations in the waste fluid quantity and pollutant concentration, and instrument and human errors in the measurement.

(c) Consider possible environmental problems caused by the residual S, the products of the decomposition of S, or other components of the plant waste; human errors or deliberate sabotage; changes in the quantity or composition of the waste; changes in the tank conditions (such as temperature); accidents in the plant; and natural disasters (earthquakes, hurricanes, etc.). In the reflection step, consider alternative waste treatment processes and possible ways to get rid of S as part of the manufacturing process so that it never leaves the plant.

9.3.4 Implement the plan

Once the solution plan has been formulated, the next step is to carry it out. The process is usually not as neatly linear as the strategy implies, however, because something unforeseen almost always comes up when solving complex problems that requires revising the exploration and planning responses and possibly the problem definition. Nevertheless, the initial attempts at definition, exploration, and planning can be invaluable in avoiding the false starts and blind alleys that usually result from skipping those steps and jumping directly to a solution.

An illustrative solution of the waste treatment problem is shown in the chapter appendix.

9.3.5 Reflect on the solution

When your students turn in the solution to a complex problem, ask them to include answers to all questions in Table 9.3–1 (next page) that are appropriate in the context of the problem.

Novice problem solvers tend to accept unquestioningly the expressions they derive and the numbers they get from calculators and programs such as MATLAB and Excel, whereas experts routinely perform checks. If students get into the habit of asking Questions 2 and 3, they have progressed toward expertise. (Deducting points for failing to ask those questions or not catching serious mistakes when they do ask can be a good motivation for them to get into the habit of asking.) Question 5 is also important

Table 9.3–1. Questions for Reflection

1. Does the problem solution satisfy all of the conditions and constraints and include all deliverables specified in the problem statement?
2. Do the numerical values of all the quantities I have calculated make physical sense?
3. Do the mathematical functions I have derived behave in the expected way as independent variables approach limiting values (e.g., when $t = 0$ and as $t \to \infty$)? What other evidence of their validity can I produce?
4. Might a better solution exist? If so, how might I go about trying to find it?
5. What have I learned from this problem?

in that it moves the student away from simple mechanical calculation to metacognition, one of the core characteristics of expert problem solving. An illustrative reflection is shown in the chapter appendix.

9.4 Problem-Based Learning

The McMaster strategy is best suited to large, authentic (real-world), open-ended problems that require students to exercise high-level thinking skills. An instructional method built entirely around such problems is *problem-based learning (PBL)* (Barrett & Moore, 2011; Boud & Feletti, 1997; Duch et al., 2001; Eberlein et al., 2008; Prince & Felder, 2006). Solving PBL problems may require literature searching, laboratory experimentation, process or product design, computer programming or research and may take a significant amount of time (from several days to an entire semester). Students usually work in teams to find the solution, and they have the primary responsibility for doing the work. They hypothesize solutions, test them, identify the need for information that the instructor may or may not provide, and try different solutions if they find previous ones unacceptable until they finally converge on a solution and write and turn in their final report. The instructor provides guidance and feedback as needed.

PBL is powerful, and there is extensive evidence that it promotes long-term retention of knowledge and a broad range of thinking and problem-solving skills in the subject being taught (Albanese & Dast, 2014; Prince & Felder, 2006; Severiens & Schmidt, 2009; Strobel &

van Barneveld, 2009). It is not without its drawbacks, however. Students encountering PBL for the first time tend to find it intimidating. Many resent their instructor for (in their view) abandoning the responsibility to teach and making the students do everything for themselves, and their end-of-course evaluations may reflect that resentment. If the instructors don't get discouraged and continue to use PBL, their ratings usually rebound and the students' attitudes about PBL end up positive, but that first experience can be rough.

If you want to use problem-based learning, go for it, but we strongly suggest taking a gradual approach if you don't already have a lot of experience with learner-centered teaching methods. First use active learning (Chapter 6), doing so until you feel comfortable with the method and know how to minimize or eliminate student resistance to it. Then introduce cooperative learning (Chapter 11) into your courses, doing it often enough to encounter and successfully deal with the logistical and interpersonal problems that student project teams often run into. Then, and only then, venture into PBL.

When you do decide to take the leap, don't feel that you have to create everything from scratch. Marra et al. (2014) and the references cited near the beginning of this section offer a wealth of suggestions for implementing problem-based learning and dealing with problems that often arise with it. PBL problems in chemistry, physics, engineering, and many other fields, and guidance on how to use them, are given by Duch et al. (2001) and on a site maintained at the University of Delaware PBL Clearinghouse (n.d.).

9.5 Ideas to Take Away

- Expert problem solvers differ from novices in four ways: they routinely (1) *classify* problems based on their underlying principles and key attributes and quickly select appropriate solution strategies; (2) practice *metacognition* during the solution process; (3) exhibit *automaticity*, solving routine problems with little apparent effort; (4) feel *self-efficacy* in their problem-solving ability.
- Instructors should provide (a) modeling, practice, and feedback in problem classification and metacognition, (b) sufficient and sufficiently spaced repetition of solution methods to lead to automaticity, and (c) interleaving (alternating solution strategies in different contexts) to develop students' flexibility in problem solving. The instructors should also minimize problem-solving speed as

a factor in determining grades and take other measures to promote students' self-efficacy in the methods and skills being taught.

○ Instructors who plan to include complex open-ended real-world problems in their course should consider teaching the students to use the *McMaster problem-solving strategy* (define, explore, plan, implement, reflect). Practice and feedback should be provided in the explore and reflect steps, which help students progress toward the metacognitive thinking that characterizes expert problem solving.

○ Problem-based learning is a powerful technique for helping students develop high-level problem-solving and self-directed learning skills, but instructors planning to use it should first become comfortable with less-demanding learner-centered teaching methods such as active and cooperative learning.

9.6 Try This in Your Course

○ Work through a difficult problem in class, verbalizing your thinking process as you plan your solution strategy, proceed from one step to the next, and check yourself along the way and at the end. (This approach contrasts with the usual one of presenting a perfectly worked-out solution with no hint about the type of thinking that led to it.)

○ Prepare a problem and worked-out solution as a class handout, leaving gaps for critical steps in the solution. Have the students work through it in pairs using the TAPPS (thinking-aloud pair problem solving) active learning structure described in Chapter 6. Generalize particularly important solution strategies. ("Under what circumstances would you do this when solving problems of this type?")

○ Use either or both of the two preceding approaches to illustrate the McMaster problem-solving strategy.

Appendix: Steps 4 and 5 of the Waste Treatment Problem Solution

Waste Treatment Problem: Step 4 (Implement the plan)

(a)

$$
\left[
\begin{array}{c}
V\,(\text{L})\,,\ C_s(t)\,(\text{g S/L}) \\[4pt]
r_{dS}\left(\dfrac{\text{g S decompose}}{\text{L}\cdot\text{hr}}\right) = 2.05C_s \\[4pt]
C_s(0) = 0.425\,\text{g S/L}
\end{array}
\right]
$$

Applying the law of conservation of mass to the S in the tank yields

$$\left[\begin{array}{l} \frac{dC_s}{dt} = -2.05C_s \\ t = 0, \ C_s = 0.425\,\text{g}\,\text{S/L} \end{array}\right]$$

Separate variables and integrate:

$$\int_{0.425}^{C_s} \frac{dC_s}{C_s} = \int_0^t -2.05dt \Rightarrow \ln\left(\frac{C_s}{0.425}\right) = -2.05t$$

$$\Rightarrow t(\text{hr}) = \frac{\ln(0.425/C_s)}{2.05} \tag{1}$$

$$\Rightarrow C_s(\text{g}\,\text{S/L}) = 0.425\,\exp(-2.05t) \tag{2}$$

Check: $t = 0 \xrightarrow{\text{Eq.}\,(2)} C_s = 0.425\,\text{g}\,\text{S/L}$ ✓

$$\text{Eq.}\,(2) \Rightarrow \frac{dC_s}{dt} = -2.05[0.425\,\exp(-2.05t)] = -2.05C_s \ \checkmark$$

From Eq. (1), $C_s = 0.005\,\text{g}\,\text{S/L} \Rightarrow [t_{.005} = 2.17\,\text{hr}]$

(b) List three probable explanations for the difference between the decomposition time calculated in Part (a) and the value that would be measured in a test in the plant. Prioritize your list in order of likelihood and explain your reasoning.

1. The decomposition rate was determined in a chemistry laboratory under ideal conditions [ultrapure chemicals, clean reaction vessel, perfectly controlled temperature]. In the plant, the reaction is probably taking place in a waste fluid containing hundreds of chemical species, any of which could interfere with the S decomposition reaction, as could impurities (such as rust) on the tank walls, and conditions in the tank are undoubtedly far from the perfectly controlled ones in the laboratory. There is no reason to expect the same decomposition rate.

2. The analytical procedure used to measure C_S could be affected by many species in the waste.

3. The technician who carried out the measurement made a mistake in the instrument calibration, sampling of the reactor contents, or conversion of the raw data to concentration of S.

(c) Suppose the calculated and measured decomposition times are almost the same. Brainstorm up to thirty possible ways the proposed system might still fail.

1. The volume and composition of the waste stream vary considerably from one day to another and from one shift to another on a given day.
2. The catalyst degrades in the plant waste and becomes inactive.
3. The assumption of perfect mixing in the tank is far off.
4. The plant process changes or something goes wrong in the plant so that much more S emerges in the waste stream.
5. The S decomposition products are as toxic as S.
6. The catalyst is more of an environmental hazard than S was.
7. The waste corrodes the tank, leading to leaks.
8. A technician operating the process makes a mistake or a process control computer fails causing a disastrous release of S to the environment.
9. Someone sabotages the process (e.g., a disgruntled employee or a group protesting company policies) with a similar disastrous result.
10. The instrument that measures the concentration of S in the waste stream is defective so that the actual outlet concentration is much greater than anyone realizes.
11. An increased plant production rate is required by a rise in demand for the plant products so that the number of tanks is inadequate to handle the waste production.
12. Something (a truck, a forklift, a plane, a meteorite) smashes into a tank, spilling the contents and requiring the plant to shut down while a lengthy cleanup is conducted.
13. An earthquake causes the tanks to break.
14. The river floods.
15. The EPA reduces the permissible discharge rate by another factor of ten.
16. . . .

Waste Treatment Problem: Step 5 (Reflect)

Deliverables.

The final solution includes the differential equation $(dC_S/dt = \ldots)$ and initial condition, the solution for $C_S(t)$ and two checks of its validity, the value of $t_{0.005}$, three possible reasons for a discrepancy between the calculated and measured values of $t_{0.005}$, and a list of possible ways the process might fail.

Possible better solution.

Use a reactor other than an old tank. Find a more effective catalyst. Store waste in a lagoon rather than treating it. Consider a separation process (absorption, adsorption, crystallization-filtration) to remove and recover S, and try to find a commercial application for S so it can be sold instead of disposed of. Try to find a way of reacting or separating S within the process so it doesn't emerge in the plant waste.

Lessons learned.

Don't automatically believe any formula or correlation you read in a journal, even a prestigious journal: test it under the anticipated conditions of operation of your system before you use it as the basis for a large system design and construction. Don't accept the first process design you think of—think of possible ways it can fail and figure out how to keep them from happening.

INTERLUDE. MEET YOUR STUDENTS: DAVE, MEGAN, AND ROBERTO

Three classmates are heading for lunch after a test on artificial organs and implants. Megan and Roberto are discussing the test, and Dave is silent and grim.

Megan: OK, so Problems 1 and 2 were pretty much out of the book, but Problem 3 was typical Brenner—he gives us a hemodialyzer design and in Part (b) asks us to criticize it. I said the design might be too expensive and they probably needed to add something to prevent clotting, but we could say anything and he couldn't tell us we're wrong.

Roberto: Sure he could—it was an awful design. They were putting blood through super-narrow fibers so you'd have trouble getting the flow you need and probably get red blood cell damage, and the dialyzing solution had some ions you probably wouldn't want diffusing into blood, and ...

M: Maybe, but it's not like there's a right answer—it's just a matter of opinion in questions like that. It's like my English teacher taking off points because of awkward expression or something when anyone with half a brain would know exactly what I was saying.

R: Come on, Megan—most real problems don't have just one solution, and he's trying to ...

M: Yeah, yeah—he's trying to get us to think critically, and I'm okay with that game as long as I don't lose points if my opinion isn't the same as his. What do you think, Dave?

Dave: I think that problem sucks! Which formula are you supposed to use for it?

M: It's not that kind of question—not everything has a formula you can ...

D: OK, so when did he tell us the answer? I memorized every freaking word he said after I bombed that last test, and not one had anything to do with ...

R: It's a thinking question—you have to try to come up with as many ...

D: &%#%&! I already know how to think—I'm here to learn medical devices.

M: Dave, not everything in the world is black and white—some things are fuzzy.

D: Yeah, in those lame humanities courses, but not in medicine—those questions have answers and Brenner's job is to teach them to me, not to play guessing games ... and that's not all—on Monday Roberto asked him that question about the best valve replacement material, and he starts out by saying "it depends" ... I'm paying tuition for the answers, and if this bozo doesn't know them he shouldn't be up there.

R: Look, the teachers don't know everything ... you have to get information wherever you can and then evaluate it and decide for yourself, and then you can ...

D: That's a crock of ...

M: Um, what did you guys do with that weird Part (c) of the problem? He tells us that a blood clot forms during a dialysis and the patient gets a pulmonary embolism and then asks us who the patient should sue and why we think so. I said the hospital and I'm pretty sure that's right, because hospitals are always cutting corners and my gut tells me that they used a faulty device, but knowing Brenner, he was probably looking for something else.

R: I said I couldn't make that judgment without more information, like how the device was tested and whether it was hooked up properly and whether they injected an anticoagulant before starting the dialysis and ...

M: Whoa—he never talked about anything like that in class.

D: I say we go straight to the dean!

These three students illustrate three stages of the *Perry model of intellectual development* (Perry, 1970/1998). The model is a hierarchy of levels that fall into several broad categories:

Dualism.

Knowledge is black and white; every question has only one correct answer and every problem only one correct solution; the authority (in school, the teacher) has the answers and solutions, and the individual's job is to memorize and repeat them.

Multiplicity.

Some questions and problems are ambiguous; supporting evidence may be used to determine answers and solutions, but preconceptions and "gut feelings" are perfectly acceptable as evidence, and the answers and solutions shouldn't have a significant effect on grades.

Relativism.

"Knowledge" depends on context and individual perspective rather than being objective and externally based. Using data, validated theory, and logic to reach and support conclusions becomes habitual and not just something teachers want students to do.

At higher levels, people begin to realize the need for commitment to a course of action even in the absence of certainty, basing the commitment on critical evaluation rather than on what external authorities say. Many entering college students are dualists, most graduate at multiplicity, and a few make it to or beyond relativism (Felder & Brent, 2004b). Dave is a dualist, Megan illustrates multiplicity, and Roberto is a relativist. Most successful STEM professionals have learned to function at or above relativism.

In Chapter 10 we discuss methods of equipping students with critically important skills in communications, creative thinking, and self-directed learning. STEM students are often resistant to instruction in such areas, particularly if the students are low on the Perry scale. Chapter 10 offers suggestions for overcoming the resistance, and Chapter 12 describes Perry and several other intellectual development scales in greater detail and proposes teaching methods that facilitate students' advancement on those scales.

PROFESSIONAL SKILLS

10.0 Introduction

As the first interlude in the book noted, much current STEM education is dedicated to preparing students for jobs that are rapidly becoming obsolete. Surveys of employers of STEM graduates note serious gaps between skills their workforces need and skills their new employees have. When asked to rate the importance of eleven intellectual and practical skills, the respondents in one survey ranked oral communication, teamwork, written communication, critical thinking, analytical reasoning, complex problem solving, information literacy, and innovation and creativity substantially higher than technological skills and quantitative reasoning (Association of American Colleges & Universities, 2015). Similar results were reported by Adecco Staffing USA (2013) and Prichard (2013).

Educational leaders have been aware of this situation for several decades, and some have identified learning outcomes future graduates will need to succeed professionally (e.g., Accreditation Board for Engineering and Technology, n.d.). Some of the outcomes involve technical knowledge and methods traditionally associated with STEM fields, whereas others deal more with more general topics such as global and societal issues, lifelong learning and learning how to learn, teamwork, and, above all, communication. The skills required to succeed in the last set of outcomes have often been somewhat disparagingly labeled *soft skills,* incorrectly suggesting that they impose lower intellectual demands than the *hard* skills of mathematics and science, and are now more appropriately labeled *professional skills.*

Not all faculty members and students are enthusiastic about the idea of integrating professional skills into STEM curricula—especially into core courses, where instruction in professional skills has its greatest impact on students. STEM professors tend to worry about having to teach skills they've never been trained in and aren't sure they're that good at themselves, and they also fear that teaching those skills will require new instructional methods that will take too much of their time to learn and too much class time away from important technical content. Many STEM students are also hostile to professional skill instruction, viewing it as a distraction from the *real* science, math, and engineering that they came to college to learn. (Dave in the preceding interlude speaks for those students.)

Discussing all important professional skills and methods for helping students develop them would require a much larger book than this one. We propose, however, that five skill areas encompass a significant fraction of the abilities that future employers of our graduates say their employees need: *communications, creative thinking* (finding innovative solutions to problems when existing approaches prove inadequate), *critical thinking* (making and supporting evidence-based judgments and decisions), *self-directed learning* (taking the initiative to identify one's learning needs, finding the resources needed to meet the needs, and doing the learning), and *teamwork*. Ways to facilitate students' development of skills in the first four areas are discussed in this chapter, and teamwork skills are examined separately in Chapter 11.

This chapter addresses the following questions:

○ How can I integrate communication, creative thinking, critical thinking, and self-directed learning skills into my courses? How can I do it without sacrificing other important course content?
○ How do students' levels of intellectual development (preceding interlude) affect their responses to instruction in professional skills? How can I create a supportive environment for professional skill development and deal with resistance when it occurs?

10.1 How Can Professional Skills Be Developed

Skills are developed in only one way. You acquired whatever skills you have—walking, reading, riding a bicycle, speaking a new language, solving algebra problems, or doing differential topology or quantum physics or genetic engineering—like this:

1. You did something that required the skill for the first time. It probably didn't go well.
2. You reflected on the experience, perhaps got feedback from someone else, and tried again.

The more cycles you went through, the more skillful you became, up to a point where you either stopped practicing that skill or—less likely—reached the limit of your ability. So, if you want to help students in your course develop a professional skill, a good place to start would be to identify a task you might assign that requires that skill and provide practice and feedback in it.

Elbow and Sorcinelli (2014) propose that assignments may be classified as *low-stakes* (primarily formative and usually fairly short) and *high-stakes* (having an impact on course grades). Table 10.1–1 lists activities and assignments that promote development of professional skills, along with some of the learning outcomes they might address. Some of the tasks are clearly low-stakes, others are equally clearly high-stakes, and still others can be either one.

Table 10.1–1. Activities and Assignments That Promote Professional Skill Development

A—Improve communication (writing and speaking) skills
B—Stimulate retrieval and reinforcement of prior knowledge
C—Motivate interest in course content
D—Broaden and deepen understanding of course content
E—Improve metacognitive thinking skills
F—Improve critical thinking skills
G—Improve creative thinking skills

Task	Outcomes addressed
Low-stakes	
Speculate on when in your life or future career might you either need or want to [identify a plant, apply a hypothesis test, speak persuasively before a group].	A, C, D
Explain [induction, this Java code, what counts as cheating in this course].	A, B, D
Explain [why you took, how you checked] each step of your solution.	A, B, D, E
List possible reasons why the value you calculated might be much different than a measured value of the same variable.	D, E, F, G

(Continued)

Table 10.1–1. (*Continued*)

List [up to ten, as many ways as you can in two minutes] to [explain ____, measure ____, do ____].	B, D, G
Reflect [in an e-mail message, in a journal] on [what you know about ____, what you learned from the video in the last assignment, how you might prepare better for the next exam].	A, B, D, E
Low-stakes or high-stakes	
In [a short paragraph, no more than two pages] summarize what you know about [messenger RNA, the big bang, proof by induction].	A, B
Draft a message to [your project team, your boss, a technician] summarizing the outcome of [your calculation, the experiment, the project].	A, D, E
Prioritize a list of alternative [process, product, or experiment designs, procedures, computer codes, approaches to a problem, causes of failure] in order of probable [quality, effectiveness, market potential, likelihood], and explain your reasoning.	A, D, E, F
[Make up, make up and solve] a real-world problem suitable for the next exam.	A, B, C, D, G
High-stakes	
Use what you have learned in this course to write an analysis of the following [controversy, ethical dilemma, article, case study].	A, B, C, D, F
Critique the following [problem solution, lab report, journal article].	A, B, D, F
[Plan, plan and give] a [lecture, seminar, workshop] on ____.	A, B, C, D, G
Prepare a case for a specified point of view in a controversy, and present it in a [talk, debate].	A, B, D, F, G
Design [an experiment, a process, a device, an algorithm, a protocol, a computer code] to ____.	A, D, F, G

10.2 Communication Skills

Many articles and books have been written about writing coherently and persuasively, speaking effectively, and preparing good presentation graphics (Alley, 1996, 2013; Alred et al., 2011; Markel, 2014; Pfeiffer, 2010). You can draw on such references to teach good communication techniques and formulate grading criteria for writing and speaking assignments. We will confine ourselves here to suggesting ways to integrate communication skill development into your STEM courses.

If you look again at Table 10.1–1, you'll see that every task we suggested for facilitating professional skill development involves writing or speaking, and so improves communication skills by providing practice and either formal or informal feedback. Following are some additional ideas.

Low-stakes assignments

Low-stakes tasks can be class activities or homework. Several examples are shown in Table 10.1–1, and more suggestions are given by Brent and Felder (1992).

Active learning (Chapter 6) provides low-stakes training in technical speaking and possibly writing. When students turn to a classmate and explain a concept or the next step in a problem solution, they are doing technical oral communication and getting immediate feedback from their partner, who either understands or doesn't. When you then call on students to report out to the class after a small-group activity, they practice speaking before a group. They get technical writing practice if, say, they individually write a short explanation of a term or concept or problem solution, then form pairs, compare their explanations, and collaborate to produce a better one.

Low-stakes writing assignments may also be included in homework assignments as separate problems or additions to existing problems. For instance, Part (a) of a problem may have the common "Given _____, calculate _____" structure. Here are some low-stakes possibilities for part (b):

- Suppose the calculation of Part (a) was part of a job assignment. Write a memo of no more than 150 words explaining your calculations and results to your project team leader (who gets upset by poor writing).
- Explain the meaning of the result of Part (a) in terms that an average high school senior could understand.

❏ Suppose the system is built and run exactly as specified in the problem statement, and the measured value of _____ is 35% lower than the value you calculated in Part (a). List at least ten possible reasons for the discrepancy, considering possible sources of error in both the calculation and the measurement.

What about grading low-stakes writing and speaking exercises? If they are done as in-class activities, no grading is necessary—just make sure the students get feedback through in-class discussion or from classmates in small groups. If the exercises are part of larger homework assignments, count them for a small percentage of the total assignment grade and don't spend much time providing detailed feedback.

High-stakes assignments

In most STEM curricula, reports on projects of any kind—labs, case study analyses, research, or work done in internships—play a major role in determining course grades, which by definition makes them high-stakes. The ability of projects to improve students' understanding and skills depends on how the projects are structured and assessed. Section 10.6 gives suggestions that apply to development of any skill. The remainder of this section focuses strictly on communication skills.

In Section 8.4 we recommended evaluating project reports using rubrics or checklists that list explicit evaluation criteria. Make sure at least one (and ideally more) of your criteria have to do with the quality of the writing or the oral presentation (e.g., grammar and spelling, style, organization, visual appearance, coherence of explanations, persuasiveness, completeness and format of literature citations, etc.).

Once you've drafted the grading form, get feedback on it from one or two knowledgeable colleagues and one or two students. Also, most large campuses and many smaller ones have staff consultants who help students and faculty members improve their writing and speaking skills. If your campus has such consultants, ask one of them to review your draft grading form and suggest improvements. See Section 8.4 for more ideas about how to use grading forms for assessment and training.

10.3 Creative Thinking Skills

The toughest problems facing our society—such as how to provide all citizens with adequate and affordable food, housing, and medical care, efficient and economical transportation, and clean and safe energy—are not likely to be solved by easy or conventional methods. If they could be, they would have been by now. To tackle these problems successfully, STEM professionals will need the creativity to improve or replace existing processes and products.

Many methods have been proposed for helping students in technical disciplines improve their creative problem-solving skills (Felder, 1985, 1987, 1988; Fogler et al., 2014; Heywood, 2005, Ch. 11). Table 10.3–1 lists four types of creative thinking exercises. The first three can be used in any STEM course, and the fourth one would generally be used in a course that includes a major project among its requirements.

You don't have to give exercises of each type in every course you teach. Start with a few that address the creative thinking skills you want your students to develop, and increase the number you assign if they seem to be getting the desired results.

Table 10.3–1. Illustrative Creative Thinking Exercises

Brainstorming or brainwriting.
Make the longest list you can of _____. The goal is quantity and variety of ideas, not quality (quality comes later in the process), and far-fetched ideas are strongly encouraged.

Explain unexpected results.
Describe an observation or measurement that differs from predictions or calculations and ask the students to suggest possible causes of the discrepancy. Troubleshooting defective processes and products falls into this category.

Make up a problem.
[Make up, make up and solve] a word problem related to material covered in [Chapter 6 of your text, this week's lectures, this week's lectures and material in another course you are currently taking]. The problem should not be a close version of one in the text.

Create something.
Design an original [product, process, procedure, experiment, research study, algorithm, computer code] that meets specified criteria. The assignment might also call on the student to demonstrate the feasibility, effectiveness, or optimality of the design, and to discuss potential drawbacks or unintended consequences.

10.3.1 Brainstorming and brainwriting

In the education most STEM students get, from first grade through their last graduate course in STEM, the following messages are never (well, hardly ever) conveyed:

○ The more possible solutions you think of for a complex problem, the more likely you are to come up with the best solution.
○ Sometimes a solution that at first sounds foolish leads to the best solution.
○ To be wrong is not necessarily to fail, as Thomas Edison clearly realized when he was trying to invent a functioning light bulb. He said, "I have not failed ten thousand times. I have successfully found ten thousand ways that will not work."

Instead of being taught to apply these messages to problem solving, most STEM students only confront problems that are well defined and have unique correct answers that their job is to find. It can be a shock to their systems when they graduate and realize that the game has changed—problems in the workplace are rarely well defined (often the hardest part of the problem is figuring out exactly what the problem is), and the goal is usually not to find the best solution in an ideal sense but rather to find the best solution obtainable with limited time and resources to devote to the search.

Brainstorming is a problem-solving technique in which many possible solutions to difficult problems are quickly generated. The solutions are then evaluated, and the best of them is identified and accepted (at least tentatively). The technique—which was invented by advertising executive Alex Osborn (1963)—is widely used in industry, and teaching STEM students to do it can be an important step in preparing them for their future careers.

A typical brainstorming assignment to student groups in a class looks like this:

> Working as a team, with all team members proposing ideas and one of them writing down all the suggestions, make the longest list you can of ____. Don't discuss or criticize the ideas, but build on them to generate more ideas. Ideas that are far-fetched, funny, and even impossible are particularly valuable.

If you decide to give a prize, it might go to the team member who comes up with the most innovative contribution.

This assignment integrates four criteria that Osborn proposed for brainstorming to be effective:

1. **Focus on quantity.** Thomas Edison articulated the reasoning behind this condition in the quote near the beginning of this section. The goal of the idea-generation phase is to generate as many ideas as possible, be they good, bad, ridiculous, or illegal. The more ideas there are, the more likely the best one is to occur.
2. **Withhold criticism.** Creative ideas flow best in a relaxed environment, and nothing kills a sense of relaxation more than trashing ideas as soon as they are raised. Once people start worrying about being criticized, the flow of ideas shuts down. If you think an idea is bad, don't criticize it—just come up with a better one (or possibly an even worse one if it has entertainment value).
3. **Combine and improve ideas.** The power of brainstorming lies in the fact that hearing ideas often stimulates people to think of related but different ideas.
4. **Welcome unusual ideas.** A seemingly absurd idea can serve two vitally important purposes. It can move the idea-generation process in a new and unexpected direction, possibly leading to good ideas that otherwise might not have come up. In addition, it can lead to laughter (approving, not mocking) and possibly serve as an incentive to come up with an even more far-fetched idea. Eventually the ideas may start flowing as fast as anyone can write them down.

When brainstorming is done in an academic setting, an upper limit should be imposed on the time spent generating ideas or the number of ideas generated to keep overachievers in the class from neglecting other important things they need to be doing.

Brainstorming has some limitations. "Verbal traffic jams" may occur in which ideas are lost because too many people are talking at once, individuals may withhold ideas out of fear of being judged, and dominant individuals may keep others with possibly better ideas from contributing (Heslin, 2009). An alternative to brainstorming that helps avoid these limitations is *brainwriting* (VanGundy, 1983). Students are given the same type of prompt, but instead of contributing ideas orally, each person writes a list of ideas. The lists are compiled and shared with the whole group, which then brainstorms additional ideas.

Heslin (2009) describes several different brainwriting formats and recommends conditions under which each one might be used.

Felder (1988) and Fogler et al. (2014, Ch. 7) suggest a variety of STEM-related brainstorming exercises. Felder (1987) describes an undergraduate transport course in which two brainstorming problems were assigned. In the students' response to the first prompt (list possible ways a given experimental waste disposal system might fail), the average number of listed possibilities was roughly four, the minimum was one (the holding tank might leak), the maximum was ten, and the total number of different ideas was thirty-four. The complete list was shared with the class and discussed. The second problem was to list independent ways to measure the velocity of a fluid in a large pipeline not equipped with a flowmeter, with ports permitting injection of tracers, withdrawal of samples, and suspension of devices in the flowing stream. With the practice and feedback of the first exercise behind them, the students came up with more than two hundred methods, with an average of twenty-six, a minimum of five, a maximum of fifty-three, and a wide variety of ingenious, humorous, and altogether fantastic devices. Table 10.3–2 suggests some additional exercises.

Every brainstorming exercise can be followed by a second exercise in which the students prioritize their lists or choose the top three items according to some specified criterion (such as importance, likelihood, or level of threat). The latter exercises require *critical thinking*, which we discuss in Section 10.4.

Table 10.3–2. Illustrative Brainstorming and Brainwriting Exercises

List:

- o ways to verify a [calculated value, derived formula]
- o ways that could be used to determine a physical property or variable [with no constraints, with no required instrument calibrations, as a function of one or more other variables, involving a stuffed bear]
- o uses for [any object, something that would usually go to waste]
- o ways to improve a [process or product, experiment, computer code]
- o real-world applications of a [theory, procedure, formula]
- o safety and environmental concerns in this [experiment, process, plant]
- o flaws in a proposed [design, procedure, code, grading rubric]

10.3.2 Explaining unexpected results

An insightful remark attributed to a variety of people (including—of course—Yogi Berra) is "In theory, there is no difference between theory and practice; in practice, there is." This statement strongly applies to science and engineering, in which determining what should happen in an experiment or process under specified conditions is only part of the problem—often the easy part. The harder and more interesting part is *troubleshooting*—trying to figure out why things didn't happen the way they were supposed to.

Successful scientists and engineers routinely troubleshoot. They brainstorm possible explanations for discrepancies between predicted and observed system behavior, such as faulty assumptions in the model used to make the predictions, defective materials of construction or impure raw materials or environmental contamination, and human errors in operations, measurements, and calculations. Once they have the list, they prioritize it in order of likelihood and check to see if any of the explanations account for the discrepancy. If none does, they search for less obvious explanations.

As fundamental as troubleshooting is in the practice of science and engineering, however, it seldom shows up in curricula in those disciplines, and it's not because troubleshooting is hard to integrate into courses. For example, an exercise in a statics course might look like this:

> In Part (a) of this problem, you determined that the cantilever support should fail when the applied load reaches 5.5×10^4 N. Suppose a test is run and the support fails at a load of only 2.1×10^4 N. List at least ten possible reasons, including three or more that involve assumptions made in the calculation.

Similar exercises could easily be integrated into problem sets and labs in any science or engineering course. Students might be called on to brainstorm possible reasons why the projectile didn't land in the predicted spot, the prescribed medical or pharmaceutical treatment failed to cure the ailment, the reactor exploded, the cells in the bacterial culture didn't survive, the amplifier output voltage was 35% greater than expected, the enzyme-catalyzed reaction product yield was 35% lower than expected, a major thunderstorm occurred on a day that was supposed to be sunny, the landing module crashed on the planet surface, the fish downstream of the plant began dying in record numbers, everyone who sat in the ergonomically designed chair for more than an hour developed a backache, and so on.

Unexpected results are not always negative: major scientific break-throughs and innovations in technology have occurred when something puzzling happened in a laboratory or commercial facility (penicillin and Teflon come to mind). A natural human tendency is to either ignore such events or dismiss them as artifacts of experimental error. To help your students develop as STEM professionals, teach them to treat unexpected results as opportunities for improved understanding—and possibly for major achievements.

10.3.3 Formulating problems

One of the hardest things STEM instructors have to do is create good problems that span the full range of course learning objectives, from straightforward exercises that require only basic knowledge to substantive challenges that call for high-level thinking and problem-solving skills. When the instructors devise, solve, and polish problems, they improve their own mastery of the required skills and also exercise their creativity, if the problems call for it. If students are assigned to create and solve problems themselves, they gain the same improved skills and creativity. An illustrative problem-formulation assignment is shown below, along with recommendations for giving such assignments.

Problem Formulation Assignment

Make up [make up and solve] a problem involving material covered in lectures, readings, and assignments from [Chapter 6, the past two weeks, this course and any other course you are currently taking]. If your problem requires only simple formula substitution—"Given this, calculate that"—you will get a minimum passing grade. To get more credit, your problem should require high-level analysis or critical or creative thinking to solve.

Before you give the first assignment of this type, show your class several examples of poorly constructed problems and problems that meet your criteria. Have the students work in small groups to evaluate the problems and discuss what makes the weak ones weak and what kind of skills the good ones require, and then share your evaluations. After that exercise, most students will have a good idea of what you want them to do. Start with one or two simple exercises (*"Make up a problem based on*

Chapter 6 material.") and progress to the more complex options given in the preceding problem formulation assignment.

When students submit problems, skim through them quickly without worrying too much about whether solutions contain mistakes (save that concern for the conventional homework problems). *Don't provide detailed corrective feedback on every submission.* Doing so can be a major drain on your time, and it might not help the students that much. Section 10.3.4 suggests better ways to assess students' creative efforts and provide feedback.

As with every other skill, the ability to formulate good problems improves with practice and feedback. After several such assignments, you should see at least some of the students developing a real flair for making up clever problems, some of which you will be able to use in future assignments and exams. Another attractive feature of problem formulation assignments in engineering curricula is that when you include them in a course, you can legitimately claim that the course addresses all three parts of the ABET Engineering Criteria outcome relating to the ability to "identify, formulate, and solve engineering problems" (ABET, n.d.). Traditional curricula do little or nothing to meet the *identify* and *formulate* parts of that outcome.

Felder (1985) describes a major problem formulation exercise used in a first-year graduate course. The last midterm exam of the semester was a five-week take-home assignment to make up and solve a final examination for the course that required the exam-takers to demonstrate the three higher-level thinking skills of Bloom's Taxonomy (analyzing, evaluating, and creating). The students received preliminary training in a low-stakes assignment to make up but not solve a problem that met the stated criteria and then submitted worked-out exams that ranged from good to spectacular. At the end of the course, several students commented that in trying to construct creative problems they learned the course material to a depth they had never experienced in other courses.

Thought Question

An instructor heard a suggestion to ask students to make up creative homework problems, liked the idea, and had her students do it on a midterm exam. The results were dreadful. What might have gone wrong, and what might she do next time to get better outcomes?

10.3.4 *Assessing creative thinking*

Creative thinking is no exception to the rule that the assessment drives the learning. No matter how many sermons you deliver in class about the importance of creativity, if you only assess basic knowledge and problem-solving skills, don't expect to see much improvement in your students' creativity. Once you decide which types of creative thinking you want to help them develop, include problems that require them in your learning objectives, assignments, projects, study guides, and exams. During class, show examples of good and bad responses to creativity exercises and explain how you would grade them.

Grading brainstorming and brainwriting, troubleshooting, and problem-formulation exercises can be done efficiently: a quick inspection of the students' responses (or in the case of brainstorming and brainwriting, a quick count) is generally enough to award points. However, if a creativity exercise is part of a large problem or project, assessment is more challenging. The first step is to identify elements of creativity that you consider important and then to either find or design a creativity assessment instrument (e.g., Kaufman et al., 2008; Torrance, 1966a, 1966b), or a rubric or checklist (Section 8.4), that addresses those elements. The following evaluation criteria are often used:

Creativity-Related Criteria for Project Evaluation

Fluency.
Number of relevant ideas or solution approaches considered

Flexibility.
Number of different categories of responses

Elaboration.
Thoroughness of exploration of ideas

Originality.
Statistical rarity of responses considered and of the final solution

---

10.4 Critical Thinking Skills

Most teachers agree that one of the goals of education should be to make students good critical thinkers, but getting to an agreement about exactly what that means is a different story. In the education literature you can find definitions of critical thinking that cover every conceivable mental activity beyond rote memorization, including analyzing, evaluating, creating, and reflecting on one's own thinking processes (metacognition).

Many authors take a more restricted view of critical thinking, taking it to mean making judgments and decisions that are supported by solid evidence and logic. A more elaborate version of this definition is that of Kurfiss (1988, p. 2), who defines critical thinking as "an investigation whose purpose is to explore a situation, phenomenon, question, or problem to arrive at a hypothesis or conclusion about it that integrates all available information and that can therefore be convincingly justified. In critical thinking, all assumptions are open to question, divergent views are aggressively sought, and the inquiry is not biased in favor of a particular outcome." True critical thinkers have the ability and the tendency to conduct such explorations.

Most in-class activities and assigned problems in STEM courses are versions of "list ___," "define ___," "explain ___," "draw ___," "given ___, calculate ___," "design ___," and "derive an expression for ___." To promote critical thinking, supplement those structures with some that call for critical analysis and evaluation. Table 10.4–1 offers examples that may easily be modified to fit any STEM subject.

In most core STEM courses the focus should be on basic content, so you don't have to include problems like the ones in Table 10.4–1 in every class session and assignment. Just identify the kinds of critical thinking tasks you'd like your students to be able to perform and provide modeling and practice in those tasks. You won't turn all of the students into expert critical thinkers that way, but that's all right—many competent professionals don't qualify for that title. Your job is just to move your students in that direction. Several strategies for doing so follow, most of them drawn from the work of Condon and Kelly-Riley (2004), Fogler et al. (2014), Lynch and Wolcott (2001), and van Gelder (2005).

10.4.1 Make expectations clear

In Chapter 2, we proposed the common sense principle that the better your students understand what you expect them to do, the more likely they are to learn to do it. We also observed that an effective way to communicate expectations is to state them as learning objectives and give them to the students in the form of study guides for tests. If you plan to use exercises like those in Table 10.4–1 in your course, include the required skills as learning objectives in your study guides. Then use some of the

Table 10.4–1. Illustrative Critical Thinking Exercises

- ○ Following are [two strategies for solving this problem, two computer codes for executing this task, three alternative designs, three possible interpretations of experimental data]. Select the best one and justify your choice.
- ○ [The statement I just made, Equation 23 on p. 247 of your text, one of the arguments in the attached editorial] is wrong. Identify and correct the error(s).
- ○ The following scenario describes the case of [an employee who knows about an unethical and possibly illegal incident involving his supervisor, a graduate student who finds that her research advisor altered experimental data]. List and discuss possible courses of action, and make and justify a recommendation.
- ○ A student who took this course submitted the attached [project report, analysis, design, essay]. Give it a grade and summarize your reasoning.
- ○ Read the attached [article from a popular scientific journal, front-page story or op-ed column in yesterday's paper, transcript of a televised interview] and critique it. Your critique should include an evaluation of the accuracy and persuasiveness of the opinions expressed and should identify stated and hidden assumptions, misleading statements, unproven claims, and anything else that could help nonexpert readers understand the piece and decide how much credibility to give it.

---

exercises in low-stakes class activities and assignments. At that point the students will be ready to deal with similar tasks on high-stakes assignments and exams.

10.4.2 Provide structure, modeling, and practice

Students unfamiliar with critical thinking can benefit from being given a structure for evaluating a publication, proposition, or written or spoken position on a controversial issue. An effective one is *structured critical reasoning* (Fogler et al., 2014, pp. 42–43), which we outline in Table 10.4–2.

Whether you teach this structure or some other critical thinking procedure, describe it and give examples of its applications, hand out sample documents or presentations and have the students apply the procedure in class activities and homework, and then include similar exercises on tests.

Table 10.4–2. Structured Critical Reasoning

When critiquing a document or presentation, do the following:

o Summarize all of the author's (or speaker's) claims.
o Examine and evaluate the author's *reasons* (justifications) and compile external *evidence* (facts, observations, research data, scientific and logical principles) that supports or negates the conclusions.
o Identify and evaluate the author's stated and unstated assumptions and biases.
o Draw conclusions about the validity of the author's claims.

10.4.3 Assessing critical thinking

If you have included critical thinking skills in your list of desired learning outcomes for your students, how can you know how well they have achieved those outcomes? Following are two commonly used types of assessment tools:

Checklists and rubrics

Exhibit 10.4–1 shows an illustrative checklist for evaluating students' critiques of an article or essay. Notice the last item in the checklist, which calls for the students to reflect on what they did well and what they might do to improve next time. This type of reflective self-evaluation (a form of metacognition) is an important step in developing strong critical thinking skills.

Having a checklist like the one shown in Exhibit 10.4–1 helps make grading more consistent and efficient and dramatically clarifies your expectations. A rubric (Section 8.4), which rates each criterion on a numerical scale (e.g., 1 through 5) and explicitly states what a response at each level would look like, can provide equally good feedback on what needs improvement and how to achieve it. Critical thinking rubrics are described by Blue et al. (2008), Condon and Kelly-Riley (2004), and Lynch and Wolcott (2001), and seven different ones are given at Association for the Assessment of Learning in Higher Education (n.d.). In one study, the average critical thinking scores in courses that used a rubric to provide regular feedback were up to 3.5 times higher than the scores in courses that did not (Condon & Kelly-Riley, 2004). That result doesn't necessarily prove that the rubrics led to the higher scores, but it adds to the large body of evidence that making expectations clear increases the likelihood that the expectations will be met.

Exhibit 10.4–1. Grading Checklist for Critical Evaluation

Student: _____

Date: _____

Article evaluated: _____

Criterion	Max. Points	Score	Comments
Understanding of document content (25%)			
Summarized author's purpose, main ideas, and conclusions	15		
Fairly represented author's viewpoint	10		
Critical analysis (40%)			
Identified author's assumptions and biases	10		
Identified strong, supported, and persuasive arguments and conclusions	10		
Identified weak and unsupported arguments	10		
Stated and persuasively justified a conclusion about the validity of the author's position	10		
Presentation (25%)			
Neat and well formatted	5		
Used correct grammar and good style	10		
Wrote clearly and persuasively	10		
Reflection (10%)			
Identified strong and weak points in this critique (including self-bias) and steps that could strengthen it	10		
Total Score	100		

Standardized instruments developed specifically to assess critical thinking skills

Examples of standardized critical thinking assessments include *Tasks in Critical Thinking* (Erwin & Sebrell, 2003), the *California Critical Thinking Skills Test* and *California Critical Thinking Disposition Index* (Phillips et al., 2004), and the *Watson-Glaser Critical Thinking Appraisal* (Watson & Glaser, 1980). Using a standardized instrument can be expensive and cumbersome, and you cannot tailor the assessment to fit your particular learning objectives. Because such instruments are validated and normed, however, they are the best measures to use for formal research studies of general critical thinking skill development.

10.5 Self-Directed Learning Skills

In the first interlude in the book we nominated attributes that STEM professionals will need in the coming decades. The ability to keep acquiring new knowledge and skills without the help of teachers was high on the list—which is to say, the professionals will have to be *self-directed learners.*

Many definitions of self-directed learning have been advanced. We will use the classic one: "In its broadest meaning, 'self-directed learning' describes a process by which individuals take the initiative, with or without the assistance of others, in diagnosing their learning needs, formulating learning goals, identifying human and material resources for learning, choosing and implementing appropriate learning strategies, and evaluating learning outcomes" (Knowles, 1975, p. 18). Following are actions you might tend to take if you are a self-directed learner:

A. **Diagnose learning needs.**

The first stage of the self-directed learning process is to ask the questions, *"What do I need to learn?"* and *"What conditions are most likely to help me learn it?"* Answering the first question means identifying the factual information you want to know, the procedures and methods you want to be able to carry out, and the concepts you want to understand. Answering the second one involves identifying the teaching media and methods that you've found most useful (books, articles, lectures, seminars, demonstrations, hands-on labs, videos, simulations, screencasts, tutorials, one-on-one or group discussions or online discussion forums, etc.), and the people who might be most helpful (colleagues, consultants).

It's also useful to identify the conditions that either don't help you or interfere with your learning. (Can you sense metacognition poking its nose under the tent?)

B. **Formulate learning goals.**

Your initial specifications of what you want to learn are likely to be somewhat general and vague (*"I want to learn to diagnose skin disorders in invertebrates"* or *"I want to understand multivariate analysis of variance"*). Because achieving such goals may require anything from a few hours on the Internet to getting a PhD, a narrower and more detailed list of goals will be much more useful. In this stage of the process, you ask, *"What's the next thing I have to learn?"* Learning an entire subject is an intimidating goal that can stop many people dead in their tracks, but simply taking the next step is usually manageable. If it isn't, break the step into smaller chunks.

C. **Identify and assemble learning resources.**

The next question you might ask is, *"Of the kinds of resources I identified in Step A [print resources, online resources, and human resources], which specific ones should I seek, and where should I look for them?"*

D. **Choose and implement learning strategies.**

Read the books and articles, sit through the lectures and seminars, watch the videos and screencasts and tutorials, participate in the discussions, and get your hands on the equipment and simulations. Act as if you're preparing for an exam and follow the test preparation strategies we suggested in Chapter 8.

E. **Evaluate learning outcomes.**

The operative questions here are, *"How well did I learn what I wanted to learn? If I need to go back and try again on any of it, what should I do differently?"* (You can't get away from metacognition if you want to be a self-directed learner.) If your answer to the first question was *"As well as I need to know it,"* then go back to Step B and do another cycle—unless you're finished with the broad learning goal you identified in Step A, in which case congratulate yourself and move on to whatever you'd like to learn next.

Suggestions for helping students learn to do all that are given in Table 10.5–1. Many of them are based on or supported by literature

Table 10.5–1. Assignments That Promote Self-Directed and Lifelong Learning

A—Diagnose learning needs.
B—Formulate learning goals.
C—Identify and assemble learning resources.
D—Choose and implement learning strategies.
E—Evaluate learning outcomes.

Have students:	Attributes addressed
Identify teaching resources and methods they believe they learn best from.	A,C,D
Formulate learning objectives, study guides, and problems.	B
Do a web search for relevant books and papers on a specified topic.	C
Given a substantial open-ended problem, state in detail what they know, what they need to determine, and how they would begin (inductive learning, Sects. 3.6, 9.4, 12.2).	A–D
Use appropriate rubrics to evaluate their own and one another's products (Ch. 8).	E
Use appropriate rubrics to evaluate the performance of their project team and each of its members, including themselves.	E
Analyze case studies of realistic situations in which individuals had to make hard choices and decisions. State what they would have done and give their reasons.	A–E
Exercise choice in their learning tasks and how they are graded (choose their own project types and topics, substitute projects for assignments and exams, designate weighting toward the final grade given to different course components).	A–E
Conduct independent research studies and projects.	A–E
Take classes in which learner-centered teaching methods are used, particularly active, cooperative, project-based learning, and problem-based learning (Chs. 6, 11; Sects. 9.4, 10.6, 12.2).	A–E
Learn about the processes of learning and metacognition (Sect. 9.2, Ambrose et al. [2010]; Oakley [2014]; University of California, San Diego [2014]).	A–E

on self-directed learning (Guglielmino, 2013; Hiemstra, 2013) and the related topics of metacognition (Tanner, 2012) and lifelong learning (Knapper & Cropley, 2000). There are some distinctions between the three topics, but when students graduate with self-directed learning skills, they are essentially equipped to be metacognitive thinkers and lifelong learners.

The first suggestion in the table is for the students to identify the types of teaching resources that tend to work best for them. The idea is not for them to demand those resources from their instructors (generally not an effective strategy) but to find them elsewhere if they are not being provided in the class.

10.6 Project-Based Learning

Whatever a STEM professional's job description may be, there's a good chance that it involves working in teams on large projects. The projects usually require creative and critical thinking: if scientists and engineers only had routine tasks to perform and they never had to make important judgment calls, they would sooner or later be replaced by computers or technicians. The team members must take individual responsibility for doing their parts and share collective responsibility for the project outcome, and their abilities to communicate effectively with one another may have a strong bearing on the outcome. In other words, most STEM professionals need all of the skills discussed in this chapter (and in Chapter 11, which deals with teamwork).

The ideal academic setting for professional skill development is one that resembles the workplace where the skills will be needed, so projects are an important component of STEM education. In *project-based learning,* projects provide the bulk of the motivation and context for the acquisition and development of targeted skills. The literature provides extensive discussions of general project-based learning (Capraro et al., 2013; Kolmos & de Graaf, 2014; Prince & Felder, 2006, 2007) and of projects that specifically involve case study analysis (Davis & Yadav, 2014; Herreid et al., 2012; National Center for Case Study Teaching in Science, n.d.); community service (*service learning*) (Engineering Projects in Community Service [EPICS], n.d.; Jacoby, 2014); engineering design (Atman et al., 2014; Dym et al., 2005, 2013); and undergraduate research (Laursen et al., 2010).

Some of the references just cited report on assessments of the instructional effectiveness of projects. Relative to traditionally taught students, students who participated in project-based learning did as well or slightly better on tests of content knowledge and significantly better on assessments of conceptual understanding, metacognitive skills, motivation to learn, communication and teamwork skills, and understanding how to apply their learning to complex realistic problems. To make projects as instructive as possible, require and provide detailed feedback on intermediate submissions such as a preliminary plan of work, periodic progress reports, and a rough draft of the final report. Provide only minimal feedback on the final report because there will be no more opportunities for revision and resubmission, and so detailed feedback is likely to be ignored. You might also schedule one or two meetings with student teams during the semester to hear and comment on how their projects are going. For information on assessing and evaluating projects in your course and using your assessment instrument to teach students project report-writing skills, review Section 8.4.

10.7 Creating a Supportive Environment for Professional Skill Development

Many STEM students don't like being taught and tested in professional skills, especially writing and speaking, and some push back hard against it. One of Rich's students once said that the reason he went into engineering was to get away from that crap!

Students' attitudes toward professional skill development are likely to be inversely associated with their *level of intellectual development* (Baxter Magolda, 1992; Felder & Brent, 2004b, 2004c; Perry, 1970/1998), a concept defined in the interlude preceding this chapter. Many students—such as Dave in the interlude—enter college as *dualists* on Perry's model of intellectual development (Perry, 1970/1998). They believe that their instructor's job is to state known facts and demonstrate well-defined methods, and their job is to reproduce the facts and methods on exams. Dualist students may be bewildered and resentful when teachers confront them with creative and critical thinking challenges that require more than memorization and don't have unique solutions, especially if the students' responses are judged not only on technical merits but also on grammar and style. Students who have moved up the ladder of intellectual development to *multiplicity* (such as Megan in the interlude) are willing to acknowledge that some questions may not have uniquely correct answers; however, they may take that to mean that any answer to an open-ended question is as good as any other as long as the method used to get it is correct. If their grades are affected by an instructor's negative judgment of the quality of their response, they may also resent it. Only when students reach the level of *relativism* (such as Roberto in the interlude) do they accept that even though some problems may not have unique correct solutions, alternatives may still be subjected to rigorous evaluation criteria, and some solutions are better than others.

As the interlude noted, two conditions must be met to help students progress along the intellectual development spectrum: *challenge* and *support* (Felder & Brent, 2004c). Students are unlikely to change the beliefs that characterize their current levels if those beliefs are not challenged. Those who believe that all knowledge is certain and all problems have unique solutions should be challenged with unresolved issues and open-ended problems. Those who believe that when knowledge is uncertain all judgments are equally valid must be challenged to produce evidence to support their judgments, and their work should be evaluated based on the quality of the evidence.

Challenge isn't enough, however. Students whose fundamental beliefs about knowledge are challenged are likely to feel threatened and often either remain at their current developmental levels or retreat to lower ones. To avoid those outcomes, support must accompany challenge. It may take the form of formative assessment (Sect. 3.6.6), clear summative evaluation criteria (Sect. 2.1, Ch. 8), any of the measures to bolster students' self-efficacy suggested in Section 9.2, or any of the ideas suggested in the remainder of this section.

Using active learning is a powerful way to support students. If you ask high-level questions in class and cold call on individual students to respond, fear of being wrong and looking foolish is likely to shut down their thinking. It's safer for them if they first work in small groups, where they can try ideas out in relative privacy. You might also let them work in pairs on their first few creative or critical thinking homework assignments.

When you ask high-level questions, acknowledge good responses and point out what makes them good if it's not obvious; also acknowledge responses that are not quite correct but come close, perhaps suggesting or asking the class to suggest improvements. Don't allow wrong answers to stand, but don't disparage them either. If you make students look bad in class if they answer a question incorrectly, they may never volunteer answers again or even try to think of them. In addition, high-level thinking usually involves coming up with many ideas before finding a good one. Unless you're sure a question has only one right answer, get several responses instead of stopping at the one you had in mind. Doing so can show the students that holding off on premature acceptance of an idea can lead to better ideas and sometimes the best one.

Finally, after you grade students' first two or three assignments that require unfamiliar professional skills, let the students revise and resubmit.

The first time you do it, either let the second grade replace the first one or use a weighted average of the two grades. Next time, count the first grade more heavily. By the third or fourth assignment, the learning benefits of second chances probably won't justify the additional required grading time required, so just permit a single submission.

10.8 Ideas to Take Away

o Development of professional skills is facilitated by instructors defining relevant learning objectives, formulating clear criteria for assessing mastery of the objectives, including the criteria in grading forms (checklists or rubrics), and using the forms for both grading student products and helping the students understand the instructors' expectations.

o *Low-stakes assignments* are brief formative writing and speaking exercises that count negligibly toward course grades, and *high stakes assignments* are exercises that count significantly. Instruction in a professional skill should begin with low-stakes assignments, and high-stakes assignments should then be used to continue and evaluate skill development.

o Creative thinking skills can be enhanced by brainstorming, brain-writing, problem formulation, and troubleshooting exercises, and assignments that explicitly require creativity. Critical thinking (making evidence-based judgments and decisions) is promoted by calling on students to choose from alternative strategies, solutions, or designs; prioritize items on a list; and critique documents or presentations using clearly defined evaluation criteria.

o Students' self-directed learning skills can be improved by asking them to formulate clear learning goals, identify and assemble resources to address those goals, choose and implement learning strategies, and evaluate learning outcomes. Self-directed learning is also promoted by learner-centered teaching methods, including active learning, cooperative learning, and project- or problem-based learning.

o A supportive environment for professional skill development can be established by showing models of good work, acknowledging good responses and suggesting how inadequate ones could be improved, collecting and evaluating outlines and rough drafts of major project reports in addition to final submissions, and providing chances for revision and resubmission of products that require professional skills.

10.9 Try This in Your Course

○ Use one or more of the low-stakes writing assignments listed in Table 10.1–1 as active learning exercises, and include similar exercises in assignments, study guides, and exams.

○ Conduct one of the brainstorming or brainwriting exercises in Table 10.3–2 (or an equivalent exercise) as a class activity. Follow it with a critical thinking activity in which the students select their top three responses according to a criterion you specify (likelihood, feasibility, order in which to try, etc.) and justify their selections. Include similar exercises in assignments, study guides, and exams.

○ After a conventional "Given _____, calculate _____" problem on an assignment, add a troubleshooting part in which the students are asked to list possible explanations if measured variable values differ significantly from the calculated values. Include similar problems on study guides and exams.

○ Include one or more problem-formulation exercises in your assignments, following the model shown in Section 10.3.3.

○ Include one or more critical thinking exercises of the types listed in Table 10.4–1 in in-class activities, assignments, and exams. Have students use structured critical reasoning (Table 10.4–2) if an exercise involves critiquing a document or presentation.

○ Assign one of the exercises in Table 10.5–1 for helping students develop self-directed learning skills.

INTERLUDE. SERMONS FOR
GRUMPY CAMPERS

As we've noted several times, if you use a teaching method that makes students take more responsibility for their own learning than they're used to, some of them may not be too enthusiastic about it. Active learning (Chapter 6), cooperative learning (Chapter 11), and inductive teaching and learning (Chapter 12) fall into this category. If you can make the case that you're not using the method for your own devious purposes but to try to improve the students' learning and grades, the class will go much more smoothly.

Following are several mini-sermons designed to help make the case. You can use variants of them when you first introduce the methods and in response to any critical questions and comments students may subsequently raise.

Student: Those group activities in class are a waste of time. I'm paying tuition for you to teach me, not to trade ideas with students who don't know any more than I do!

Professor: I agree that my job is to teach you, but to me that means making learning happen, not just putting out information. I can show you a stack of research that says people don't learn much by listening to someone telling them what they're supposed to know. You learned most of what you know by doing things, seeing how they went, getting feedback or learning from your mistakes, and doing them again. What you're doing in those short activities are the same things you'll have to do in the homework and exams— the hard parts. The difference is that now when you get to the homework you will already have practiced those parts and gotten instant feedback, so the homework will go a lot faster and you'll probably do better on the exams. By the way, let me know if you'd like to see that research.

S: I really hate working on homework in groups—why can't I work by myself?

P: I get that you're unhappy and I'm sorry about it, but I've got to be honest with you—my job here is not to make you happy but to prepare you to for your career. Here's what's not going to happen on your first day at work. They're not going to say, "Welcome to the company, Mr. or Ms. Jones. Tell me how you like to work—by yourself or with other people?" No. The first thing they'll do is put you on a team, and your success will depend more on how you work with that team than on how you solve differential equations and run tensile tests. Because teamwork is a big part of what you'll be doing there, my job is to teach you how to do it here, and that's what I'll be doing.

S: Okay, but I don't want to be in a group with those idiots you assigned me to. Why can't I work with my friends?

P: Sorry—also not an option. Another thing that won't happen on that first day is someone saying, "Here's a list of everyone in the company. Tell me who you'd like to work with." What will happen is they'll tell you who you'll be working with, and you won't have a vote on it. I can show you a survey in which engineering alumni who had been through extensive group work in college were asked what in their education best prepared them for their careers [Felder, 2000]. The second most common response was "the homework groups." (Number one was all that tough homework.) One of them said, "When I came to work here, the first thing they did was put me on a team, and you know those annoying teammates back in college who never pulled their weight—it turns out they're here, too. The difference between me and people who came here from other colleges is that I have some idea what to do about those slackers." In this class you're going learn what to do about those slackers.

At one point the instructor offered to share the research supporting her claims that learner-centered teaching leads to greater learning and higher grades. Good sources to cite are Freeman et al. (2014) for active learning, Springer et al. (1999) for cooperative learning, and Prince and Felder (2006) for inductive teaching and learning.

And that's that. Our suggestion is to put your own spin on those sermonettes and trot them out when the right occasion presents itself. Although we don't guarantee that they will immediately convert all students into believers—in fact, we guarantee they won't—our experience is that at least they'll keep student resistance down enough for most students to see that the instructor was telling them the truth.

TEAMWORK SKILLS

11.0 Introduction

Working in a STEM profession means working in teams, like it or not. Most difficult problems in plants and research labs are complex and multidisciplinary, and it is rare to find individuals with broad enough expertise to solve the problems entirely by themselves. In surveys in which employers of STEM graduates are asked to list the skills they have found most lacking in their recent hires, teamwork is one of the skills mentioned most frequently, along with the communication, creative thinking, and critical thinking skills discussed in Chapter 10 (CBI, 2008; Hart Research Associates, 2010; Lang et al., 1999).

The only meaningful way to teach students to work well in teams is to give them team assignments, teach them teamwork strategies, assess their performance, and provide constructive feedback. If you're like the average STEM instructor, however, the thought of students working in groups does not give you warm fuzzy feelings. When you were a student and worked on assignments or projects in groups, it may not have been all that enjoyable. Maybe some team members didn't pull their weight and stuck you with extra work, or there was incessant squabbling, or you just preferred to work alone. If you've given teamwork assignments as an instructor, you've undoubtedly seen similar patterns, only now you had to deal with a parade of dysfunctional groups and unhappy team members complaining to you. The kvetching in the last interlude is not purely hypothetical: every instructor who has ever worked with student teams has heard it, and many in that situation have thought, "Who needs these headaches?" Thinking of the ubiquity of teamwork in STEM and those employer surveys inevitably leads to the answer, "We all do."

Team assignments do much more than teach teamwork. Research has repeatedly shown that they can promote almost every conceivable learning outcome. The promotion is not automatic, however: putting students to work in teams can do more harm than good if the teams are not formed, managed, and guided properly. In this chapter we outline principles of *cooperative learning,* an instructional approach that equips students to function effectively in teams and to avoid problems that often arise in poorly-structured group work. This chapter answers the following questions:

○ What is cooperative learning? What are its benefits to students and instructors?
○ How can I use teams effectively in my lecture, lab, and project-based courses?
○ How should I form teams? What's wrong with letting students form their own teams?
○ How can I evaluate individual team members' performance? How can I hold each team member accountable for understanding all of the team's work?
○ What problems should I anticipate when I put students to work in teams? How can I minimize those problems and deal with them effectively when they occur?

11.1 Cooperative Learning

There are many forms of teaching that involve students working in groups, with names that include *active learning* (which in this book denotes brief course-related in-class activities); *cooperative, collaborative,* and *team-based learning; inquiry-based, problem-based,* and *project-based learning; peer instruction; peer-led team learning;* and *process-oriented guided-inquiry learning.* They are all described and compared in an encyclopedic pair of issues of the *Journal on Excellence in College Teaching* (vol. 25, nos. 3 and 4, 2014), with articles written by most of the world's leaders in team-based methods in higher education.

Several thousand research studies have shown that relative to students taught with teacher-centered lectures and individual assignments, students working in groups on assignments and projects under certain conditions generally exhibit higher academic achievement, greater persistence through graduation, better high-level reasoning skills, lower levels of anxiety and stress, greater intrinsic motivation to learn and achieve, more positive and supportive relationships with peers, and higher self-esteem (Hattie, 2009, Ch. 10; Johnson et al., 2000, 2014; Smith et al., 2005; Springer et al., 1999; Terenzini et al., 2001). Moreover, these benefits are observed for all categories of students, including at-risk minorities (Lichtenstein et al., 2014). Before you rush out tomorrow morning to form student teams and give them assignments, however, recall that little qualifier early in this paragraph: group work leads to many learning benefits *under certain conditions*. Lots of things can go wrong with student teams, a number of which were listed in the introductory section. Unless you take steps to minimize their occurrence and teach students to deal with them when they occur, the students could end up learning less than they would have if they had worked on their own.

A team learning approach used widely with great success in STEM education is *cooperative learning (CL)*. According to a CL model developed by David Johnson and Roger Johnson of the University of Minnesota (Felder & Brent, 2007; Johnson et al., 2006; Millis & Cottell, 1998; Smith et al., 2005), cooperative learning is instruction that involves students working on team assignments with five conditions in place:

1. **Positive interdependence.** Team members must rely on one another to achieve the instructor's learning goals.
2. **Individual accountability.** All students in a team are held accountable for doing their share of the work and for mastering all of the material covered in the assignments.
3. **Promotive interaction.** Although some of the assigned work may be parceled out and done individually, some is done interactively. In the interactions, team members provide one another with feedback, debate solution strategies and conclusions, and most important, teach and encourage one another.
4. **Development an appropriate use of teamwork skills.** The students are helped to develop the skills required for high-performance teamwork, such as communication, leadership, decision making, time management, and conflict resolution.
5. **Regular self-assessment of team functioning.** The students set team goals and periodically assess their progress toward meeting the goals, identify what they are doing well and where they may be falling short, and decide on changes they will make to function more effectively in the future.

In this chapter we present a number of suggestions for establishing and maintaining those conditions. First, though, a piece of advice if the students in your class are unaccustomed to team assignments. Before you put them to work, follow the recommendation in the last interlude to let them know what you plan to do and why you'll be doing it. If you don't, the student resistance you may initially encounter could be intense, and it might take a lot of time and effort to overcome it before you start to see the research-proven benefits of cooperative learning.

11.2 How Should Teams Be Formed?

When you set out to give assignments to student teams, you immediately confront two questions: (1) Should I form the teams or let the students choose their own? (2) If I form them, how should I do it?

11.2.1 Form teams yourself

When you use active learning for brief in-class exercises (Chapter 6), students in adjacent seats should quickly cluster themselves into groups. For more extended team assignments and projects, you should form the teams.

Research comparing the performance of instructor-formed teams with that of self-selected teams tends to support the former approach (e.g., Fiechtner & Davis, 1985; Oakley et al., 2004), although the effect sizes of the differences are generally small. There are several other compelling arguments for instructor formation, however. When students select their own teams, the top students in the class often find one another and so put weaker students at an unfair disadvantage, and underrepresented minority students may be left out or isolated. Instructor formation of teams can help avoid those situations. Instructor formation also simulates the professional workplace: STEM professionals almost always work in teams, and they generally have no choice about who their teammates will be.

11.2.2 Criteria for team formation

We propose four criteria for team formation in Table 11.2–1 and elaborate on them in the paragraphs that follow. You may decide to use other criteria as well, including distributing students with critical skills (such as computer skills) among teams and putting students with common interests together.

Table 11.2–1. Criteria for Team Formation

1. Form teams of three or four students for most group assignments and projects.
2. Make teams heterogeneous in ability.
3. If assignments require work being done outside class, form teams whose members have common blocks of time to meet.
4. Avoid forming teams containing a single student from an underrepresented or at-risk minority group in the first two years of college.

Form teams of three or four students for most group assignments and projects.

When students work in pairs, there is no natural mechanism for resolving conflicts, and dominant members are likely to win almost every argument, whether they are right or wrong. Larger teams provide more of the diversity of ideas and approaches that lead to many of the benefits of teamwork, but they also make project management more unwieldy. Members of large teams are more likely to be disengaged or marginalized (Aggarwal & O'Brien, 2008). Teams of three or four tend to be optimal for most assignments and projects. If you do form larger teams, the responsibilities of individual team members should be carefully spelled out. (See Michaelson et al. [2004] for a good model of cooperative learning with teams of six.)

Make teams heterogeneous in ability.

The unfairness of forming a team with only weak students is obvious, but teams with only strong students are also problematic. The members of such teams tend to divide up assignments, rely on one another to do their parts correctly and may not even look at what their teammates did, and only truly understand the parts they were personally responsible for. In mixed-ability teams, the weaker students gain from seeing how the stronger students approach problems and from getting one-on-one tutoring, and the stronger students gain a deeper understanding of the subject by teaching it to others.

Warning, however. Teams that are heterogeneous in ability may also be heterogeneous in learning goals and work ethics, which can lead to conflict. If you plan to form the mixed-ability teams we recommend, consider also adopting the measures we will suggest to help students learn to manage conflicts.

Make sure that students in a team have common blocks of time to work together outside class.

Among classes, jobs, and extracurricular activities, most college students have packed calendars. If you form teams randomly, the members of some of them may be unable to find times when they can conveniently meet to work on assignments. You can avoid that problem—or at least minimize it—by finding out in advance when students in your class are available to meet and forming teams of students with common free times. A questionnaire can be used to get the required information (an example is available at Felder and Brent [n.d.]), as can the online program *CATME Team-Maker* [CATME Smarter Teamwork, n.d.], which we will describe later.

Another way to deal with the team-meeting problem is to help the students set up online team interactions. Tools such as Google Hangouts, Skype, and FaceTime can enable meetings when in-person sessions are impractical or impossible (such as in online courses).

Don't isolate a single student in an underrepresented or at-risk minority group in the first two years of college.

Certain student populations are underrepresented in STEM disciplines or historically at risk for failing STEM courses, leaving STEM curricula, or dropping out of college. Students in those populations are liable to be marginalized or to adopt passive roles when they are isolated in teams (Felder et al., 1995; Heller & Hollabaugh, 1992; Rosser, 1998), which leads to our recommendation not to do that. As a rule, though, if those students can survive the first two years of college, they have a good probability of finishing the degree program. Your focus should then shift to preparing them for their postgraduation workplaces, where no one will be protecting them from being isolated in groups, and so you may drop this criterion.

11.2.3 Team-forming procedures

Here are four ways to carry out team formation, starting with the one we recommend most highly:

1. Use *CATME Team-Maker* (Layton et al., 2010), **an online team-forming program that is part of the *CATME Smarter Teamwork* system (CATME, n.d.).** You first select the sorting criteria from a comprehensive list of common choices (including those in Table 11.2–1) or create your own criteria. Team-Maker queries students and collects and stores the required information—e.g.,

grades in prerequisite courses and times available to work outside class on assignments—into a database. When the students in the class have all responded, Team-Maker sorts the students into teams at the click of a button.

2. **Collect team formation data from the students and use it to form teams manually.** Once you decide what sorting criteria you wish to use, prepare a corresponding questionnaire and administer it on Day 1 of the class. A sample questionnaire is available at Felder and Brent (n.d.).

3. **Form practice teams randomly that function for the first two or three weeks of the course. Give a fairly challenging quiz during that period, and form permanent teams using the quiz grades as the measure of ability.**

4. **Let students self-select into groups, stipulating that no group may have more than one student who earned As in one or two specified prerequisite courses.** This method is a reasonable approach if you are reluctant to form teams yourself. Although not ideal, it avoids teams of exclusively top students.

11.2.4 Dissolving and reforming teams

A frequently asked question is how long assignment and project teams should remain together. One argument for frequent dissolution and reformation of teams is that students on those teams will experience fewer conflicts than members of long-standing teams. Although we concede the validity of that argument, we take the opposite viewpoint about team reformation and recommend that teams remain together for extended periods of time. One objective of using team assignments is to have students experience and learn to overcome the scheduling and interpersonal problems that teams often confront in the workplace. For this learning to occur, the teams must remain together long enough to get past the phase when everyone is on his or her best behavior.

A reasonable policy is to dissolve all teams once during the semester and form new ones for the remainder of the course. (Obviously, this wouldn't work for a course with a single semester-long project.) We have had success with the following strategy:

o Announce when teams are first formed that they will be dissolved roughly halfway through the semester and reformed, *unless* each member of a team submits a request for the team to remain together, in which case that team will not be dissolved.

o At the designated time, teams that did not unanimously ask to stay together are dissolved and new teams are formed.

What generally happens is that one or two seriously dysfunctional teams fail to submit those requests, and they are consequently dissolved and either shuffled into new teams or distributed among teams of three to form teams of four. Other teams may have had problems but they managed to work through them, with or without the instructor's help, thereby achieving an important outcome of cooperative learning.

11.3 What Can Teams Be Asked to Do?

Team assignments in STEM courses are generally either problem sets or projects (including labs). This section outlines several different *structures* (the cooperative learning term for formats of team assignments and activities) in each category. For additional ideas, see Johnson et al. (2006) and Millis and Cottell (1998).

11.3.1 Problem sets

Students in lecture courses work in teams on some assignments, submitting only one solution set per team. The teams are strongly encouraged to include only the names of actual participants on their submissions. Several recommendations follow.

Use a mixture of individual and team assignments in a lecture course rather than having all assignments completed by teams.

As professionals the students will have individual and team responsibilities, and assignments of both types will help prepare them to work in both ways. If there is a lot of dropping and adding in the first few weeks of a course, consider giving only individual assignments until the class enrollment stabilizes, and then form teams and give them assignments.

Have each team submit only one complete solution set, but encourage or require all team members to outline problem solutions individually (no detailed calculations) before meeting to work out the details.

There are several reasons for requiring a single team solution. Most important, it emulates the professional workplace. In addition, requiring the students to submit individual solutions simply forces them to spend a lot of time copying and learning little in the process, and it increases the grading load by a factor of three to four.

So why ask team members to outline problem solutions individually before meeting to work out the details? If the students jump directly into a group problem-solving session, the fastest problem solver on the team is likely to begin almost every solution. The other team members can then avoid figuring out for themselves how to begin solutions until they take the individual exam, which could be disastrous for them. We suggest that on your first few assignments you require team members to prepare, sign, and hand in their outlines with the completed assignment to help them get into the habit.

Periodically assess the individual performance of each team member and use the assessments to adjust the team assignment grade for each member.

Many of the interpersonal conflicts commonly associated with student teamwork arise when all team members—workers and slackers alike—get the same grade. This recommendation helps avoid that problem.

Most people who hear the recommendation have questions that are variants of "How do you do that assessment?" We're going to hold off on answering for the moment: first, because we will make the identical suggestion in the next section, and second, because the answer is a long story which we'll tell in Section 11.4.5.

11.3.2 Team projects and jigsaw

Some courses are built around major team projects that may take several weeks or months to complete. Cooperative learning is ideally suited to such courses. Teams hand in only one report for each project, but as with assignments, individual team member performance is assessed and the team project grade is adjusted for each team member.

A powerful structure called *jigsaw* (Aronson et al., 1978) applies to team projects that call for expertise in several distinct areas. In a science laboratory experiment the areas might be background, experimental design, data collection, and data analysis and interpretation, and an engineering design project could involve conceptual design, mechanical design, instrumentation and control, and economic analysis.

Suppose you identify three areas of expertise for a team project in your class. Form teams of three or more and designate an area of expertise for each team member, making sure that each team has at least one expert in each area. Convene expert groups (groups containing all the experts on a specific topic), and give each group instruction in its area of expertise. The instruction may take the form of a handout or a training session conducted by you or a knowledgeable colleague, graduate student, or advanced undergraduate. The experts then return to their home teams, which complete the projects and submit reports.

Jigsaw promotes positive interdependence, because each team member is responsible for contributing to the team's effort with knowledge that no other team member possesses. If an expert does a poor job, the overall quality of the work suffers. If in addition you give tests covering every aspect of the project, all team members are then held accountable for the work everyone did and not just the parts for which they were principally responsible (individual accountability), and also for teaching the others what they learned in their training (more positive interdependence).

11.3.3 TBL, PLTL, and POGIL

In this section we briefly describe three team learning formats that have been widely used in STEM education and shown to produce good learning outcomes. They may or may not be variants of cooperative learning, depending on whether the five defining conditions of CL are in place.

In *team-based learning (TBL)* (Haidet & McCormack, 2014; Michaelson et al., 2004; Roberson & Franchini, 2014), a course instructor forms teams of five to seven students with diverse skills. The teams remain together through the entire course. The students submit completed assignments before the first day of each major content unit, take a short individual readiness assessment test at the beginning of the next class, then retake it in their teams and get immediate feedback on the correct answers. The test results show the instructor which content needs to be stressed in subsequent lessons and which has been mastered by the students on their own. The teams also carry out application exercises in class activities and longer out-of-class projects. Contributions to team efforts are assessed, and points are rewarded or withheld based on the results. TBL has had its greatest rate of adoption in the health professions.

Peer-led team learning (PLTL) (Eberlein et al., 2008; Gosser et al., 2001; Peer-Led Team Learning [PLTL], n.d.; Sarquis et al., 2001; Tien et al., 2002) supplements lectures with weekly two-hour workshops in which students work in six- to eight-person groups to solve problems under the guidance of trained student peer leaders. The course instructor creates problems and instructional materials, leads the training and supervision of peer leaders, and monitors progress in the workshops. The materials prompt students to reflect on ideas, confront misconceptions, and apply what they know to the solution process. The peer leaders clarify goals, facilitate engagement of the students with the materials and one another, and provide encouragement, but don't lecture or provide answers and solutions. The method was initially developed and used in chemistry education, and it subsequently spread to other STEM disciplines.

Process-Oriented Guided Inquiry Learning (POGIL) (Douglas & Chiu, 2013; Eberlein et al., 2008; Moog & Spencer, 2008; Process-Oriented Guided Inquiry Learning, n.d.) has students work in small groups in a class or laboratory on instructional modules, followed by leading questions designed to guide them toward formulation of their own conclusions. The instructor serves as facilitator, working with student groups if they need help and addressing classwide difficulties in mini-lectures when necessary. The POGIL website contains reports of implementations on several campuses, instructional materials for different branches of chemistry, and a video showing an implementation of the method in an introductory chemistry class.

Eberlein et al. (2008) compare key features of problem-based learning (which we discussed in Chapter 9), PLTL, and POGIL to help those new to these approaches select the one that will best fit their needs. To find references to applications in specific disciplines, enter "PBL _____," "PLTL _____," or "POGIL _____" (where _____ denotes the desired discipline) into a search engine.

11.4 Turning Student Groups into High-Performance Teams

Just putting your students into teams and telling them to complete an assignment or project together is no guarantee that you'll see all the knowledge and skill gains promised in the literature and previewed in Section 11.1. This section outlines several steps you can take to increase the chances that you will.

11.4.1 Establish team policies and expectations

Once teams have been formed, your first step in helping them function smoothly is to establish and explain your teamwork policies. Illustrative policies for team assignments and projects are given in Felder and Brent (n.d.). It's not that your policies should look like ours—yours may be quite different. The point is that whatever your policies are, they should be made explicitly clear to the students from the outset of the course and then followed consistently throughout the course.

After you've established your teamwork policies, a good next step is to have the teams formulate goals and expectations for themselves. An illustrative assignment of this type is shown in Felder and Brent (n.d.), and examples of a *team charter* (an expanded version of the goals assignment) are described by Hunsaker et al. (2011). After three to four weeks of teamwork, ask the teams to discuss how well they are adhering to their expectations and how they might improve. (Remember, self-assessment is the fifth defining feature of cooperative learning.)

11.4.2 Promote positive interdependence

Positive interdependence (sometimes referred to as *group cohesion*) means that team members have the sense that they are in it together—the team's success depends on all of them doing their jobs to the best of their ability (Johnson et al., 2006). Teamwork is time-consuming and poses a lot of problems to students. You can tell your students that it's good preparation for their future careers, but that can be a hard message to sell—especially to the brighter students—if they think they could have done just as well with fewer disruptions by working individually. Without positive interdependence, that's exactly what many of them are likely to think.

Here are several ways to establish positive interdependence.

Make team assignments too challenging for most students to complete comfortably by themselves in the allotted time.

Many students who confront team assignments for the first time are not enthusiastic about them. If your team assignments are simple enough that most students could easily complete them individually, the resentment we just spoke about is certain to appear. Making the assignments challenging minimizes or eliminates this problem. This suggestion should be viewed as a fundamental principle of cooperative learning.

Don't increase the challenge simply by making the assignments longer, however. Teamwork takes time, and if you just give team assignments that are twice as long as they would be if they were given to individual students, you will experience more resentment and resistance rather than less. Instead, incorporate more tasks at the higher levels of Bloom's Taxonomy—problems that require high-level analytical, critical, and creative thinking. (See Section 2.2 and Chapters 9 and 10 for examples.)

Define distinct roles for team members.

Positive interdependence is fostered if each team member has a unique *management role* critical to the success of the team effort. Management roles are designed to ensure that the team operates smoothly and effectively and produces a high-quality product in a timely manner. Table 11.4–1 shows four common roles. The division of labor among the roles is fuzzy, and all team members are generally involved in some or all of them, but the team member who officially serves in a role is responsible for seeing that the tasks associated with the role are completed.

Management roles should be rotated among team members, because one of the goals of teamwork is to help students develop a full range of teamwork skills, including leadership and project management

Table 11.4–1. Possible Management Roles on CL Teams

Coordinator.

Reminds team members of when and where they should meet, keeps everyone on task during team meetings, and makes sure everyone knows who is supposed to do what before the next meeting.

Recorder.

Assembles the product [problem solution set, interim or final project report] to be turned in for grading and passes it on to the checker. Generating some product components—such as drawings, charts, and computer-generated graphics—may be the responsibility of someone else on the team, but it is the recorder's job to collect and incorporate all components into the final product.

Checker.

Double-checks the final product, making sure it is complete, error-free, and turned in on time.

Process monitor.

Makes sure every team member understands every part of the final product and can explain how everything was done. In teams of three, the coordinator (or any other team member) may also assume the duties of the monitor.

(coordinator), report preparation (recorder), and quality assurance (checker for the product, monitor for the team learning). In courses with regular team homework assignments, the management roles should be rotated often—as frequently as every week. In project courses, each team member should serve as coordinator at least once during the project, and the other roles should mainly come into play in the periods before intermediate and final products are due. When assignments and reports are turned in, the roles played by each team member should be indicated next to their names.

Use jigsaw.

Jigsaw, the structure in which project team members are assigned different areas of expertise and given supplementary training in those areas, is an excellent vehicle for promoting positive interdependence. The teams must rely on all of their members to bring their expertise to bear in completing the project.

Give bonus points for good team performance on tests.

Before a course test, announce that all members of teams with an average test grade above (say) 80 percent will get bonus points added to their grade—perhaps two or three points for a hundred-point test. Don't require each person on the team to get the criterion grade, which would put unreasonable pressure on weaker members of the team and make it impossible for teams with a very weak student to ever get the bonus. Linking the bonus to the team average grade gives all team members an incentive to get the highest grade they can and motivates the stronger students to tutor their teammates.

If oral team reports are to be given, arbitrarily assign team members to report on different parts of the projects.

When teams give final oral reports on their projects, the students usually report on the parts for which they were principally responsible. Instead of letting that happen, a short time before the report presentation (from an hour to a day), designate who will report on which part of the project. (Your intention to do this should be known to the students from the beginning of the course.) All team members must then make sure their teammates can explain every part of the project, because any of them might have to report on any part and their grades depend on the quality of those reports. This technique also promotes individual accountability.

11.4.3 Establish individual accountability

A depressingly common problem in group work is *hitchhiking* (also known as *free riding* and *social loafing*), when students do little of the required work, don't understand and may not even have looked at the submitted problem set or project report, and still get the same grade that their more responsible teammates earned. This problem can usually be traced directly to a failure to hold individual team members accountable for doing their share of the work and understanding the work everyone else did. The paragraphs that follow suggest effective techniques for establishing individual accountability.

Give individual tests on assignment and project content.

The most effective way to ensure individual accountability is to give individual tests that cover the full content of the team assignments or projects. In courses with regular team problem-solving assignments, count the test grades toward the final course grade by a significant amount. Also, consider requiring a student's average grade on the tests to be at the passing level or higher for the team assignment grades to count.

In project-based courses (including labs), give individual exams on the projects and count them enough so that they can affect the course grade if they are really low. Keeping hitchhikers from getting high course grades they don't deserve goes a long way toward eliminating the resentment and conflicts that often arise in unstructured group work.

Monitor every team member's understanding.

One of the suggested team management roles is *process monitor*. The team member who holds this responsibility should make sure each team member understands the solution of each problem in an assignment or the content of each part of a project report. The process monitor could ask the team members to answer questions about the solution or report when the whole team is present so that all of the members can contribute to any explanations or clarifications that may be required. The questioning may be performed at the last team meeting before the assignment or report is handed in or in a study session before a test on the assignment or project.

As the instructor, you have no control over whether the team takes this task seriously, and left to their own devices students are very likely to skip it in their haste to complete the work and move on. (They are almost guaranteed to skip it in a project course with no individual tests.) The best you can do is let them know that checking for understanding benefits them: it leads to higher grades on the tests, and if they do it before they hand in the assignment or project report, they will probably find errors or omissions they can correct to get better grades.

Give credit only to active participants.

On the first day of a course announce a policy that only contributors' names should go on assignments and reports, and remind students about this policy when they come to you complaining about hitchhikers on their teams. Most students are inclined to cut their teammates some slack, but if hitchhikers keep failing to do what they're supposed to do, eventually their teammates should get tired of being exploited and begin to implement this policy, particularly if you didn't allow friends to select one another as teammates. Once hitchhikers receive one or two zeroes because their name was not on the submitted assignments, their sense of responsibility could undergo a dramatic reawakening.

Use peer ratings to adjust team project grades for individual performance.

The most frequent complaint about project teams is that some team members do most of the work and everyone on the team gets the same grade. A common method of avoiding this situation is to adjust team project grades for individual team member performance, using peer ratings as the basis for the adjustment. A good peer rating system can be a powerful tool for helping students develop good teamwork skills.

Peer rating criteria fall into two broad categories. Some are related to students' ability, such as their command of project-related knowledge and skills, and the percentage of the total work contributed by each team member. Other criteria are related to "team citizenship," irrespective of ability. These criteria might include reliability (showing up for team meetings, doing what they're supposed to do when they said they'd do it), level of cooperation in team activities, and commitment to the team's success.

We recommend focusing heavily or entirely on team citizenship in peer ratings. Ability-related criteria usually favor the brighter team members, who already enjoy (appropriately) advantages in their courses. The primary goal of peer rating should not be to provide one more assessment of ability but to promote cooperation, responsibility, and commitment, all attributes of high-performance teamwork. If the brightest students automatically get the highest ratings, the latter goals are unlikely to be achieved.

In a fairly simple but effective peer rating system called *autorating,* team members rate themselves and one another on specified criteria for team citizenship, and the ratings are used to compute multipliers of the team project grade for individual team members that may range from 1.05 (for team members who go above and beyond what is expected of them) down to 0 (for team members who do none of the work required to complete the assignments or project). The original version of the system was developed by Robert Brown (1995) of the Royal Melbourne Institute of Technology, and a variant was developed, class-tested, and described in detail by Kaufman et al. (2000). A powerful online peer rating system originally based on autorating is part of the teamwork support program called *CATME,* which we describe later in this section.

Provide last-resort options of firing and quitting.

When a team has an uncooperative member and everything else has been tried unsuccessfully (including a team meeting with the instructor to try and work things out), the other team members may notify the hitchhiker in writing that he or she will be fired if cooperation is not forthcoming, sending a copy of the memo to the instructor. If there is no improvement after a week, or if there is temporary improvement and the behavior soon resumes, they may send a second memo (copy to the instructor) that the hitchhiker is no longer with the team. Students who are fired must find a team of three willing to accept them, otherwise they get zeroes for the remaining assignments or the project. A similar policy may be implemented allowing students whose team members are not cooperating to quit the team.

In our experience, firing and quitting rarely occur if the measures we have suggested for obtaining positive interdependence and individual accountability are in place. Before things reach a state where the first memo is sent, the student in danger of being fired and the teammates of the one threatening to quit are likely to recognize that something bad is about to happen and start cooperating. As a rule, the only students who get fired or allow their responsible teammate to quit are those who have basically given up: they are failing the exams, don't anticipate passing the course no matter what they do, and see no reason to keep spending all that time on the team assignments or projects.

11.4.4 Get teams to monitor their own performance

An essential component of cooperative learning is regular team self-assessment, in which team members identify what the team is doing well (communication, time management, leadership, etc.) and what needs improvement. One benefit of self-assessment is that it gets team members to identify potential conflicts early and start to work on resolving them, as opposed to sweeping them under the rug until resentments become serious enough to cause the team to explode.

To implement self-assessment, every two to four weeks have teams respond in writing to these (or similar) questions:

○ How well are we addressing the goals and expectations we agreed on?
○ What are we doing well?
○ What needs improvement?
○ What (if anything) will we do differently from now on?

After you give this assignment for the first time, consider having a short debriefing session in class. Teams may get good ideas from other teams.

You don't have to spend much time reviewing the self-assessments, and don't grade them unless they are not submitted, in which case some penalty should be imposed. Just glance through them looking for warning signs of existing or potential serious conflicts. If you see any, you might call the team in for a discussion, perhaps using *active listening* to help work out a resolution (see Section 11.5.2).

11.4.5 CATME—An online teamwork support program

An online suite of programs, *CATME Smarter Teamwork* (www.catme .org), provides assistance with a variety of aspects of student team assignments and projects (Loughry et al., 2007, 2014; Ohland et al., 2012). CATME began as a peer rating system called *Comprehensive Assessment of Team Member Effectiveness* and subsequently added other tools. To use it, first go to the CATME website and open an account for yourself (it's free). Upload a file with the names and e-mail addresses of students enrolled in your course, and specify the information you will need from each student to form teams (such as GPA or grades in prerequisite courses, computing or writing skills, times available to work outside class on team assignments, and other options you can select or create). CATME then prompts the students to log in and enter the requested information and notifies you when they have all done so. You may then access and use the following resources:

Team-Maker (described in Section 11.2.).

With a single click, the program forms teams using the criteria you specified. You may then have to make minor adjustments to team compositions but generally far fewer than if you form the teams manually.

Rater calibration.

Before your students carry out their first peer evaluation, CATME describes several hypothetical team members, and the students rate them using the same rubric they will later use to evaluate their own teammates. You then show and discuss the ratings you would give.

Peer rating.

As often as you request, the students are prompted to rate their teammates and themselves on any or all of five criteria of high-performance teamwork: contributing to the team's work, interacting with teammates, keeping the team on track, expecting quality, and having course-relevant knowledge and skills. (We recommend not using the last criterion, which focuses on ability and not team citizenship.) Once all team members have completed and submitted their ratings, CATME (1) provides a factor that can be used to adjust team project grades for individual team members based on their average ratings; (2) reports the individual ratings and adjustments to the instructor; (3) flags suspicious patterns of ratings (such as significantly different ratings of the same team member by different teammates), alerting the instructor to investigate rather than simply accepting the adjusted grades for those teams; (4) reports to students their average ratings from their teammates and the average score for the entire team, and suggests how they might improve their ratings in subsequent evaluations.

Since CATME first appeared in 2005, its frequency of use has been growing exponentially. By mid-2015 it had been used by roughly 370,000 students and 7,500 faculty members at 1,200 institutions in 64 different countries.

11.5 Dealing with Difficulties

This section reviews some problems that commonly occur in teamwork and suggests ways to deal with them.

11.5.1 Defusing student resistance

As we suggested in the interlude preceding this chapter, if you confront students with *any* unfamiliar learner-centered teaching method, some may conclude that you are either shirking your job by making them teach themselves or running some kind of experiment with them as the guinea pigs. They are not happy either way (Felder & Brent, 1996; Weimer, 2013).

Students forced to take major responsibility for their learning go through a sequence of stages psychologists associate with trauma and grief.

Stages of Student Responses to Learner-Centered Teaching

1. **Shock:** "I don't believe it—we have to do homework in groups and I can't choose my own teammates?"
2. **Denial:** "Dr. Parker can't be serious about this—if I ignore it, it will go away."
3. **Strong emotion:** "I can't do it—I'd better drop the course and take it next semester" or "Dr. Parker can't do this to me—I'm going to complain to the department head!"
4. **Resistance and withdrawal:** "I'm not going to play this dumb game—I don't care if Parker fails me."
5. **Surrender and acceptance:** "OK, I think it's stupid but I'm stuck with it, and I might as well give it a shot."
6. **Struggle and exploration:** "Everybody else seems to be getting this—maybe I need to do things differently to get it to work for me."
7. **Return of confidence:** "Hey, I may be able to pull this off after all—I think it's starting to work."
8. **Integration and success:** "YES! This stuff is all right—I don't know why I had so much trouble with it before."

Sources: Felder and Brent (1996); Woods (1994).

Just as some people have an easier time than others in moving through the grieving process, some of your students may quickly adapt to teamwork and short-circuit many of the eight steps, and others may have difficulty getting past the negativity of Stages 3 and 4. The idea is to remember that resistance is a normal part of students' progression from dependence on authorities to independent thinking. If you deal with it effectively early in the course, it will shrink or disappear for most students. However, if you don't take steps to counter it quickly, it can become a serious distraction to you and limit the effectiveness of the class.

Our primary suggestion for overcoming student resistance to teams is to explain why you are requiring teamwork and particularly what's in it for the students. We offered suggestions for how to do it in the interlude. Once the students recognize that working in teams is in their best interests, they may still be unhappy, but most will keep an open mind long enough to see that you are telling them the truth.

Another way to reduce student resistance to teamwork is to ask about it in your midterm evaluation, following the procedure suggested for active learning near the end of Section 6.6. If you have been doing cooperative learning effectively, most students in the class will express positive or neutral feelings about it, and when the unhappy students discover that they are only a small minority, you are not likely to hear any more complaints from them. However, if many students are still negative about group work after a month of doing it, you may be violating one of the guidelines we have recommended. Review this chapter and see if you can spot something you need to change.

11.5.2 Dealing with dysfunctional teams

As irritating as student resistance to group work may be to instructors, teams with members who can't stand each other can be even worse. "*Who signed up for this?*" asks the instructor, after listening to the third or fourth student complaint that week about obnoxious teammates. "*I'm supposed to teach genetics—playing therapist to a bunch of irresponsible whiners is not in my contract.*"

The instructor's exasperation is understandable, and many professors would agree with the point of view that they were not trained in team dynamics or conflict resolution and so should not have to deal with those things as part of their job. There is another point of view, however. We propose that our primary job as instructors is not simply to teach course content and evaluate students' learning (Peter Elbow's "gatekeeper" function) but to help equip our students with the skills they will need to succeed as professionals and educated citizens (Elbow's "coach" function). Those skills include the technical skills traditionally taught in STEM curricula, the professional skills discussed in Chapter 10, and the interpersonal skills needed to function effectively in teams. Fortunately, you don't have to be a trained counselor to teach teamwork skills. The rest of this section outlines several simple but effective methods of helping students learn to deal with common team problems.

Hold in-class crisis clinics.

Two to three weeks after group work has begun, you will probably start hearing complaints about troublesome team members, such as hitchhikers or dominant students who insist on discounting everyone else's viewpoints and doing everything their way. Use those characters as subjects of brief *crisis clinics* in class, in which the students brainstorm and then prioritize possible group responses to specified offensive behaviors (Felder & Brent, 2001).

For example, after you've gotten a few complaints about hitchhikers, you might do this:

1. **Come into class one day and mention that groups sometimes have trouble with team members not pulling their weight—failing to do what they were supposed to do, showing up unprepared for work sessions, or not showing up at all.** Then tell the class that you want to spend a few minutes talking about ways to deal with those individuals.
2. **Put the class into small groups and give them a few minutes to brainstorm actions hitchhikers' teammates might take—not just good strategies but also bad and even illegal ones.** Students generally have a good time with this exercise, thinking of reasonable ideas (have the whole team or one team member talk to the hitchhikers, give them specific assignments, partner them with a productive team member, warn them about consequences if they don't start cooperating, leave their names off future assignments, and fire them from the team) and not so reasonable ideas (short-sheet their beds, report them to their mothers, etc.).
3. **Stop the brainstorming after about a minute or two and call on groups to report their ideas.** Write the ideas on the board, adding one or two of your own if you have some that no one else thought of.
4. **Put the students back in their groups for another two minutes to try and reach consensus on (a) the best first response, (b) what to do if that doesn't work, and (c) what to do as a last resort.** After a few minutes, stop the groups and list their ideas on the board, telling the class to copy the lists for themselves.

At that point the clinic is finished. Tell the students to take the ideas seriously and use them when necessary, and then go on with your class. The students will leave class with an arsenal of good strategies for dealing with hitchhikers, and the hitchhikers will know that in the future their irresponsibility is likely to have consequences they may not enjoy, which might induce them to change their ways. One or two weeks later you can make the aggressively dominant individual (or another troublesome team member) the subject of another clinic.

Use active listening to mediate conflicts.

Even if you do everything you can think of to avoid conflicts in your student teams, not everything is under your control, and in every class there may be one or more teams in which major conflicts arise. *Active listening* is powerful tool for conflict resolution (Rogers & Farson, 1987).

Here's how active listening works in the context of teamwork (it has many other applications). Suppose you learn that one of the teams in your class is conflicted to an extent that hampers the members' ability to work together. Get all team members to meet with you in your office or a conference room, and have one faction (Side 1, the complainer or complainers) state their case. Side 2 (those being complained about) must listen without commenting or attempting to rebut the complaints. When Side 1 has finished, Side 2 must repeat Side 1's story, point for point, still without commenting or rebutting. If Side 2 gets something wrong, Side 1 corrects them and they repeat the correction and resume. If Side 2 does anything but repeat what Side 1 said, you jump in and stop them, reminding them that they'll get their turn. Then, Side 2 presents their case, which Side 1 must repeat without commenting or rebutting. All that remains after that is for the team members to work out—either by themselves or with some help from you—how they will proceed for the rest of the course.

What makes active listening so effective? In most conflicts, as each side presents its case, the other side is too busy framing counterarguments to really listen to what their opponents are saying. In active listening, after each side has been forced to listen to and then repeat the other side's position, every student at least understands what the conflict is really about. Once that point has been reached, the battle is three-quarters over. The last step of the process usually goes surprisingly smoothly, with very little input from the instructor needed. Once students have gone through this process, they are equipped with a strategy they can use to resolve professional and personal conflicts for the rest of their lives.

Don't get discouraged.

Whatever you do, don't let occasional problems blind you to the successes of the method. Consider Rich's story of an experience he once had.

A colleague who had taken a workshop from me came up and said that he had used student teams in the previous semester, and it had been a disaster. Here's how the dialogue went from there.

Rich: I'm sorry to hear it. What happened?

Colleague: I had fourteen teams in the class, and one of them was the team from hell! The stuff they turned in was always sloppy, full of mistakes, and late, and the team members were constantly arguing and complaining to me about each other—I was afraid they'd end up in a fistfight. I'm sure not going to try teams again.

Rich: That must have been a pain to deal with. How about the other thirteen teams?

Colleague: Oh, they were fine. In fact, I got the best work I had ever seen in that course from them.

Rich: Really? So help me understand how thirteen student teams do the best work you've ever seen, one is dysfunctional, and it counts as a disaster.

Colleague: Um . . .

The sad truth is that no matter how well you implement teamwork, you can't count on a 100% success rate. No instructional method is guaranteed to work well for all students at all times—too many uncontrollable factors affect students' performance in a course and on a team. But just as a few failing students in a traditional class don't prove that the teaching was poor, having a few dysfunctional student teams in a class is not a sign that teamwork failed. Next time the problem students are part of a work team—in school or in their careers—they may have some vivid memories of the consequences of poor teamwork, and their experience might have been unpleasant enough that they decide not to do whatever got them into trouble the first time.

In short, cooperative learning is not trivial, and you are likely to experience some annoying problems when you first implement it. If you follow the recommended procedures, however, and have the patience and confidence to work through the problems, your students will reap the rewards of more and deeper learning and better preparation for their future jobs. It's worth dealing with a few annoyances to do that.

Thought Question

Think of yourself as the inexperienced instructor you once were (and may still be), and imagine that you were assigned to teach a course in which student teams would be working on weekly homework assignments. What would you have been worried about? (Don't just brainstorm a list of possible concerns—answer for yourself as that instructor.)

Now imagine yourself to be an experienced instructor who has been successful with cooperative learning. How would you respond to the new instructor's concerns?

11.6 Ideas to Take Away

- *Cooperative learning* (according to the model developed by Johnson and Johnson) is group work carried out under conditions that ensure *positive interdependence, individual accountability, promotive interaction, development and appropriate use of teamwork skills,* and *regular self-assessment of team functioning.* Thousands of research studies have shown that when these conditions are in place, group work has a positive effect on most learning outcomes.
- Instructor-formed teams of three to four students generally work best for group projects. The team members should be heterogeneous in ability and have common blocks of time to meet outside class. In the first two years of the curriculum, students who belong to underrepresented or at-risk minorities should not be isolated in teams.
- One product (problem solution set or lab or project report) should be collected per team, but the team grade should be adjusted for individual team member performance. The *CATME* Smarter Teamwork suite of online tools provides an excellent basis for the adjustment (as well as for forming teams using instructor-specified criteria). Also consider giving individual tests covering all aspects of team projects.
- Students unaccustomed to group work may exhibit considerable resistance to it. To minimize or eliminate it, explain how and why you will be doing it (the interlude before this chapter suggests an

effective way to explain) and provide teams with devices (such as crisis clinics) for dealing with uncooperative members and strategies (such as active listening) for resolving conflicts.

11.7 Try This in Your Course

- o If you've never tried teamwork, give a relatively limited team assignment in the next course you teach, maybe one lasting two to three weeks. Form the teams yourself using the guidelines we've suggested, and use a peer rating tool to assess individual team member performance. If it goes well, consider trying a full-scale implementation in a future class.
- o If you teach a class with project or lab teams, identify one method for improving positive interdependence and one method for increasing individual accountability that you have not previously tried, and try them.
- o Several weeks after teamwork starts, conduct a crisis clinic in class.
- o Get a CATME account and use it for team formation and development and to conduct peer ratings.

LEARNER-CENTERED TEACHING REVISITED

12.0 Introduction

In Chapter 1, we stated that the pedagogical framework for this book is *learner-centered teaching (LCT)*, an approach that puts more responsibility for students' learning on the students than traditional teacher-centered methods do. We didn't say much about LCT explicitly in the next ten chapters but we also never left the subject, because almost every teaching method we've discussed qualifies as learner-centered teaching. In this chapter, we'll make the connections more explicit and introduce several more LCT concepts and methods.

A learner-centered teacher has the dual roles of *gatekeeper* (setting and enforcing high standards) and *coach* (doing as much as possible to help all qualified students meet or exceed those standards) (Elbow, 1986). The gatekeeper's job is to certify that students who pass a course have the necessary knowledge and skills to enroll in subsequent courses, and that students who get high grades have met specified high-level learning objectives. All faculty members are familiar with the gatekeeper role and pursue it with varying levels of success. Being coach is another matter. Many faculty members never experienced meaningful coaching as students and either don't know how to do it or don't view it as their responsibility.

In competitive sports and corporate training, the first thing good coaches do is learn about the people they are coaching—their strengths and weaknesses and what motivates them to do their best. Armed with that knowledge, the coaches devise strategies for building the strengths, overcoming the weaknesses, and providing the appropriate motivation.

It works the same way in learner-centered teaching. As we observed in Chapter 3, one of your first goals as coach should be to learn about your students—their prior knowledge, interests, learning gaps and misconceptions, and to the extent possible, their names. Thereafter, your goal should be to identify and implement teaching strategies that connect new material to the students' prior knowledge and interests, fill in gaps in their knowledge, correct their misconceptions, and promote their mastery of the knowledge and skills specified in your learning objectives.

This chapter overviews two additional topics related to the coach's role: *student diversity* (identifying and addressing ways in which students differ that may affect their attitudes and performance in a course), and *inductive teaching and learning* (beginning instruction of a course topic with a challenge and teaching the topic content in the context of addressing the challenge). In previous chapters we discussed several aspects of diversity and two of the most common inductive teaching methods—problem-based learning and project-based learning. In this chapter, we'll address the following questions:

○ How can I meet the widely varying learning needs and preferences of students in different demographic diversity categories with different approaches to learning, levels of intellectual development, and learning styles?

○ What do different inductive teaching methods have in common and how do they differ? What does research say about their effectiveness? How should I determine which ones (if any) I should use in a given class?

○ Which learning strategies presented in this book qualify under the general heading of learner-centered teaching? Where in the book and outside it can I find information on how to implement the strategies effectively?

○ How should I make the transition from traditional teaching to learner-centered teaching?

12.1 Aspects of Student Diversity

As every student knows—and as you know from having been a student—teaching methods vary considerably from one instructor to another. Some instructors mainly lecture and others spend considerable time on demonstrations and activities, some focus on principles and others on applications, some emphasize memory and others understanding, some are all business in their interactions with students and others are warm and approachable. How much a student learns in your class is governed in large measure by that student's native ability, prior preparation, motivation to learn what you will be teaching, and work ethic, but also by the compatibility between how you teach and the student's learning needs and preferences.

Taking a learner-centered approach to teaching does not mean trying to teach each student exclusively in the way he or she might prefer. For one thing, it's not possible to determine all of the factors that affect a student's learning, much less to address all of them. Also, even if you knew the optimal teaching approaches for every student (which would not necessarily coincide with the ways they would prefer to be taught), it would be impossible to implement those approaches simultaneously in a class of more than two.

But if attempting to tailor instruction to each individual student is futile, adopting a teaching approach that fits no one is even worse. Unfortunately, the teaching method that has dominated higher education for centuries—the professor lectures and the students attempt to absorb the lecture content and reproduce it in examinations—is such an approach. As we have repeatedly shown, nonstop lecturing violates every principle of effective instruction established by modern cognitive science and empirical classroom research. Any other approach designed to fit a certain type of student is likely to be more effective than that one, but it would still be ineffective for most other students. So, if completely individualized instruction is impractical and one-size-fits-all is ineffective for most students, attempting to balance the different needs and preferences of students must be the best we can do. The question then becomes, what are those different needs and preferences?

Several forms of diversity are useful to consider when designing instruction, including differences in race and ethnicity, gender identity and expression, cultural and educational background, other demographic categories, and three other student attributes mentioned briefly in earlier chapters: *approaches to learning, levels of intellectual development*, and *learning styles* (Felder & Brent, 2005). The next four subsections survey the challenges to instructors posed by these forms of student diversity in their classrooms, and Section 12.3 reviews teaching strategies that address the challenges.

12.1.1 Demographic diversity

Certain groups have historically under-enrolled in STEM curricula, and some of those groups have experienced relatively high attrition from STEM, resulting in their underrepresentation in the STEM workforce (National Academy of Sciences, National Academy of Engineering, & Institute of Medicine, 2011; Ohland et al., 2008, 2011; Schneider et al., 2015; US Department of Commerce, 2011). Several different approaches to reducing attrition from STEM curricula have been explored, including summer bridge and first-year support programs for incoming students (Burke & Mattis, 2007; Chubin et al., 2005; Jain et al., 2009; Johri & Olds, 2014, Chs. 16–18; National Science Foundation, 2009). Successful programs tend to be characterized by the learner-centered teaching strategies listed in Section 12.3 implemented in an inclusive environment in which all students are welcomed and their contributions valued.

Researchers have carried out extensive studies of the effects of the classroom environment on underrepresented minority students. Experiences that encourage students to engage with diversity promote student learning (Pascarella & Terenzini, 2005), and creating an inclusive environment has been shown to have a powerful impact on the intellectual and social development of *all* students (Gurin, 1999; Reason et al., 2010; Smith et al., 2010).

Measures to make the academic environment inclusive and supportive of underrepresented groups have been described in the literature (Baitz, 2006; Beemyn, 2005; Busch-Vishniac & Jarosz, 2007; Evans, 2002; Goodman et al., 2002; Lichtenstein et al., 2014; Poynter & Washington, 2005; Rankin et al., 2010; Rosser, 1997; Weber & Custer, 2005). Stephanie Farrell (personal communication, June 29, 2015) offers the following suggestions based in part on those descriptions:

1. **Examine your assumptions.** Instructors often make subconscious assumptions that they and their students have similar cultural backgrounds, and that the students come from traditional families, have parents who attended college, and are heterosexual, all of which can make students outside the majority feel marginalized. Become aware of any such assumptions you hold and do your best to avoid using language or behavior that reflects them.
2. **Avoid stereotypes and combat stereotype threat.** Be particularly wary of stereotypes that assign certain traits, skills, or weaknesses to members of a particular group (Latinos are _____, Asians are _____, women are_____, etc.), and take steps to minimize *stereotype threat* (students' fear of inadvertently confirming a

negative stereotype about one's own group) (Steele, 2010). Make sure to create equal opportunities for all students to participate in class discussions and answer questions, and avoid actions that suggest a belief in low-ability stereotypes, such as asking women less-challenging questions. Eschenbach et al. (2014) present a comprehensive review of the literature on the impact of stereotype threat in engineering education and best practices for reducing it.

3. **Use inclusive language.** For example, avoid using only masculine pronouns (*he, him, his*) to refer to both men and women.

12.1.2 Approaches to learning

In the interlude preceding Chapter 8 you met Michelle, Ryan, and Alex, who illustrate three approaches students may take toward studying and learning. Michelle tends to take a *deep approach,* pushing beyond the instructor's minimal requirements in an effort to truly understand what is being taught. She is motivated by interest, and if she doesn't think a subject is particularly important she may not make the effort necessary to get a high course grade. Ryan is more inclined toward a *surface approach,* relying primarily on memorization of facts and formulas and satisfied with a passing course grade. Alex takes a *strategic approach.* He goes for the top grade, whatever it takes to get it—staying on the surface if he can, digging deep when he has to. A deep approach has been found to correlate with attainment of most learning outcomes other than memorizing factual information and implementing routine procedures (Felder & Brent, 2005, p. 64).

Approaches to learning are tendencies, not fixed behavior patterns, and certain teaching strategies can induce Michelle, Alex, and sometimes even Ryan to take a deep approach. The strategies are reviewed in Chapter 8 and listed in Section 12.3.

12.1.3 Levels of intellectual development

The interlude before Chapter 10 introduced you to three other students—Dave, Megan, and Roberto—who illustrate three different stages of *Perry's model of intellectual development* (Perry, 1970/1998). Students similar to Dave are in what Perry called *dualism* and Kroll (1992) refers to as a state of *ignorant certainty.* They believe that knowledge is certain, beliefs are either right or wrong and not contextually dependent, author- ities (such as teachers and textbook authors) have the answers to all questions, and the student's job is to memorize those answers and repeat them on tests. Many entering college students hold those beliefs (Felder & Brent, 2004b).

As college students gain experience, most (such as Megan) progress to higher levels of the Perry scale when they recognize that some knowledge is contextually dependent, and some students (like Roberto) reach a state that Perry calls *relativism* and Kroll calls *intelligent confusion,* in which they recognize that all knowledge is contextual. In that progression, students take increasing responsibility for making their own judgments on the basis of evidence rather than relying on the word of authorities, and they become increasingly sophisticated at gathering and interpreting evidence from a wide range of sources. Students like Roberto, who consistently use evidence-based decision-making practices in a domain of knowledge (e.g., science), have begun to think like experts in that domain. Relatively few college students get there by the time they graduate.

Perry's model was criticized for having been developed entirely from interviews with men. Belenky et al. (1986/1997) developed and validated an alternative model applicable to women, and Baxter Magolda (1992) subsequently formulated a model that synthesized Perry's and Belenky's models, with gender-specific subcategories for several levels. The descriptions of the levels for all of the models are quite similar (Felder & Brent, 2004b).

The key to helping students move up the developmental scale on any of the models is to provide an appropriate balance of challenge (a gatekeeping function) and support (a coaching function), occasionally posing problems one or two levels above the students' current position, modeling the type of thinking required to solve the problems, and providing supportive feedback on the students' initial efforts (Felder & Brent, 2004c). Although doing those things won't guarantee that all of our students will reach Perry's relativism level or higher by the time they graduate, the more we move them in that direction, the better we will be doing our job. Strategies for providing effective challenge and support are suggested in Chapter 10 and included in Section 12.3.

12.1.4 Learning styles

Students have different *learning styles*—preferences for certain types of information and methods of teaching. Some STEM students like to focus on facts, data, and real-world applications; others are more comfortable with concepts, theories, and mathematical models. Some gravitate toward visual forms of information, such as pictures, diagrams, and schematics; others prefer verbal forms—written and spoken explanations. Some tend to learn actively and interactively; others are more inclined to work introspectively and individually. A student's preferences for one form of instruction over another fall on a continuum from very strong to almost nonexistent and may vary from one subject and classroom environment to another, and the strength of each preference (and possibly the preference itself) is likely to change as the student matures. Aisha and Rachel (interlude preceding Chapter 6) and Stan and Nathan (interlude preceding Chapter 9) illustrate students with contrasting learning style preferences.

Approaches to learning, levels of intellectual development, and learning styles have several features in common (Felder & Brent, 2005). They are all context-dependent patterns of behavior rather than invariant human attributes and are based on extensive observation of students rather than brain physiology. Some individuals almost always follow a particular pattern, others follow a pattern with a moderate level of predictability, and still others are almost as likely to follow one pattern as its opposite. Models have been proposed to identify categories in each domain (e.g., surface, deep, and strategic approaches to learning; dualism, multiplicity, and relativism in Perry's model of intellectual development; and sensing and intuitive learners in Jung's theory of psychological types and the Felder-Silverman learning styles model), and instruments have been developed for each model to assess the strength of a student's inclination toward one or another category. The models have been used extensively and effectively to categorize patterns of students' behavior and to design instruction that promotes learning for students in all categories.

Unlike approaches to learning and levels of intellectual development, however, learning styles have periodically come under heavy attack in the psychology literature (e.g., Coffield, 2012; Riener & Willingham, 2010; Rohrer & Pashler, 2012). Most of the criticisms are variants of those of Riener and Willingham (2010), who propose that no evidence has been found to support the following claims: (1) *"Learners have preferences about how to learn that are independent of both ability and content and have meaningful implications for their learning."* (2) *"Learning can be improved by matching instruction to students' learning styles."* The second claim has been labeled the *matching hypothesis or meshing hypothesis* by several of the critics.

We agree that research does not definitively support those two assertions; however, the assertions do not reflect current conceptions of learning styles (Felder, 2010). Similar to approaches to learning, learning style preferences are commonly acknowledged to be context-dependent, with the strength of a preference and possibly the preference itself changing with time and experience. The second assertion—the matching hypothesis—may or may not be correct (a lack of definitive supporting evidence is not proof of invalidity), but its validity is not required by current learning styles theory and in fact is irrelevant. *Even if teaching could be perfectly matched to each student's learning style preferences, it shouldn't be.* The goal should instead be balanced instruction that does not heavily favor one learning style preference over its opposite (in Kolb's [1984] terminology, *teaching around the cycle*).

The value of learning styles in instructional design stems from the fact that each learning style category is associated with certain skills and attitudes, all of which can be important for professional success. For example, STEM professionals should at some times be practical, methodical, and attentive to details (as sensing learners tend to be), and at other times be innovative, quick, and thoughtful about possible meanings and implications of observations and data (as intuitive learners tend to be). They should habitually reflect and seek more information before making decisions and taking action prematurely (a characteristic of introverted and reflective learners) but also be prepared to take decisive action (like extraverted and active learners) rather than continually delaying in hope of more information. They have to extract meaning from visual information (visual learners) and verbal information (verbal learners). And so on. When instruction is balanced, all students are sometimes taught in their preferred manner (so they are not too uncomfortable to learn) and sometimes in their less preferred manner (so they develop important skills they might not develop if instruction always matched their preferences). Section 12.3 lists strategies that promote the attainment of such balance.

12.1.5 Teaching to address diversity

There is no evidence that students in any diversity category described in the preceding sections are inherently less capable of succeeding in STEM than any other students, and students in every category have in fact succeeded brilliantly in all STEM disciplines. Our goal should be to teach in an inclusive manner that helps as many students as possible to succeed.

How can we achieve that goal? That question will bring us back to learner-centered teaching, but we have one topic left to address before we get there. One of our suggestions for implementing LCT will be to "use inductive teaching and learning." We have scattered discussions of several inductive methods throughout the book but haven't really defined induction or discussed what those methods have in common and how they differ. We will fill in these gaps in the next section, then overview LCT methods that address different forms of diversity, and finally offer a few inspirational (we hope) words to close out the book.

12.2 Inductive Teaching and Learning

The traditional approach to STEM instruction is *deductive*, moving from general principles to specific examples and applications. You start with the appropriate underlying principle for what you plan to teach—conservation of mass, a fundamental axiom of geometry, the theory of evolution, or whatever it may be—and deduce your way to the relationship or method or application you're heading for. The traditional STEM curriculum is also heavily deductive. The first two or three years are devoted almost entirely to fundamental mathematical and scientific principles and methods, with the students repeatedly being assured that those things will be vitally important later in the curriculum or after graduation. The assumption is that the students cannot deal with real processes and systems until they have mastered all the foundational knowledge and skills.

That assumption is wrong. When deductive teaching is done well, it is efficient and sometimes elegant, which may explain why it has dominated STEM education for centuries. It is not how people usually learn, however. We learn most of what we know by connecting new information to relevant cognitive structures in our long-term memories (no relevant structures ⇒ no learning), and by trying things, getting corrective feedback and learning from our mistakes, and trying again. In Chapter 4 we introduced *inductive teaching and learning,* an approach to teaching that matches this form of learning. The instructor begins each new topic with a challenge—a question to answer, a problem to solve, a case study to analyze, or an observation of a natural phenomenon or experimental outcome to explain. The challenges are carefully designed to help the students relate new course content to their prior knowledge, and meeting the challenges requires carrying out tasks specified in course learning objectives. Students grappling with the challenges are led to recognize the need to know certain facts and procedures, at which point the instructor provides the needed information or helps the students acquire it for themselves.

12.2.1 What can students be asked to do?

There are innumerable possibilities for inductive exercises, many of which have been suggested in earlier chapters. For example, students may be called on to do the following:

- ○ **Explain observations** (Sect. 4.5). Ask students to speculate on why foam forms on espresso, leg muscles tremble after a long run, we are comfortable in still air at 20°C and freezing in water at the same temperature, or why any of the thousands of familiar devices and phenomena discussed in *How Stuff Works* (n.d.) function as they do.
- ○ **Answer conceptual questions** (Sect. 8.2). Pose ConcepTests (multiple-choice questions that include common misconceptions among the distractors) to the class, and use clickers or smartphones with polling software to collect and display the responses. Address the misconceptions while teaching the relevant course material.
- ○ **Make predictions about experimental outcomes or the behavior of a physical system or the output from a computer code** (Sect. 4.5, Table 6.1-1). Describe an experiment or an action that will be taken on a real or simulated system or a treatment that will be administered to a patient with specified symptoms and have the students predict the outcome. Present a spreadsheet or computer code and ask the students to predict the output when the program is run.
- ○ **Troubleshoot.** Present the results of an experiment or the behavior of a system or the response of a patient or the output of a computer program that did not match what was supposed to happen, and have the students speculate on or figure out reasons for the discrepancy.
- ○ **Formulate a plan of attack for an open-ended real-world problem** (Sects. 3.6.2 and 9.4). Present a problem that will require course material to solve and have the students outline what they know, what they need to find out, and where they would begin. Then provide instruction that helps the students get the solution started, and if the complete solution has not been obtained, repeat the exercise to take the next step. For relatively simple problems that can be solved in a short time, this structure is an example of inquiry-based learning, and for major problems that require multiple steps over a long period of time (up to an entire semester), it is problem-based learning.

12.2.2 Inductive teaching methods

Prince and Felder (2006, 2007) survey inductive methods, outline their strengths and weaknesses, summarize the research that affirms their effectiveness, and offer suggestions for implementing them. Table 12.2–1 lists

Table 12.2–1. Inductive Teaching Methods

Method → Feature ↓	Inquiry	Problem-based	Project-based	Case-based	Discovery	Just-in-time teaching
Questions or problems provide context for learning.	1	2	2	2	2	2
Complex, ill-structured, open-ended real-world problems provide context for learning.	4	1	3	2	4	4
Major projects provide context for learning.	4	4	1	3	4	4
Case studies provide context for learning.	4	4	4	1	4	4
Students discover course content for themselves.	2	2	2	3	1	2
Students complete and submit conceptual exercises electronically; instructor adjusts lessons according to their responses.	4	4	4	4	4	1
Primarily self-directed learning	4	3	3	3	2	4
Active learning	2	2	2	2	2	2
Collaborative and cooperative (team-based) learning	4	3	3	4	4	4

Note: 1—by definition, 2—always, 3—usually, 4—possibly.

the defining and secondary attributes of the most common methods. All of the methods but inquiry-based learning have unique defining characteristics, whereas the definition of inquiry is simply that it is inductive. Any inductive method that does not fall into one of the other categories may therefore be considered a form of inquiry.

Although the quality of research data supporting the different inductive methods is variable, evidence that inductive teaching on average works better than traditional deductive teaching is conclusive (Prince & Felder, 2006). Relative to deduction, however, induction poses greater planning and management challenges to instructors and is more likely to provoke student resistance and resentment. Inductive methods that involve team projects introduce additional challenges, including students receiving credit for work they didn't do and don't understand and interpersonal problems that often arise when people work in teams (see Chapter 11). If you fail to provide appropriate support when you start teaching inductively, your students' natural resistance to learner-centered teaching can escalate to hostility, and their learning and your teaching evaluations could be worse than they were when you taught traditionally. The tips that follow should enable you to avoid this situation.

12.2.3 Implementation tips

Ease into induction.

Prince and Felder (2007) propose a hierarchy of levels of challenge of different inductive methods, ranging from minor (inquiry, ConcepTests and peer instruction, small individual projects, and case study analyses) to moderate (more extensive projects, just-in-time teaching) to considerable (any project-based method that involves cooperative learning) to major (problem-based learning). If you have never used an inductive teaching method, we suggest starting with inquiry or one of the other relatively easy ones. Do it often enough to become comfortable with it, and then consider moving to a more challenging method, such as cooperative learning (Chapter 11). Once you can do that successfully, if you want to take on full-scale problem-based learning, have at it.

Check the literature before starting to use an inductive method, and use existing resources—including human resources—to the greatest possible extent.

You can spend a staggering amount of time and effort making up and evaluating ConcepTests, inquiry exercises, case studies, simulations, interactive multimedia tutorials for just-in-time teaching and flipped classrooms, and open-ended real-world problems for problem-based learning. Before you set out to create such materials from scratch, search the literature to find existing materials you can use, either as is or with minor modifications. Be sure to find out from the literature what the potential problems are with a method and how to deal with them if and when you encounter them. A reasonable starting point might be references cited in Prince and Felder (2006, 2007) and in Sections 4.3 (inquiry, case-based instruction), 9.4 (problem-based learning), and 10.6 (project-based learning). Those references also give sources of questions, PBL problems, and case studies in all STEM disciplines that can be used as focal points for inductive exercises.

The literature can only take you so far in figuring out how to deal with the difficulties that may arise in inductive teaching. When you are trying either to anticipate and avoid those difficulties or to deal with one that has arisen, seek experienced colleagues or teaching consultants on your campus who can offer guidance.

Set the stage.

Whenever you teach in a way that deviates from the usual "I show you how to do something and then ask you to do it on the test" model, some students are likely to be unhappy and push back. That statement applies to active learning (Chapter 6) and cooperative learning (Chapter 11), and it's especially true for inductive teaching and learning. The more you require students to figure things out for themselves, the more resistance you're likely to encounter, with problem-based learning generating the most resistance of any method you'll encounter in this book. (If it's done well it will probably also generate the deepest learning.) Before you launch into an inductive method, explain to the students what you'll be doing, why you'll be doing it, how they will benefit from it, and what the research says about its effectiveness. Even if you do all that, you'll still experience resistance, but it will be far milder and shorter-lived than you can expect if you don't do it.

12.3 Learner-Centered Teaching Strategies

Weimer (2012, 2013) defines learner-centered teaching as teaching that has the first five attributes listed in Table 12.3–1. We propose adding the sixth one. The table lists teaching methods that address each attribute and pointers to where in the book the methods are discussed.

The teaching methods listed in Table 12.3–1 have all been found to correlate with one or more of the following outcomes: improved student learning, improved academic performance, fewer dropouts in general and specifically of underrepresented groups, motivating students to adopt a deep approach to learning, promoting intellectual development, and balancing the needs and preferences of students with different learning styles (Busch-Vishniac & Jarosz, 2007; Felder & Brent, 2004c, 2005; Rosser, 1997; Svinicki & McKeachie, 2014; Weber & Custer, 2005).

Table 12.3–1 should not be viewed as a recipe for good teaching—a list of necessary and sufficient conditions of instruction that collectively guarantee achievement of all learning objectives by all students. There is no such recipe. You can name any teaching strategy, from straight lecturing to the most radical learner-centered approach, and you will find instructors

Table 12.3–1. Learner-Centered Teaching Attributes and Methods

---

A. **Engages students in the hard, messy work of learning**
   - ❏ Vary question and problem types (closed-ended and open-ended, quantitative and qualitative, well and poorly defined, all levels of Bloom's Taxonomy) in class activities, assignments, and tests (Chs. 2, 8–10).
   - ❏ Use active learning (Chs. 3–6) and cooperative learning (Ch. 11).
   - ❏ Teach inductively (Sect. 12.2).

B. **Motivates and empowers students by giving them some control over their education**
   - ❏ Give students a voice in setting policies regarding course grading (Sect. 3.4), cheating (Sect. 3.6), and project topics (Ch. 10).

C. **Encourages collaboration among students**
   - ❏ Use small-group active learning (Chs. 3–6) and cooperative learning (Ch. 11).

D. **Promotes students' reflection about what and how they are learning**
   - ❏ Use thinking-aloud pair problem-solving exercises that require students to explain critical steps in problem solutions (Sect. 6.4).
   - ❏ Give low-stakes and high-stakes writing assignments that call for reflection (Sect. 10.2), including metacognitive reflection (Sect. 9.2).

E. **Includes explicit skills instruction**
   - ❏ Write learning objectives that explicitly cover technical and professional skills (Chs. 2, 10) and knowledge and skills at all levels of Bloom's Taxonomy (Ch. 2), and include them in study guides for tests (Chs. 2, 8).
   - ❏ Include tasks that address the objectives in assignments and tests (Ch. 8), and model the required procedures in lectures and class activities (Chs. 2, 4, 6–10).

F. **Clearly conveys a sense of caring about students and their learning**
   - ❏ Establish good communications and rapport with the students (Sects. 3.6, 7.3).
   - ❏ Be inclusive and attentive to helping all students feel that they belong and can succeed. Avoid stereotyping and combat stereotype threat (Sect. 12.1).
   - ❏ Take measures to provide a supportive environment when students are challenged with high-level thinking tasks (Sect. 10.6) and address students' concerns about learner-centered instruction (Chs. 6, 11, "Sermons for Grumpy Campers" interlude).
   - ❏ Teach in a manner that addresses the learning needs and preferences of all students (Chs. 2–11, "Meet Your Students" interludes, Sect. 12.1).

---

who use it and who have deserved and won teaching awards. But if you seek a set of strategies that give you an excellent chance of equipping most of your students with the knowledge, skills, and values your course is designed to promote, Table 12.3–1 might be a good place to start.

12.4 Last Words

If you have managed to make your way through this entire book—or if you just read selected parts and jumped back here to see our final message—and you are intimidated by the sheer volume of information and suggestions we have thrown at you, who could blame you? Let us remind you, however, of several pieces of advice we gave you in Chapter 1.

First, to be a good teacher, you don't have to take every suggestion in this book. You may be a good teacher right now. If you are, and you continue doing whatever you've been doing without adopting a single idea from the book, you'll still be a good teacher—and if you adopt even a few of the ideas you'll probably be a better teacher.

Second, don't be too radical when you move toward learner-centered teaching. Don't, for example, jump directly from straight lecturing to full-scale problem-based learning in a flipped classroom, or set out to implement every method in Table 12.3–1 (or any other collection of methods) starting next Monday. You might get away with it if you're an extraordinarily talented teacher, but the chances are much greater that if you try to do too much too soon, the combination of your uncertainty and your students' resistance could be toxic, discouraging you from ever again trying anything new in your classes. Your goal should simply be to steadily improve your teaching. Make only two or three changes in your course at any one time, and you should see improvement in your students' performance from the last time you taught the course, at which point you should declare victory and start thinking about what you might do to make the course even better next time. If there is such a thing as a recipe for a successful and satisfying academic career, that last sentence could be it. It's a worthwhile and rewarding journey. Enjoy it.

REFERENCES

Accreditation Board for Engineering and Technology (ABET). (n.d.). Retrieved from http://www.abet.org/accreditation/

Active Learning. (1998). *Active learning with Dr. Richard Felder* [Video]. North Carolina State University. Retrieved from www.youtube.com/watch?v=1J1URbdisYE

Adecco Staffing USA. (2013). Lack of soft skills negatively impacts today's US workforce. Retrieved from www.adeccousa.com/about/press/Pages/20130930-lack-of-soft-skills-negatively-impacts-todays-us-workforce.aspx

Aggarwal, P., & O'Brien, C. L. (2008). Social loafing on group projects: Structural antecedents and effect on student satisfaction. *Journal of Marketing Education, 30*(3), 255–264.

Albanese, M. A., & Dast, L. (2014). Problem-based learning: Outcomes evidence from the health professions. *Journal on Excellence in College Teaching, 25*(3&4), 239–252.

Allen, D., & Tanner, K. (2006). Rubrics: Tools for making learning goals and evaluation criteria explicit for both teachers and learners. *CBE Life Sciences Education, 5*(3), 197–203. Retrieved from www.lifescied.org/content/5/3/197.full

Alley, M. (1996). *The craft of scientific writing* (3rd ed.). New York: Springer.

Alley, M. (2013). *The craft of scientific presentations: Critical steps to succeed and critical errors to avoid* (2nd ed.). New York: Springer.

Alred, G. J., Brusaw, C. T., & Oliu, W. E. (2011). *Handbook of technical writing* (10th ed.). Boston: St. Martin's Press.

Ambrose, S. A., Bridges, M. W., DiPietro, M., Lovett, M. C., & Norman, M. K. (2010). *How learning works: Seven research-based principles for smart teaching.* San Francisco: Jossey-Bass.

American Institute of Chemical Engineers. AIChE Concept Warehouse. (n.d.). Retrieved from jimi.cbee.oregonstate.edu/concept_warehouse

Anderson, L. W., & Krathwohl, D. R. (Eds.). (2001). *A taxonomy for learning, teaching and assessing: A revision of Bloom's taxonomy of educational objectives; Complete edition* (pp. 67–68). New York: Longman.

Angelo, T. A., & Cross, K. P. (1993). *Classroom assessment techniques: A hand-book for college teachers* (2nd ed.). San Francisco: Jossey-Bass.

Arnold, L., Willoughby, L., Calkins, V., Gammon, L., & Eberhart, G. (1981). Use of peer evaluation in the assessment of medical students. *Journal of Medical Education, 56*(1), 35–42.

Aronson, E., Blaney, N., Stephan, C., Sikes, J., & Snapp, M. (1978). *The jigsaw classroom.* Beverly Hills, CA: Sage.

Association of American Colleges & Universities. (2015). Falling short? College learning and career success. Retrieved from www.aacu.org/leap/public-opinion-research/2015-survey-falling-short

Association for the Assessment of Learning in Higher Education (AALHE). (n.d.). Retrieved from course1.winona.edu/shatfield/air/rubrics.htm

Astin, A. W. (1993). *What matters in college: Four critical years revisited.* San Francisco: Jossey-Bass.

Atman, C. J., Eris, O., McDonnell, J., Cardella, M. E., & Borgford-Parnell, J. L. (2014). Engineering design education: Research, practice and examples that link the two. In A. Johri & B. M. Olds (Eds.), *Cambridge handbook of engineering education research* (pp. 201–226). New York: Cambridge University Press.

Baars, B. J., & Gage, N. M. (Eds.). (2007). *Cognition, brain, and consciousness: Introduction to cognitive neuroscience.* Amsterdam: Elsevier.

Baitz, I. (2006). Strategies for inclusion of lesbian, gay, bisexual and transgender learners in discipline-based programs. *International Journal of Pedagogies & Learning, 2*(3), 52–60.

Bandura, A. (1977). Self-efficacy: Toward a unifying theory of behavioral change. *Psychological Review, 84*(2), 191–215.

Barkley, E. F. (2009). *Student engagement techniques: A handbook for college faculty.* San Francisco: Jossey-Bass.

Barrett, T., & Moore, S. (2011). *New approaches to problem-based learning: Revitalising your practice in higher education.* New York: Routledge.

Baxter Magolda, M. B. (1992). *Knowing and reasoning in college.* San Francisco: Jossey-Bass.

Beemyn, G. (2005). Making campuses more inclusive of transgender students. *Journal of Gay and Lesbian Issues in Education, 3*(1), 77–87.

Belenky, M. F., Clinchy, B. M., Goldberger, N. R., & Tarule, J. M. (1986/1997). *Women's ways of knowing: The development of self, voice, and mind.* New York: Basic Books.

Bellanca, J. (1992). *The cooperative think tank II: Graphic organizers to teach thinking in the cooperative classroom.* Palatine, IL: Skylight Publishing.

Benton, S. L., & Cashin, W. E. (n.d.). Student ratings of teaching: A summary of the research and literature. IDEA Paper 50. Summary of research through 2010. The IDEA Center, Kansas State University. Retrieved from ideaedu .org/sites/default/files/idea-paper_50.pdf

Biggs, J. (1999). *Teaching for quality learning at university.* Buckingham, UK: SRHE and Open University Press.

Biggs, J., & Tang, C. (2011). *Teaching for quality learning at university* (4th ed.). Maidenhead, UK: Open University Press.

Bligh, D. A. (1998). *What's the use of lectures?* San Francisco: Jossey-Bass.

Bloom, B. S., & Krathwohl, D. R. (1956). *Taxonomy of educational objectives: The classification of educational goals by a committee of college and university examiners. Handbook 1. Cognitive domain.* New York: Addison-Wesley.

Blue, J., Taylor, B., & Yarrison-Rice, J. (2008). Full cycle assessment of critical thinking in an ethics and science course. *International Journal for the Scholarship of Teaching and Learning, 2*(1). Retrieved from digitalcommons .georgiasouthern.edu/cgi/viewcontent.cgi?article=1078&context=ij-sotl

Boettcher, J. V., & Conrad, R. M. (2010). *The online teaching survival guide: Simple and practical pedagogical tips.* San Francisco: Jossey-Bass.

Boice, R. (1990). *Professors as writers.* Stillwater, OK: New Forums Press.

Boice, R. (2000). *Advice for new faculty members.* Needham Heights, MA: Allyn Bacon.

Boud, D., & Feletti, G. I. (Eds.). (1997). *The challenge of problem-based learning* (2nd ed.). London: Kogan Page.

Bransford, J., Brown, A., & Cocking, R. (2000). *How people learn: Brain, mind, experience and school.* Washington, DC: Commission on Behavioral and Social Science and Education, National Research Council. Retrieved from www.nap.edu/catalog/9853/how-people-learn-brain-mind-experience-and-school-expanded-edition

Brent, R., & Felder, R. M. (1992). Writing assignments—Pathways to connections, clarity, creativity. *College Teaching, 40*(1), 43–47. Retrieved from www.ncsu.edu/felder-public/Papers/Writing_Paper.pdf

Brent, R., & Felder, R. M. (2012). Learning by solving solved problems. *Chemical Engineering Education, 46*(1), 29–30. Retrieved from www.ncsu.edu/felder-public/Columns/WorkedSolutions.pdf

Brown, P. C., Roediger III, H. L., & McDaniel, M. A. (2014). *Make it stick: The science of successful learning.* Cambridge, MA: Belknap Press.

Brown, R. W. (1995). Autorating: Getting individual marks from team marks and enhancing teamwork. *1995 Frontiers in Education Conference Proceedings* (November). Pittsburgh, PA: IEEE/ASEE.

Brownell, S. E., Kloser, M. J., Fukami, T., & Shavelson, R. (2012). Undergraduate biology lab courses: Comparing the impact of traditionally based "cookbook" and authentic research-based courses on student lab experiences. *Journal of College Science Teaching, 41*(4), 36–45.

Bullard, L. G., & Melvin, A. T. (2011). Using a role-play video to convey expectations about academic integrity. *Advances in Engineering Education, 2*(3), 1–12.

Bunce, D. M., Flens, E. A., & Neiles, K. Y. (2010). How long can students pay attention in class? A study of student attention decline using clickers. *Journal of Chemical Education, 87*(12), 1438–1443.

Burke, R. J., & Mattis, M. C. (Eds). (2007). *Women and minorities in science, technology, engineering and mathematics: Upping the numbers.* Cheltenham, UK: Edward Elgar.

Busch-Vishniac, I. J., & Jarosz, J. P. (2007). Achieving greater diversity through curricular change. In R. J. Burke & M. C. Mattis (Eds.), *Women and minorities in science, technology, engineering and mathematics: Upping the numbers* (Chap. 11). Cheltenham, UK: Edward Elgar.

Capraro, R. M., Capraro, M. M., & Morgan, J. R. (2013). *STEM project-based learning: An integrated science, technology, engineering, and mathematics (STEM) approach* (2nd ed.). Rotterdam: Sense Publishers.

Carl Wieman Science Education Initiative. (n.d.). Retrieved from www.cwsei.ubc .ca/resources/clickers.htm#questions

Carpenter, D. D., Harding, T. S., & Finelli, C. J. (2010). Using research to identify academic dishonesty deterrents among engineering undergraduates. *International Journal of Engineering Education, 26*(5), 1156–1165.

Carpenter, D. D., Harding, T. S., Finelli, C. J., Montgomery, S. M., & Passow, S. J. (2006). Engineering students' perceptions of and attitudes toward cheating. *Journal of Engineering Education, 23*(4), 181–194.

Case, J. M., & Marshall, D. (2009). Approaches to learning. In M. Tight, K. H. Mok, J. Huisman, & C. C. Morphew (Eds.), *The Routledge international handbook of higher education* (pp. 9–22). New York: Routledge.

CATME Smarter Teamwork. (n.d.). Retrieved from info.catme.org

CBI. (2008). *Taking stock: CBI education and skills survey 2008.* London: Confederation of Business Industry.

Cedefop (European Centre for the Development of Vocational Training). (2009). *The shift to learning outcomes: Policies and procedures in Europe.* Luxembourg: Office for Official Publications of the European Communities.

Chi, M. T. H. (2005). Common sense conceptions of emergent processes: Why some misconceptions are robust. *Journal of the Learning Sciences, 14,* 161–199.

Cho, K., & MacArthur, C. (2010). Student revision with peer and expert reviewing. *Learning and Instruction, 20,* 328–338.

Chubin, D. E., May, G. S., & Babco, E. L. (2005). Diversifying the engineering workforce. *Journal of Engineering Education, 94*(1), 73–86.

Clark, R. C., & Mayer, R. E. (2003). *e-Learning and the science of instruction.* San Francisco: Pfeiffer.

Coffield, F. (2012). Learning styles: Unreliable, invalid and impractical and yet still widely used. *Bad education: Debunking myths in education.* Berkshire UK: Open University Press.

Cohen, P. A. (1984). College grades and adult achievement: A research synthesis. *Research in Higher Education, 20*(3), 281–293.

Condon, W., & Kelly-Riley, D. (2004). Washington State University critical thinking project: Improving student learning outcomes through faculty practice. *Assessing Writing, 9*(1), 56–75.

Cornelius, T. L., & Owen-DeSchryver, J. (2008). Differential effects of full and partial notes on learning outcomes and attendance. *Teaching of Psychology, 35*(1), 6–12.

Cowan, N. (2010). The magical mystery four: How is working memory capacity limited, and why? *Current Directions in Psychological Science, 19*(1), 51–57.

Crooks, T. J. (1988). The impact of classroom evaluation practices on students. *Review of Educational Research, 58*(4), 438–481.

Croxton, R. A. (2014). The role of interactivity in student satisfaction and persistence in online learning. *Journal of Online Learning and Teaching, 10*(2), 314–325. Retrieved from jolt.merlot.org/vol10no2/croxton_0614.pdf

Dansereau, D. F., & Newbern, D. (1997). Using knowledge maps to enhance teaching. In W. E. Campbell & K. A. Smith (Eds.), *New paradigms for college teaching* (pp. 127–147). Edina, MN: Interaction Book Company.

Davis, C., & Yadav, A. (2014). Case studies in engineering. In A. Johri & B. M. Olds (Eds.), *Cambridge handbook of engineering education research* (pp. 161–180). New York: Cambridge University Press.

DeMars, C. (2010). *Item response theory.* Oxford: Oxford University Press.

Deslauriers, L., Schelew, E., & Wieman, C. (2011). Improved learning in a large-enrollment physics class. *Science, 332*(6031), 862–864.

Dewey, J. (1910). *How we think.* Lexington, MA: D. C. Heath.

Donhardt, G. L. (2004). In search of the effects of academic achievement in post-graduation earnings. *Research in Higher Education, 45*(3), 271–284.

Douglas, E. P., & Chiu, C. C. (2013). Implementation of process oriented guided inquiry learning (POGIL) in engineering. *Advances in Engineering Education, 3*(3), 1–16. Retrieved from advances.asee.org/wp-content/uploads/vol03/issue03/papers/aee-vol03-issue03–03.pdf

Duch, B. J., Groh, S. E., & Allen, D. E. (Eds.). (2001). *The power of problem-based learning.* Sterling, VA: Stylus.

Dunlosky, J., Rawson, K. A., Marsh, E. J., Nathan, M. J., & Willingham, D. T. (2013). Improving students' learning with effective learning techniques: Promising directions from cognitive and educational psychology. *Psychological Science in the Public Interest, 14*(1), 4–58.

Dweck, C. (2006). *Mindset: The new psychology of success.* New York: Ballantine Books.

Dym, C. L., Agogino, A. M., Eris, O., Frey, D. D., & Leifer, L. (2005). Engineering design, thinking, teaching, and learning. *Journal of Engineering Education, 94*(1), 103–120.

Dym, C. L., Little, P., & Orwin, E. (2013). *Engineering design: A project-based introduction* (4th ed.). Hoboken, NJ: Wiley.

Eberlein, T., Kampmeier, J., Minderhout, V., Moog, R. S., Platt, T., Varma-Nelson, P., & White, H. G. (2008). Pedagogies of engagement in science: A comparison of PBL, POGIL, and PLTL. *Biochemistry and Molecular Biology Education, 36*(4), 262–273.

Elbow, P. (1986). *Embracing contraries: Explorations in learning and teaching.* New York: Oxford University Press.

Elbow, P. (1998). *Writing without teachers.* Oxford: Oxford University Press.

Elbow, P., & Sorcinelli, M. D. (2014). Using high-stakes and low-stakes writing to enhance learning. In M. D. Svinicki & W. J. McKeachie (Eds.), *McKeachie's teaching tips: Strategies, research, and theory for college and university teachers* (14th ed., pp. 213–231). Belmont, CA: Wadsworth Cengage.

Ellis, G. W., Rudnitsky, A., & Silverstein, B. (2004). Using concept maps to enhance understanding in engineering education. *International Journal of Engineering Education, 20*(6), 1012–1021.

Engineering Projects in Community Service (EPICS). (n.d.). Retrieved from engineering.purdue.edu/EPICS

Ericsson, K. A., Krampe, R. T., & Tescher-Romer, C. (1993). The role of deliberate practice in the acquisition of expert performance. *Psychological Review*, *100*, 363–406.

Erwin, T. D., & Sebrell, K. W. (2003). Assessment of critical thinking: ETS's tasks in critical thinking. *Journal of General Education*, *52*(1), 50–70.

Eschenbach, E. A., Virnoche, M., Cashman, E. M., Lord, S. M., & Camacho, M. M. (2014). Proven practices that can reduce stereotype threat in engineering education: A literature review. *Proceedings of the 2014 Frontiers in Education Conference*, Madrid, Spain. IEEE/ASEE.

Etkina, E., Brookes, D. T., Murthy, S., Karelina, A., Villasenhor, M. R., & Heuvelen, A. V. (2006). Developing and assessing student scientific abilities. *Proceedings of the National STEM Assessment Conference*. Washington, DC: National Science Foundation and Drury University. Retrieved from www.openwatermedia.com/downloads/STEM(for-posting).pdf

Etkina, E., Murthy, S., & Zou, X. (2006). Using introductory labs to engage students in experimental design. *American Journal of Physics*, *74*, 979–986.

European Higher Education Area. (2014). Bologna Process—European Higher Education Area. Retrieved from http://www.ehea.info/article-details.aspx?ArticleId=5

Evans, N. J. (2002). The impact of an LGBT safe zone project on campus climate. *Journal of College Student Development*, *43*(4), 522–539.

Exam wrappers. (n.d.). Eberly Center, Carnegie Mellon University. Retrieved from www.cmu.edu/teaching/designteach/teach/examwrappers

Fassinger, P. A. (1995). Understanding classroom interaction: Students' and professors' contributions to students' silence. *Journal of Higher Education*, *66*(1), 82–96.

Feisel, L. D., & Rosa, A. J. (2005). The role of the laboratory in undergraduate engineering education. *Journal of Engineering Education*, *94*(1), 126–130.

Felder, R. M. (1985). The generic quiz: A device to stimulate creativity and higher-level thinking skills. *Chemical Engineering Education*, *19*(4), 176–181, 213–214. Retrieved from www.ncsu.edu/felder-public/Papers/Generic.pdf

Felder, R. M. (1987). On creating creative engineers. *Journal of Engineering Education*, *77*(4), 222–227. Retrieved from www.ncsu.edu/felder-public/Papers/Creative_Engineers.pdf

Felder, R. M. (1988). Creativity in engineering education. *Chemical Engineering Education*, *22*(3), 120–125. Retrieved from www.ncsu.edu/felder-public/Papers/Creativity(CEE).pdf

Felder, R. M. (1994). Any questions? *Chemical Engineering Education, 28*(3), 174–175. Retrieved from www.ncsu.edu/felder-public/Columns/Questions .pdf

Felder, R. M. (1995). A longitudinal study of engineering student performance and retention. IV. Instructional methods and student responses to them. *Journal of Engineering Education, 84*(4), 361–367. Retrieved from www .ncsu.edu/felder-public/Papers/long4.html

Felder, R. M. (1999). Memo to students who are disappointed with their last test grade. *Chemical Engineering Education, 33*(2), 136–137. Retrieved from www.ncsu.edu/felder-public/Columns/memo.pdf

Felder, R. M. (2000). The alumni speak. *Chemical Engineering Education, 34*(3), 238–239.

Felder, R. M. (2007). Sermons for grumpy campers. *Chemical Engineering Education, 41*(3), 183–184. Retrieved from www.ncsu.edu/felder-public/ Columns/Sermons.pdf

Felder, R. M. (2010). Are learning styles invalid? (Hint: No.) *On-Course Newsletter,* September 27. Retrieved from www.ncsu.edu/felder-public/Papers/LS_ Validity(On-Course).pdf

Felder, R. M. (2011a). Hang in there: Dealing with student resistance to learner-centered teaching. *Chemical Engineering Education, 45*(2), 131–132. Retrieved from www.ncsu.edu/felder-public/Columns/HangInThere.pdf

Felder, R. M. (2011b). How to stop cheating—or at least slow it down. *Chemical Engineering Education, 45*(1), 37–38. Retrieved from www.ncsu.edu/ felder-public/Columns/Cheating.pdf

Felder, R. M., & Brent, R. (1996). Navigating the bumpy road to student-centered instruction. *College Teaching, 44,* 43–47. Retrieved from www.ncsu.edu/ felder-public/Papers/Resist.html

Felder, R. M., & Brent, R. (1997). Objectively speaking. *Chemical Engineering Education, 31*(3), 178–179. Retrieved from www.ncsu.edu/felder-public/ Columns/Objectives.html

Felder, R. M., & Brent, R. (2001). Effective strategies for cooperative learning. *Journal of Cooperation and Collaboration in College Teaching, 10*(2), 69–75. Retrieved from www.ncsu.edu/felder-public/Papers/ CLStrategies(JCCCT).pdf

Felder, R. M., & Brent, R. (2003). Designing and teaching courses to satisfy the ABET Engineering Criteria. *Journal of Engineering Education, 92*(1), 7–25. Retrieved from www.ncsu.edu/felder-public/Papers/ABET_Paper_ (JEE).pdf

Felder, R. M., & Brent, R. (2004a). Death by PowerPoint. *Chemical Engineering Education, 39*(1), 28–29. Retrieved from www.ncsu.edu/felder-public/Columns/PowerPoint.pdf

Felder, R. M., & Brent, R. (2004b). The intellectual development of science and engineering students. 1. Models and challenges. *Journal of Engineering Education, 93*(4), 269–277. Retrieved from www.ncsu.edu/felder-public/Papers/IntDev-I.pdf

Felder, R. M., & Brent, R. (2004c). The intellectual development of science and engineering students. 2. Teaching to promote growth. *Journal of Engineering Education, 93*(4), 279–291. Retrieved from www.ncsu.edu/felder-public/Papers/IntDev-II.pdf

Felder, R. M., & Brent, R. (2004d). A protocol for peer review of teaching. *Proceedings, 2004 Annual ASEE Conference.* Washington, DC: American Society for Engineering Education. Retrieved from www.ncsu.edu/felder-public/Papers/ASEE04(Peer-Review).pdf

Felder, R. M., & Brent, R. (2005). Understanding student differences. *Journal of Engineering Education, 94*(1), 57–72. Retrieved from www.ncsu.edu/felder-public/Papers/Understanding_Differences.pdf

Felder, R. M., & Brent, R. (2007). Cooperative learning. In P. A. Mabrouk (Ed.), *Active learning: Models from the analytical sciences.* Washington, DC: American Chemical Society. Retrieved from www.ncsu.edu/felder-public/Papers/CLChapter.pdf

Felder, R. M., & Brent, R. (2008). Student ratings of teaching: Myths, facts, and good practices. *Chemical Engineering Education, 42*(1), 33–34. Retrieved from www.ncsu.edu/felder-public/Columns/StudentRatings.pdf

Felder, R. M., & Brent, R. (2009). Active learning: An introduction. *ASQ Higher Education Brief, 2*(4). Retrieved from www.ncsu.edu/felder-public/Papers/ALpaper(ASQ).pdf

Felder, R. M., & Brent, R. (2010). Hard assessment of soft skills. *Chemical Engineering Education, 44*(1), 63–64. Retrieved from www.ncsu.edu/felder-public/Columns/SoftSkills.pdf

Felder, R. M., & Brent, R. (n.d.). Forms for cooperative learning. Retrieved from www.ncsu.edu/felder-public/CL_forms.doc

Felder, R. M., Felder, G. N., & Dietz, E. J. (2002). The effects of personality type on engineering student performance and attitudes. *Journal of Engineering Education, 91*(1), 3–17. Retrieved from www.ncsu.edu/felder-public/Papers/longmbti.pdf

Felder, R. M., Felder, G. N., Mauney, M., Hamrin Jr., C. E., & Dietz, E. J. (1995). A longitudinal study of engineering student performance and retention. III.

Gender differences in student performance and attitudes. *Journal of Engineering Education, 84*(2), 151–174. Retrieved from www.ncsu.edu/felder-public/Papers/long3.pdf

Felder, R. M., & Peretti, S. W. (1998). A learning theory-based approach to the undergraduate engineering laboratory. *American Society of Engineering Education Annual Conference Proceedings.* Washington, DC: American Society for Engineering Education. Retrieved from www.ncsu.edu/felder-public/Papers/330Lab.pdf

Felder, R. M., & Silverman, L. K. (1988). Learning and teaching styles in engineering education. *Journal of Engineering Education, 78*(7), 674–681. Retrieved from www.ncsu.edu/felder-public/Papers/LS-1988.pdf

Felder, R. M., & Stice, J. E. (2014). Tips on test-taking. *Chemical Engineering Education, 48*(1), 57–58. Retrieved from www.ncsu.edu/felder-public/Columns/TestTaking.pdf

Fiechtner, S. B., & Davis, E. A. (1985). Why some groups fail: A survey of students' experiences with learning groups. *The Organizational Behavior Teaching Review, 9*(4), 75–88.

Fink, L. D. (2003). *Creating significant learning experiences.* San Francisco: Jossey-Bass.

Fogler, H. S., LeBlanc, S. E., & Rizzo, B. (2014). *Strategies for creative problem solving* (3rd ed.). Upper Saddle River, NJ: Pearson.

Freeman, S., Eddy, S. L., McDonough, M., Smith, M. K., Okoroafor, N., Jordt, H., & Wenderoth, M. P. (2014). Active learning increases student performance in science, engineering, and mathematics. *Proceedings of the National Academy of Science,* June 10, 2014, Vol. 111, No. 23. Retrieved from www.pnas.org/content/early/2014/05/08/1319030111.full.pdf+html

Garber, A. (2001). Death by PowerPoint. Small Business Computing.com (April). www.smallbusinesscomputing.com/biztools/article.php/684871/Death-By-Powerpoint.htm

Gibbs, G., & Simpson, C. (2004–2005). Conditions under which assessment supports students' learning. *Learning and Teaching in Higher Education, 1,* 3–31.

Gikandi, J. W., Morrow, D., & Davis, N. E. (2011). Online formative assessment in higher education: A review of the literature. *Computers & Education, 57,* 2333–2351.

Goodman, I. F., Cunningham, C. M., Lachapelle, C., Thompson, M., Bittinger, K., Brennan, R. T., & Delci, M. (2002). *Final report of the women's experiences in college engineering (WECE) Project*. Cambridge, MA: Goodman Research Group. Retrieved from www.grginc.com/WECE_FINAL_REPORT.pdf

Gosser, D. K., Cracolice, M. S., Kampmeier, J. A., Roth, V., Strozak, V. S., & Varma-Nelson, P. (Eds.). (2001). *Peer-led team learning: A guidebook*. Upper Saddle River, NJ: Prentice Hall.

Gronlund, N. E. (2008). *How to write and use instructional objectives* (8th ed.). Upper Saddle River, NJ: Prentice Hall.

Guglielmino, L. M. (2013). The case for promoting self-directed learning in formal educational institutions. *SE-eDUC Journal, 10*(2). Retrieved from www-nwu-ac-za.web.nwu.ac.za/sites/www-nwu-ac-za.web.nwu.ac.za/sites/www.nwu.ac.za/files/files/p-saeduc/sdl%20issue/Guglielmino,%20L.M.%20The%20case%20for%20promoting%20self-directed%20lear.pdf

Guo, P. J., Kim, J., & Rubin, R. (2014). How video production affects student engagement: An empirical study of MOOC videos. *Proceedings of the first ACM Conference on Learning@Scale*. Atlanta, Georgia, March 4–5, 2014. Retrieved from groups.csail.mit.edu/uid/other-pubs/las2014-pguo-engagement.pdf

Gurin, P. (1999). The compelling need for diversity in education (expert report). University of Michigan. Retrieved from diversity.umich.edu/admissions/legal/expert/gurintoc.html

Haidet, P., Kubitz, K., & McCormack, W. T. (2014). Analysis of the team-based learning literature: TBL comes of age. *Journal on Excellence in College Teaching, 25*(3&4), 303–333.

Hart, J. (2015). Top 100 tools for learning. Center for Learning & Performance Technologies. Retrieved from c4lpt.co.uk/top100tools/

Hart Research Associates. (2010). *Raising the bar: Employers' views on college learning in the wake of the economic downturn*. Washington, DC: Author. Retrieved from www.aacu.org/leap/documents/2009_EmployerSurvey.pdf

Hartley, J., & Davies, I. K. (1978). Note-taking: A critical review. *Programmed Learning & Educational Technology, 15*, 207–224.

Hattie, J. (2009). *Visible learning*. New York: Routledge.

Hawk, T. F., & Lyons, P. R. (2008). Please don't give up on me: When faculty fail to care. *Journal of Management Education, 32*(3), 316–338.

Heller, P., & Hollabaugh, M. (1992). Teaching problem solving through cooperative grouping. Part II: Designing problems and structuring groups. *American Journal of Physics*, 60, 637–644.

Herreid, C. F., Schiller, N. A., & Herreid, K. F. (2012). *Science stories: Using case studies to teach critical thinking*. Arlington, VA: NSTA Press.

Heslin, P. A. (2009). Better than brainstorming? Potential contextual boundary conditions to brainwriting for idea generation in organizations. *Journal of Occupational and Organizational Psychology*, 82, 129–145.

Heywood, J. (2005). *Engineering education: Research and development in curriculum and instruction*. Hoboken, NJ: IEEE/Wiley.

Hiemstra, R. (2013). Self-directed learning: Why do most instructors still do it wrong? *International Journal of Self-Directed Learning*, 10(1), 23–34.

Hobson, E. H. (2004). Getting students to read: Fourteen tips (IDEA Paper 40). Manhattan, KS: The IDEA Center. Retrieved from ideaedu.org/research-and-papers/idea-papers/idea-paper-no-40/

How stuff works. (n.d.). Retrieved from www.howstuffworks.com/

Hunsaker, P., Pavett, C., & Hunsaker, J. (2011). Increasing student-learning team effectiveness with team charters. *Journal of Education for Business*, 86(3), 127–139.

Hutchison-Green, M. A., Follman, D. K., & Bodner, G. M. (2008). Providing a voice: Qualitative investigation of the impact of a first-year engineering experience on students' efficacy beliefs. *Journal of Engineering Education*, 97(2), 177–190.

International Engineering Alliance. (n.d.). Washington accord. Retrieved from www.washingtonaccord.org/washington-accord

Jackson, M. (1996). Making the grade: The formative evaluation of essays. In *ultiBASE* (July 3). Retrieved from trove.nla.gov.au/work/153148874?q&versionId=166904470

Jacobs, L. C. (2002). How to write better tests: A handbook for improving test construction skills. Indiana University. Retrieved from www.indiana.edu/~best/pdf_docs/better_tests.pdf

Jacoby, B. (2014). *Service-learning essentials: Questions, answers, and lessons learned*. San Francisco: Jossey-Bass.

Jain, R., Shanahan, B., & Roe, C. (2009). Broadening the appeal of engineering—addressing factors contributing to low appeal and high attrition. *International Journal of Engineering Education*, 25(3), 405–418.

Jensen, J. L., Kummer, T. A., & Godoy, D. d. M. (2015). Improvements from a flipped classroom may simply be the fruits of active learning. *CBE-Life*

Sciences Education, 14, 1–12. Retrieved from www.lifescied.org/content/ 14/1/ar5.full.pdf+html

Johnson, D. W., Johnson, R. T., & Smith, K. A. (2006). *Active learning: Cooperation in the college classroom* (3rd ed.). Edina, MN: Interaction Book.

Johnson, D. W., Johnson, R. T., & Smith, K. A. (2014). Cooperative learning: Improving university instruction by basing practice on validated theory. *Journal on Excellence in College Teaching, 25*(3&4), 85–118.

Johnson, D. W., Johnson, R. T., & Stanne, M. E. (2000). *Cooperative learning methods: A meta-analysis.* University of Minnesota, Minneapolis: Cooperative Learning Center. Retrieved from www.lcps.org/cms/lib4/ VA01000195/Centricity/Domain/124/Cooperative_Learning Methods A Meta-Analysis.pdf

Johri, A., & Olds, B. M. (Eds.). (2014). *Cambridge handbook of engineering education research.* New York: Cambridge University Press.

Journals in Higher Education (JIHE). (n.d.) Retrieved from www.cideronline.org/ jihe/view1.cfm

Just-in-Time Teaching (JiTT). (n.d.). Retrieved from jittdl.physics.iupui.edu/ jitt/

Karpicke, J. D., & Blunt, J. E. (2011). Retrieval practice produces more learning than elaborative studying with concept mapping. *Science, 331*(6018), 772–775.

Kaufman, D. B., Felder, R. M., & Fuller, H. (2000). Accounting for individual effort in cooperative learning teams. *Journal of Engineering Education, 89*, 133–140. Retrieved from www.ncsu.edu/felder-public/Papers/ Kaufmanpap.pdf

Kaufman, J. C., Plucker, J. A., & Baer, J. (2008). *Essentials of creativity assessment.* Hoboken, NJ: Wiley.

Kiewra, K. A. (1989). A review of note-taking: The encoding storage paradigm and beyond. *Educational Psychology Review, 1*(2), 147–172.

Kiewra, K. A. (2012). Using graphic organizers to improve teaching and learning. Idea Paper 51. Manhattan, KS: The Idea Center. Retrieved from ideaedu .org/research-and-papers/idea-papers/idea-paper-no-51/

King, A. (1993). From sage on the stage to guide on the side. *College Teaching, 41*(1), 30–35.

Knapper, C. K., & Cropley, A. J. (2000). *Lifelong learning in higher education.* London: Kogan Page.

Knowles, M. S. (1975). *Self-directed learning: A guide for learners and teachers.* New York: Association Press.

Kolb, D. A. (1984). *Experiential learning: Experience as the source of learning and development.* Englewood Cliffs, NJ: Prentice Hall.

Kolmos, A., & de Graaf, E. (2014). Problem-based and project-based learning in engineering education. In A. Johri & B. M. Olds (Eds.), *Cambridge handbook of engineering education research* (pp. 141–160). New York: Cambridge University Press.

Kolowich, S. (2013). The new intelligence. *Inside Higher Ed* (January 25). Retrieved from https://www.insidehighered.com/news/2013/01/25/arizona -st-and-knewtons-grand-experiment-adaptive-learning

Koretsky, M. D. (2015). Program level curriculum reform at scale: Using studios to flip the classroom. *Chemical Engineering Education, 49*(1), 47–57.

Koretsky, M. D., & Brooks, B. J. (2012). Student attitudes in the transition to an active-learning technology. *Chemical Engineering Education, 46*(1), 289–297.

Koretsky, M. D., Kelly, C., & Gummer, E. (2011a). Student learning in industrially situated virtual laboratories. *Chemical Engineering Education, 45*(3), 219–228.

Koretsky, M. D., Kelly, C., & Gummer, E. (2011b). Student perceptions of learning in the laboratory: Comparison of industrially situated virtual laboratories to capstone physical laboratories. *Journal of Engineering Education, 100*(3), 540–573.

Krathwohl, D. R., Bloom, B. S., & Massia, B. B. (1984). *Taxonomy of educational objectives. Handbook 2. Affective domain.* New York: Addison-Wesley.

Kroll, B. M. (1992). *Teaching hearts and minds: College students reflect on the Vietnam War in literature.* Carbondale, IL: Southern Illinois University Press.

Kurfiss, J. G. (1988). *Critical thinking: Theory, research, practice, and possibilities.* ASHE-ERIC Higher Education Report 2. Washington, DC: ASHE-ERIC.

Lang, J. D., Cruse, S., McVey, F. D., & McMasters, J. (1999). Industry expectations of new engineers: A survey to assist curriculum designers. *Journal of Engineering Education, 88*(1), 43–51.

Lasry, N., Mazur, E., & Watkins, J. (2008). Peer instruction: From Harvard to the two-year college. *American Journal of Physics, 76*(11), 1066–1069.

Laursen, S., Hunter, A., Seymour, E., Thiry, H., & Melton, G. (2010). *Undergraduate research in the sciences: Engaging students in real science.* San Francisco: Jossey-Bass.

Layton, R. A., Loughry, M. L., Ohland, M. W., & Ricco, G. D. (2010). Design and validation of a web-based system for assigning members to teams using instructor-specified criteria. *Advances in Engineering Education,* 2(1), 1–28.

Lee, V. S. (Ed.). (2004). *Teaching & learning through inquiry: A guidebook for institutions and instructors.* Sterling, VA: Stylus.

Lee, V. S. (Ed.). (2012). *Inquiry-guided learning new directions for teaching and learning,* No. 129. San Francisco: Jossey-Bass.

Lichtenstein, G., Chen, H. I., Smith, K. A., & Maldonado, T. A. (2014). Retention and persistence of women and minorities along the engineering pathway in the United States. In A. Johri & B. M. Olds (Eds.), *Cambridge handbook of engineering education research* (pp. 311–334). New York: Cambridge University Press.

Lightman, A., & Sadler, P. (1993). Teacher predictions versus actual student gains. *The Physics Teacher, 31,* 162–167.

Lochhead, J., & Whimbey, A. (1987). Teaching analytical reasoning through thinking-aloud pair problem solving. In J. E. Stice (Ed.), *Developing critical thinking and problem-solving abilities* (pp. 73–92). New Directions for Teaching and Learning, No. 30. San Francisco: Jossey-Bass.

Loughry, M. L., Ohland, M. W., & Moore, D. D. (2007). Development of a theory-based assessment of team member effectiveness. *Educational and Psychological Measurement, 67*(3), 505–524.

Loughry, M. L., Ohland, M. W., & Woehr, D. J. (2014). Assessing teamwork skills for assurance of learning using CATME Team Tools. *Journal of Marketing Education, 36*(1), 5–19.

Lowman, J. (1995). *Mastering the techniques of teaching* (2nd ed.) San Francisco: Jossey-Bass.

Lyman Jr., F. (1981). The responsive classroom discussion: The inclusion of all students. In A. S. Anderson (Ed.), *Mainstreaming digest.* College Park: University of Maryland.

Lynch, C. L., & Wolcott, S. K. (2001). Helping your students develop critical thinking skills (IDEA Paper 37). Manhattan, KS: The IDEA Center. Retrieved from ideaedu.org/research-and-papers/idea-papers/idea-paper-no-37/

Mager, R. F. (1997). *Preparing instructional objectives: A critical tool in the development of effective instruction.* Atlanta, GA: The Center for Effective Performance.

Markel, M. (2014). *Technical communication* (11th ed.). Boston: Bedford/St. Martin's.

Marra, R., Jonassen, D. H., Palmer, B., & Luft, S. (2014). Why problem-based learning works: Theoretical foundations. *Journal on Excellence in College Teaching, 25*(3&4), 221–238.

Marton, F., Hounsell, D., & Entwistle, N. (Eds.). (1997). *The experience of learning* (2nd ed.). Edinburgh: Scottish Academic Press.

Mastascusa, E. J., Snyder, W. J., & Hoyt, B. S. (2011). *Effective instruction for STEM disciplines: From learning theory to college teaching.* San Francisco: Jossey-Bass.

Mayer, R. E. (2003). Cognitive theory and the design of multimedia instruction: An example of the two-way street between cognition and instruction. In D. F. Halpern & M. D. Hakel (Eds.), *Applying the science of learning to university teaching and beyond* (pp. 55–72). New Directions for Teaching and Learning Science, No. 89. San Francisco: Jossey-Bass.

Mazur, E. (1997). *Peer instruction: A user's manual.* Upper Saddle River, NJ: Prentice Hall.

Means, B., Toyama, Y., Murphy, R., Bakia, M., & Jones, K. (2010). *Evaluation of evidence-based practices in online learning: A meta-analysis and review of online learning studies.* Washington, DC: US Department of Education. Retrieved from www2.ed.gov/rschstat/eval/tech/evidence-based-practices/finalreport.pdf

Meyers, S. A. (2009). Do your students care whether you care about them? *College Teaching, 57*(4), 205–210.

Michaelson, L. K., Knight, A. B., & Fink, L. D. (2004). *Team-based learning: A transformative use of small groups in college teaching.* Arlington, VA: Stylus.

Middendorf, J., & Kalish, A. (1996). The "change-up" in lectures. *National Teaching and Learning Forum, 5*(2), 1–5.

Millis, B. J., & Cottell Jr., P. G. (1998). *Cooperative learning for higher education faculty.* Phoenix: Oryx Press.

Momsen, J. L., Long, T. M., Wyse, S. A., & Ebert-May, D. (2010). Just the facts? Introductory undergraduate biology courses focus on low-level cognitive skills. *CBE Life Sciences Education, 9*(4), 435–440. Retrieved from www.lifescied.org/content/9/4/435.full

Moog, R. S., & Spencer, J. N. (Eds.). (2008). *Process-oriented guided inquiry learning.* New York: American Chemical Society.

Morris, P. E., Fritz, C. O., Jackson, L., Nichol, E., & Roberts, E. (2005). Strategies for learning proper names: Expanding retrieval practice, meaning and imagery. *Applied Cognitive Psychology, 19*(6), 779–798.

National Academy of Sciences, National Academy of Engineering, & Institute of Medicine. (2011). *Expanding underrepresented minority participation.* Washington, DC: National Academies Press. Retrieved from grants.nih .gov/training/minority_participation.pdf

National Center for Case Study Teaching in Science (NCCSTS). (n.d.). Retrieved from sciencecases.lib.buffalo.edu/cs/

National Science Foundation. (2009, January). *Women, minorities, and persons with disabilities in science and engineering.* NSF 09–305. Arlington, VA: National Science Foundation, Retrieved from www.nsf.gov/statistics/ wmpd/

Nilson, L. B. (2007). *The graphic syllabus and the outcomes map: Communicating your course.* San Francisco: Jossey-Bass.

Novak, J. D., & Cañas, A. J. (2008). The theory underlying concept maps and how to construct them. Technical Report IHMC CmapTools 2006–01 Rev 01–2008. Florida Institute for Human and Machine Cognition. Retrieved from cmap.ihmc.us/Publications/ResearchPapers/ TheoryUnderlyingConceptMaps.pdf

Oakley, B. (2014). *A mind for numbers: How to excel at math and science (even if you flunked algebra).* New York: Jeremy P. Tarcher/Penguin.

Oakley, B., Felder, R. M., Brent, R., & Elhajj, I. (2004). Turning student groups into effective teams. *Journal of Student-Centered Learning, 2*(1), 9–34. Retrieved from www.ncsu.edu/felder-public/Papers/Oakley-paper(JSCL) .pdf

O'Brien, J. G., Millis, B. J., & Cohen, M. W. (2008). *The course syllabus: A learning-centered approach* (2nd ed.). Hoboken, NJ: Wiley.

Ohland, M. W., Brawner, C. E., Camacho, M. M., Layton, R. A., Long, R. A., Lord, S. M., & Wasburn, M. H. (2011). Race, gender, and measures of success in engineering education, *Journal of Engineering Education, 100*(2), 225–252.

Ohland, M. W., Loughry, M. L., Woehr, D. J., Bullard, L. G., Felder, R. M., Finelli, C. J., Layton, R. A., Pomeranz, H. R., & Schmucker, D. G. (2012). The comprehensive assessment of team member effectiveness: Development of a behaviorally anchored rating scale for self and peer evaluation. *Academy of Management Learning & Education, 11*(4), 609–630.

Ohland, M. W., Sheppard, S. D., Lichtenstein, G., Eris, O., Chachra, D., & Layton, R. A. (2008). Persistence, engagement, and migration in engineering programs. *Journal of Engineering Education, 97*(3), 259–277.

Orpen, C. (1982). Student versus lecturer assessment of learning: A research note. *Higher Education, 11,* 567–572.

Osborn, A. F. (1963). *Applied imagination: Principles and procedures of creative problem solving* (3rd ed.). New York: Charles Scribner's Sons.

Pascarella, E. T., & Terenzini, P. T. (2005). *How college affects students: A third decade of research.* San Francisco: Jossey-Bass.

Peer-Led Team Learning (PLTL). (n.d.). Retrieved from www.pltl.org

Penner, J. (1984). *Why many college teachers cannot lecture.* Springfield, IL: Charles C. Thomas.

Perry, W. G. (1970/1998). *Forms of intellectual and ethical development in the college years: A scheme.* San Francisco: Jossey-Bass.

Pfeiffer, W. S. (2010). *Pocket guide to technical communication* (5th ed.). Upper Saddle River, NJ: Longman.

Phillips, C. R., Chesnut, R. J., & Rospond, R. M. (2004). The California critical thinking instruments for benchmarking, program assessment, and directing curricular change. *American Journal of Pharmaceutical Education, 68*(4), Article 101.

Pólya, G. (1945). *How to solve it.* Princeton, NJ: Princeton University Press.

Poynter, K. J., & Washington, J. (2005). Multiple identities: Creating community on campus for LGBT students. *New Directions for Student Services, 111,* 41–47.

Prichard, J. (2013). *The importance of soft skills in entry-level employment and post-secondary success.* Seattle: Seattle Jobs Initiative. Retrieved from www.seattlejobsinitiative.com/wp-content/uploads/SJI_SoftSkillsReport_vFINAL_1.17.13.pdf

Prince, M. J. (2004). Does active learning work? A review of the research. *Journal of Engineering Education, 93*(3), 223–231.

Prince, M. J., & Felder, R. M. (2006). Inductive teaching and learning methods: Definitions, comparisons, and research bases. *Journal of Engineering Education, 95*(2), 123–138. Retrieved from www.ncsu.edu/felder-public/Papers/InductiveTeaching.pdf

Prince, M. J., & Felder, R. M. (2007). The many faces of inductive teaching and learning. *Journal of College Science Teaching, 36*(5), 14–20. Retrieved from www.ncsu.edu/felder-public/Papers/Inductive(JCST).pdf

Prince, M. J., Vigeant, M. A. S., & Nottis, K. E. K. (2012). Assessing the prevalence and persistence of engineering students' misconceptions in heat transfer. *Journal of Engineering Education, 101*(3), 412–438.

Process Oriented Guided Inquiry Learning (POGIL). (n.d.) Retrieved from pogil.org/post-secondary

Pyc, M. A., Agarwal, P. K., & Roediger III, H. L. (2014). Test-enhanced learning. In V. A. Benassi, C. E. Overson, & C. M. Hakala (Eds.),

Applying science of learning in education: Infusing psychological science in the curriculum (pp. 78–90). Washington, DC: American Psychological Association.

Ramsden, P. (2003). *Learning to teach in higher education* (2nd ed.). New York: Routledge Falmer.

Rankin, S., Weber, G., Blumenfeld, W., & Frazer, S. (2010). *2010 state of higher education for lesbian, gay, bisexual and transgender people.* Charlotte, NC: Campus Pride. Retrieved from issuu.com/campuspride/docs/campus_pride_2010_lgbt_report_summary

Reason, R. D., Cox, B. E., Quaye, B. R. L., & Terenzini, P. T. (2010). Faculty and institutional factors that promote student encounters with difference in first-year courses. *Review of Higher Education, 33*(3), 391–414.

Renkl, A. (2014). Learning from worked examples: How to prepare students for meaningful problem solving. In V. A. Benassi, C. E. Overson, & C. M. Hakala (Eds.), *Applying science of learning in education: Infusing psychological science in the curriculum* (pp. 118–130). Washington, DC: American Psychological Association.

Riener, C., & Willingham, D. (2010). The myth of learning styles. *Change: The magazine of higher learning.* Retrieved from www.changemag.org/Archives/Back%20Issues/September-October%202010/the-myth-of-learning-full.html

Roberson, B., & Franchini, B. (2014). Effective task design for the TBL classroom. *Journal on Excellence in College Teaching, 25*(3&4), 275–302.

Roediger III, H. L., & Butler, A. C. (2011). The critical role of retrieval practice in long-term learning. *Trends in Cognitive Science, 15*(1), 20–27.

Rogers, C. R., & Farson, R. E. (1987). Active listening. In R. G. Newman, M. A. Danziger, & M. Cohen (Eds.), *Communication in business today.* Washington: Heath.

Rohrer, D., Dedrick, R., & Burgess, K. (2014). The benefit of interleaved mathematics practice is not limited to superficially similar kinds of problems. *Psychonomic Bulletin & Review, 21*, 1323–1330.

Rohrer, D., & Pashler, H. (2007). Increasing retention without increasing study time. *Current Directions in Psychological Science, 16*(4), 183–186.

Rohrer, D., & Pashler, H. (2012). Learning styles: Where's the evidence? *Medical Education, 46*, 634–635. Retrieved from onlinelibrary.wiley.com/doi/10.1111/j.1365-2923.2012.04273.x/full

Rohrer, D., Taylor, K., Pashler, H., Wixted, J. T., & Cepeda, N. J. (2004). The effect of overlearning on long-term retention. *Applied Cognitive Psychology, 19*, 361–374.

Rosen, C. (2008). The myth of multitasking. *The New Atlantis,* Spring, 105–110. Retrieved from www.thenewatlantis.com/publications/the-myth-of-multitasking

Rosser, S. (1997). *Re-engineering female friendly science.* New York: Teachers College Press.

Rosser, S. V. (1998). Group work in science, engineering, and mathematics: Consequences of ignoring gender and race. *College Teaching, 46*(3), 82–88.

Rowe, M. B. (1986). Wait time: Slowing down may be a way of speeding up! *Journal of Teacher Education, 37*(1), 43–50.

Rutledge, M. L., & Warden, M. A. (2000). Evolutionary theory, the nature of science & high school biology teachers: Critical relationships. *The American Biology Teacher, 62*(1), 23–31.

Sadler, P. M., & Good, E. (2006). The impact of self- and peer-grading on student learning. *Educational Assessment, 11*(1), 1–31.

Sarquis, J. L., Dixon, L. J., Gosser, D. K., Kampmeier, J. A., Roth, V., Strozak, V. S., & Varma-Nelson, P. (2001). The workshop project: Peer-led team learning in chemistry. In J. E. Miller, J. E. Groccia, & M. Miller (Eds.), *Student-assisted teaching: A guide to faculty-student teamwork* (pp.150–155). Bolton, MA: Anker.

Schneider, B., Blikstein, P., & Pea, R. (2013). The flipped, flipped classroom. *The Stanford Daily,* August 5. Retrieved from www.stanforddaily.com/2013/08/05/the-flipped-flipped-classroom/

Schneider, B., Milesi, C., Brown, K., Gutin, I., & Perez-Felkner, L. (2015). Does the gender gap in STEM majors vary by field and institutional selectivity? *Teachers College Record,* July 16.

Seidel, S. B., & Tanner, K. D. (2013). "What if students revolt?"—Considering student resistance: Origins, options, and opportunities for investigation. *CBE Life Sciences Education, 12,* 586–595. Retrieved from www.lifescied.org/content/12/4/586.full

Severiens, S., & Schmidt, H. (2009). Academic and social integration and study progress in problem based learning. *Higher Education, 58*(1), 59–69.

Seymour, E., & Hewitt, N. M. (1997). *Talking about leaving: Why undergraduates leave the sciences.* Boulder, CO: Westview Press.

Shank, J. D. (2014). *Interactive open educational resources: A guide to finding, choosing, and using what's out there to transform college teaching.* San Francisco: Jossey-Bass.

Shuman, L. J., Besterfield-Sacre, M., & McGourty, J. (2005). The ABET "professional skills"—Can they be taught? Can they be assessed? *Journal of Engineering Education, 94*(1), 41–55.

Silverthorn, D. U. (2006). Teaching and learning in the interactive classroom. *Advances in Physiology Education, 30,* 135–140.

Simkins, S., & Maier, M. (Eds.). (2009). *Just-in-time teaching: Across the disciplines, and across the academy.* Sterling, VA: Stylus Publishing.

Simpson, E. J. (1972). *The classification of educational objectives, psychomotor domain.* ERIC Document ED010368, Education Resource Information Center.

Singh, H. (2003). Building effective blended learning programs. *Educational Technology, 43*(6), 51–54.

Smith, H., Parr, R., Woods, R., Bauer, B., & Abraham, T. (2010). Five years after graduation: Undergraduate cross-group friendships and multicultural curriculum predict current attitudes and activities. *Journal of College Student Development, 51*(4), 385–402.

Smith, K. A., Sheppard, S. D., Johnson, D. W., & Johnson, R. T. (2005). Pedagogies of engagement: Classroom-based practices. *Journal of Engineering Education, 94,* 87–101.

Sorcinelli, M. D., & Yun, J. (2007). From mentor to mentoring networks: Mentoring in the new academy. *Change, 39*(6), 58–61.

Sousa, D. A. (2011). *How the brain learns* (4th ed.) [Kindle version]. Retrieved from http://www.amazon.com/Brain-Learns-David-Anthony-Sousa/dp/1412997976

Springer, L., Stanne, M. E., & Donovan, S. (1999). Effects of small-group learning on undergraduates in science, mathematics, engineering, and technology: A meta-analysis. *Review of Educational Research, 69*(1), 21–51. Retrieved from www.wcer.wisc.edu/archive/cl1/CL/resource/scismet.pdf

Steele, C. M. (2010). *Whistling Vivaldi: And other clues to how stereotypes affect us.* New York: W. W. Norton.

Stice, J. E. (1979). Grades and test scores: Do they predict adult achievement? *Journal of Engineering Education, 69*(5), 390–393.

Streveler, R. A., Miller, R. L., Santiago-Roman, A. I., Nelson, M. A., Geist, M. R., & Olds, B. M. (2011). Rigorous methodology for concept inventory development: Using the "assessment triangle" to develop and test the thermal and transport science concept inventory (TTCI). *International Journal of Engineering Education, 27*(5), 968–984.

Strobel, J., & van Barneveld, A. (2009). When is PBL more effective? A meta-synthesis of meta-analyses comparing PBL to conventional classrooms. *Interdisciplinary Journal of Problem-based Learning, 3*(1), 44–58.

Stuart, J., & Rutherford, R. (1978). Medical student concentration during lectures. *The Lancet, 2,* 514–516.

Svinicki, M. D. (2010). Synthesis of the research on teaching and learning in engineering since the implementation of ABET Engineering Criteria 2000. National Academies Board on Science Education. Retrieved from sites .nationalacademies.org/dbasse/bose/dbasse_080124

Svinicki, M., & McKeachie, W. J. (2014). *McKeachie's teaching tips: Strategies, research, and theory for college and university teachers* (14th ed.). Belmont, CA: Wadsworth.

Sweller, J. (2006). The worked example effect and human cognition. *Learning and Instruction, 16*(2), 165–169.

Sweller, J., Ayres, P., & Kalyuga, S. (2011). *Cognitive load theory.* Springer Science and Business Media. Available from https://books.google.com/ books/about/Cognitive_Load_Theory.html?id=sSAwbd8qOAAC.

Szpunar, K. K., Khan, N. Y., & Schacter, D. L. (2013). Interpolated memory tests reduce mind wandering and improve learning of online lectures. *Proceedings of the National Academy of Sciences, 110*(16), 6313–6317.

Tanner, K. D. (2012). Promoting student metacognition. *CBE-Life Sciences Education, 11,* 113–120.

Taylor, A. K., & Kowalski, P. (2014). Student misconceptions: Where do they come from and what can we do? In V. A. Benassi, C. E. Overson, & C. M. Hakala (Eds.), *Applying science of learning in education: Infusing psychological science into the curriculum.* Retrieved from teachpsych.org/ebooks/ asle2014/index.php

Taylor, K., & Rohrer, D. (2010). The effects of interleaved practice. *Applied Cognitive Psychology, 24*(6), 837–848.

Terenzini, P. T., Cabrera, A. F., Colbeck, C. L., Parente, J. M., & Bjorklund, S. A. (2001). Collaborative learning vs. lecture/discussion: Students' reported learning gains. *Journal of Engineering Education, 90,* 123–130.

Tien, L. T., Roth, V., & Kampmeier, J. A. (2002). Implementation of a peer-led team learning approach in an undergraduate organic chemistry course. *Journal of Research in Science Teaching, 39,* 606–632.

Tinto, V. (1993). *Leaving college: Rethinking the causes and cures of student attrition* (2nd ed.). Chicago: University of Chicago Press.

Tobias, S. (1994). *They're not dumb, they're different.* Tucson, AZ: Research Corporation.

Torrance, E. P. (1962). Creative thinking through school experiences. In S. J. Parnes & H. F. Harding (Eds.), *A source book for creative thinking* (pp. 31–47). New York: Charles Scribner's Sons.

Torrance, E. P. (1966a). Rationale of the Torrance tests of creative thinking ability. In E. P. Torrance & W. F. White (Eds.), *Issues and advances in education psychology.* Istica, IL: F. E. Peacock.

Torrance, E. P. (1966b). *Torrance test on creative thinking: Norms–technical manual.* Lexington, MA: Personal Press.

Trigwell, K., Prosser, M., & Waterhouse, F. (1999). Relations between teachers' approaches to teaching and students' approaches to learning. *Higher Education, 37,* 57–70.

Tucker, C. (2013). Mind/Shift teacher's guide to using videos. KQED and NPR. Retrieved from ww2.kqed.org/mindshift/wp-content/uploads/sites/23/2013/03/MindShift-Guide-to-Videos.pdf

University of California, San Diego. (2014). Learning how to learn: Powerful mental tools to help you master tough subjects. Retrieved from www.coursera.org/learn/learning-how-to-learn

University of Delaware PBL Clearinghouse. (n.d.). Retrieved from http://www.udel.edu/inst/clearinghouse/index.html

University of Oregon. (2014). Writing multiple choice questions that demand critical thinking. Retrieved from tep.uoregon.edu/resources/assessment/multiplechoicequestions/mc4critthink.html

US Copyright Office. (n.d.). Circular 92 107 limitations on exclusive rights: Fair use. Retrieved from www.copyright.gov/title17/92chap1.html#107

US Department of Commerce. (2011). Women in STEM: A gender gap to innovation. *ESA Issue Brief 04–11.* Washington, DC: US Department of Commerce.

van Gelder, T. (2005). Teaching critical thinking: Some lessons from cognitive science. *College Teaching, 53*(1), 41–46.

VanGundy, A. B. (1983). Brainwriting for new product ideas: An alternative to brainstorming. *Journal of Consumer Marketing, 1,* 67–74.

Velegol, S. B., Zappe, S. E., & Mahoney, E. (2015). The evolution of a flipped classroom: Evidence-based recommendations. *Advances in Engineering Education, 4*(3). Retrieved from advances.asee.org/wp-content/uploads/vol04/issue03/papers/AEE-15-Velegol.pdf

Watson, G., & Glaser, E. (1980). *Watson-Glaser critical thinking appraisal.* San Antonio, TX: The Psychological Corporation.

Weber, K., & Custer, R. (2005). Gender-based preferences toward technology education content, activities, and instructional methods. *Journal of Technology Education, 16*(2), 55–71.

Weimer, M. (2012). Five characteristics of learner-centered teaching. Faculty Focus. Magna publications. Retrieved from www.facultyfocus .com/articles/effective-teaching-strategies/five-characteristics-of-learner-centered-teaching/

Weimer, M. (2013). *Learner-centered teaching: Five key changes to practice* (2nd ed.). San Francisco: Jossey-Bass.

Wieman, C. (2014). Large-scale comparison of science teaching methods sends clear message. *Proceedings of the National Academy of Sciences (PNAS), 111*(23), 8319–8320. Retrieved from www.pnas.org/content/111/23/8319 .full

Williams, L., & Kessler, R. (2002). *Pair programming illuminated.* Boston: Addison-Wesley.

Wilson, R. C. (1986). Improving faculty teaching: Effective use of student evaluations and consultants. *Journal of Higher Education, 57*(2), 196–211.

Woods, D. R. (1985). *A strategy for problem solving* (3rd ed.). Hamilton, Ontario: Department of Chemical Engineering, McMaster University.

Woods, D. R. (1994). *Problem-based learning: How to get the most from PBL.* Waterdown, Ontario: Woods Publishing.

Woods, D. R. (2000). An evidence-based strategy for problem solving. *Journal of Engineering Education, 89*(4), 443–459.

Zeilik, M. (n.d.). Field-tested learning assessment guide (FLAG). Classroom assessment techniques: Minute paper. Retrieved from www.flaguide.org/ cat/minutepapers/minutepapers7.php

Zimarro, D. (2004).Writing good multiple choice exams. University of Texas at Austin. Retrieved from ctl.utexas.edu/sites/default/files/writing-good-multiple-choice-exams-04-28-10.pdf

INDEX

A

AALHE. *See* Association for the Assessment of Learning in Higher Education

ABET. *See* Accreditation Board for Engineering and Technology

Absolute grading. *See* Grading

Accreditation Board for Engineering and Technology (ABET). 35–36, 217

Active learning: 111–129; addressing common concerns, 125–127; avoiding common mistakes, 122–125, 129; definition, 111, 113, 128; for avoiding cognitive overload, 94; for conceptual understanding, 161–162; for problem-solving skill development, 119–120; for retrieval practice, 116–117; formats of activities, 114; illustrative activities, 113; in flipped (inverted) classrooms, 128, 143–146, 149; in online courses, 146–148; in recitations, 128; reasons for effectiveness, 116–119; research support for, 111, 116. 128; resistance of students to, 122–127, 243–244; think-pair-share, 114; to address specific outcomes and skills, 115

Active listening, 266

Approaches to learning: deep, surface, and strategic, 151–152; motivating students' adoption of a deep approach, 152–153

Assessment instruments: checklists and rubrics, 176–181, 183, 233–234; classroom assessment techniques (CATs), 103; closed-book versus open-book tests, 168; concept inventories, 164, 182; ConcepTests, 162–164, 182; minute paper, 62–63, 103–105; multiple-choice and short-answer tests, 156–160; problem-solving tests, 166–174, 200. *See also* Evaluation and Test length

Assessment. *See* Assessment instruments and Evaluation

Assignments: creative thinking, 228; critical thinking, 232; low-stakes and high-stakes, 219, 241; pre-class, 96–99, 104; problem-solving, 164–166, 182; writing and speaking, 219–222

Association for the Assessment of Learning in Higher Education (AALHE), 180

Astin, Alexander, 54

Attention span in lectures and activities, 117–119, 128

Automaticity, 192, 195, 197, 208

B

Blended (hybrid) learning. *See* Technology-assisted instruction

Bloom's Taxonomy of Educational Objectives: 30–34, 68; critical thinking in, 31; minimizing class time spent on Level 1 material, 34, 36; multiple-choice questions at different levels, 156–157; sample learning objectives at different levels, 32